HEAVEN AND HELL ON EARTH

HEAVEN AND HELL ON EARTH:

An Appreciation of Five Novels
of Graham Greene

K.C. Joseph Kurismmootil, S.J.

A Campion Book

Loyola University Press
Chicago, Illinois

Ad majorem Dei gloriam

Printed in the United States of America

186021

Library of Congress Cataloging in Publication Data

Kurismmootil, K. C. Joseph, 1949-
  Heaven and hell on earth.

Bibliography: p.
1. Greene, Graham, 1904-   —Criticism and
interpretation.   I. Title.
PR6013.R44Z643   823'.912   82-57
ISBN O-8294-0378-7   AACR2

To M. M. J.

PREFACE

This book owes a great deal to the novelist himself. Indeed it should never have gone to the press but for the open enthusiasm with which he received it. Mr. Greene has been almost lavish in his kindnesses to me; and he never left a querry unanswered even if he had to snatch precious moments on his journeys to attend to my numerous questions. He also took time out to go over my typescript and redrafts of several chapters. For all this no acknowledgment can be quite adequate. One could only wish one had a better work to show for such great favors, as one must go on cherishing the memory of his boundless generosity.

An "appreciation," I guess, is how this work is best designated; the word "criticism" might claim far more for it than I have attempted here. While with most connoisseurs of fiction, distancing—both moral and emotional—is a critical absolute, my own concern has been to enter as much, and as deeply, into the world of the various novels as is practicable. That I have succeeded herein I cannot vouch for with any certainty. Nor can I claim to any completeness of analyses. An inquiry into such complex patterns of meaning as make up Mr. Greene's fiction must perforce be somewhat tentative. And perhaps this is just as well. For after all the final judge of the worth or otherwise of a novel must be the reader. The reviewer's task is done when he has mapped out the strange contours of the region, signposted the roads, marked the major yields and the important events. Here the reader must take over. My own very modest aims will have been realized if this study should in some way challenge the reader's imagination, broaden his or her perspective, and open a way to deepened perceptions and a more enhanced enjoyment of Greene's novels.

I have enjoyed the rather unusual privilege of being guided by some persons of great literary eminence—among them, Professor D.P. Singh, Dean of the School of Languages, North-Eastern Hill

University, Shillong. With his keenly perceptive mind, and his vast erudition in such diverse fields as philosophy, psychology and other behavioral sciences spurring on the imagination, a session with him is bound to be a challenge. For me his guidance has been as much pleasurable as greatly rewarding. I also owe a great debt of gratitude to Professors Frank Kermode of King's College and Christopher Ricks of Christ's College, Cambridge; David Lodge of The University of Birmingham; Leopoldo Durán of Madrid University, Spain; Kevin Cleary, Richard Lambert and Jerome Durack all of St Xavier's, Patna for their kindness in reading and critically assessing various chapters. I am particularly bound to Professor Ricks for the care and thoroughness with which he pursued the matter. Professors Francis Smith of John Carroll University, Ohio, and Gene Phillips of Loyola University of Chicago read through the entire work in the first draft. Mrs. Elisabeth Dennys, Greene's sister, Mr. Dennis Karamitis of Wisconsin and Mr. James Kutticherry of Boston furnished me with valuable review material.

I would like to remember with gratitude Fathers Cap Miller, S.J. and the late Paul Dent, S.J. and the Jesuit Community of St Xavier's Godavari, Kathmandu who kindly offered me the hospitality of their house—a very pleasant retreat—for my work; Professor R.K. Sinha, formerly of Patna University; the late Rev. Vincent Horrigan, S.J. of Loyola University Press; Rev. Daniel Flaherty, S.J. and finally, Fr. Abraham Puthumana, S.J. who took a very personal interest in the progress of my work.

Although the perspectives are largely my own, and mine entirely the responsibility for any errors in interpretation, still these perspectives have not been shaped independently of the vast body of reviews and incidental criticism available on Greene's fiction. All direct quotations I have duly acknowledged in footnotes; and the bibliography gives a more or less complete list of literary sources I have used.

Kohima
December 8, 1981

K.C. Joseph Kurismmootil, S.J.

CONTENTS

A SORT OF BACKGROUND

Far-call'd our navies melt away—
On dune and headland sinks the fire—
Lo, all our pomp of yesterday
Is one with Nineveh and Tyre!

—Rudyard Kipling

England at the turn of the twentieth century was a scene of complex ironies. The Boer War, the bloodiest in recent memory, was not being managed to the nation's credit. England finally won the war but not without loss of face. The wild reprisals let loose on a scantily armed people could only reflect dishonor upon her fair name. Many a Briton saw the barbarity of this war as a blot not only on their sense of honor, but on the civilization for which they had posed themselves as the champions. Queen Victoria's passing away in January 1901 did not help matters at all. For more than half-a-century Victoria had remained a symbol of the security and permanence of the English nation. With her at the helm of their country's affairs Britons had no doubts they were a great people and their way of life superior to any in the world. Now she was gone, and with her death the English felt less sure of themselves.

From the Victorian Age the English had inherited a thought and sensibility that were contrary to their early twentieth-century self image. The new sensibility not merely challenged age-old traditions; it roused serious and anguished doubts in the minds of many a Briton. The crisis of identity this occasioned was disturbing enough and too widespread not to arouse concern. That the crisis took on convulsive features is no matter for surprise. What should cause some surprise is that the nation should have survived with so little loss.

The final decades of the nineteenth century, the "braggart years," had been a period of enhanced prosperity for England. It was an era of daring new ideas and liberal thought, of social and political reforms. But the many poor houses, the sprawling urban slums, and the lot of the deprived and "the submerged" (in their thousands), of farm laborers and factory hands, painted a different picture altogether. British society was not very fair to the young either. While in preaching about matters of sex and ethics, puritan ideals prevailed; in practice "concessions" to human weakness were all too frequent. All this was indicative of a state of ambiguity, of moral confusion—an apt climate for prophecy. Poet and philosopher made common cause with the reformer to try to explore what was amiss and set aright whatever might be rectified. Particularly eloquent in their prophetic utterings were T.S. Eliot, W.H. Auden and Graham Greene.

Urbanity was found to be a poor substitute for an authentic mode of being; nor might science displace true insight. England was still struggling to catch up with knowledge and its widening horizons. Darwin's theories appealed to many especially among the intellectuals. Indeed, his vision of a people free of superstition and taboo was something too dizzy. The advances in science promised a future of the utmost comfort. There would be no want that the newly grown technology could not attend to. This was the very picture of bliss. And yet neither the Victorians nor their successors were any happier for all the improvements. On the contrary, the more thoughtful among them were struck with a new dilemma. They had to redeem whatever was true and right about faith from the annihilating clutches of science. Science posed a challenge to religion, and this challenge had to be met honorably in the service of truth. It caused much heart-probing concerning life, its meaning, and ultimate ends. There was uncertainty and a sense of *angst*, which not even the most brilliant were adequate to cope with. Tennyson, Hardy, and Matthew Arnold were all victims of this strange consequence. Confusion and fear fogged the mind; left unchecked, they would clog up the very sources of human vitality.

Tennyson spoke for his own generation and the next when he questioned the "forward countenance" of knowledge that "leaps into the future chance":

> Half-grown as yet, a child, and vain—
> She cannot fight the fear of death.
> What is she, cut from love and faith,
> But some wild Pallas from the brain
>
> Of demon?[1]

To that poser no adequate answer was heard. It was not that there was no beauty in scientific knowledge. Nor did anyone deny the commendable role science played in bettering man's condition. Still, the need for restraint was widely felt. Lest "cut from love and faith" science should transform itself into a demoniac force, there was a call to redefine faith and its proper rights in the light of the new knowledge.

R.A. Scott-James has described the early decades of the present century as an "age of unease and restlessness."[2] "Mere anarchy is loosed upon the world," said Yeats of the twenties.[3] Stephen Spender complained of forced vigils:

> We cannot sleep. At night we watch
> A speaking clearness through cloudy paranoia.[4]

The whole nation shared the *angoisse*; and for being shared, it was the more difficult to define. Fear was writ large on every face in the subway and on the street. No individual escaped it; no fact of life was immune to it. Yet all this was only symptomatic of the slide down to catastrophe of which "The Great War," was the culmination.

To the English, and to the West generally, the First World War was like a suicide note; it presaged an even worse fate. It challenged Western man and his culture, with its proud achievements and manifold pretensions, which was shown up as a thing of no consequence. The War held a mirror up to the Western World, and the face it reflected was gory, the image of a mangled self. Or perhaps

A heap of broken images, where the sun beats,
And the dead tree gives no shelter, the cricket no relief,
And the dry stone no sound of water.[5]

A familiarly Arthurian landscape, it shamed a person's pride even to look about one's native land. One saw vast stretches of untilled land, parched and blown with dust. It appeared as though the fog of some divine curse brooded overhead. One even sensed fear "in a handful of dust."[6] In familiar sounds and about everyday movements there appeared a hidden menace. Such anxiety is a great stimulant. It urged the modern knights, just as it had the knights of the Holy Grail, out on the weary trail, questing for the sources of vitality.

The knights set out in every direction. D.H. Lawrence, among the loudest of modern prophets, stopped by, a short way from the start, to harken to the libido. Lawrence preached that in sex were immured the seeds of vitality. But disillusion awaited him round the final curve in the path; and in the evening of his life he would admit to having failed. Auden and Stephen Spender, among others, took a different route. It was not psychology but the economics of social change that intrigued them. In the twenties many were in fact dazzled by the Russian experiment. Many more marvelled at the changes socialism claimed to have brought about. The Russians, it appeared, had blazed a path: couldn't the rest of the world at least follow the lead? The suggestion had an appeal, particularly for the idealist. Subsequent events would, however, prove that the reports from Russia were less fact than propaganda.

Still others sought the Grail at the portals of religion. Among these were Chesterton, Ronald Knox, T.S. Eliot, Belloc, and Evelyn Waugh. Eliot became an Anglican; and the rest embraced the Catholic faith. On a wintry afternoon in January 1926 there knelt in a deserted corner of a dark little church a young man of great promise. It was Graham Greene, come for his baptism—a person and name to startle the world into new awareness and, by the sheer power of his art, hold it spellbound for decades to come.

Greene had his first novel published in 1929. He was barely 25 then. The book, titled *The Man Within*, was quite a success, enough to make him want to take up fiction as a career. Fifty years later, two dozen more novels have joined it. His other works include poems, short stories, travelogues, plays, reviews, and essays in criticism. In 1971 he published an autobiographical sketch. His works to date would add up to some fifty volumes ranging the whole gamut of literary experience. The diversity and magnitude of it all is staggering. Insatiable in his creative effort, he has a sense of vocation, a certain adventurous straining for fresh vistas, for worlds yet unconquered. Perhaps it was the sheer challenge of the new that drew him to the stage and then to the cinema. The screen he found particularly congenial, just the right sort of medium for his effects. Besides writing some remarkably good screenplays, he has had the rare satisfaction of seeing most of his novels, and several short stories, made into films.

Greene has said that "the creative writer perceives his world once and for all in his childhood and adolescence." His entire career, then, "is an effort to illustrate his private world in terms of the great public world we all share."[7] Greene was born in 1904. His father was headmaster of a well-known "public" school in Berkhamstead. While the senior Greene was a cultivated, tolerant, gentlemanly man (in *A Sort of Life* Graham Greene recalls his poetry recitals with great affection), yet in young Greene's mind this school is associated most uncannily with the unpleasant. This contrast created a certain ambiguity in the son. In this peaceful situation, his very earliest impressions are violent ones.

> The first thing I can remember at all was a dead dog at the bottom of my pram; it had been run over at a country cross roads . . . and the nurse put it at the bottom of the pram and pushed me home.[8]

"There was no emotion attached to the sight," he reports. "It was just a fact." Even in those early days he had the gift of "an admirable objectivity."

Greene also recalls witnessing an attempt at suicide. The man had rushed out of his cottage jerkily and in a rage. "He looked angry about something: he was going to cut his throat with a knife if he could get away from his neighbors, 'having no hope and without

God in the world.'"9 Later life would fill in the darkening landscape: the suburban youth with hair smarmed and scented scouting around the dusky lanes for parlor maids, the retired colonel with turned up whiskers leering at boys of a certain age. In the papers he read reports of an adolescent couple (the girl was pregnant) found headless on a railway line. Experience would futher supplement the design, but the primary sketch was there—or was it the melody?—etched on the magnetic tape of childhood memory. The scenes he did not create through phantasy; they belonged to the world of common sense and proper behavior, the adult world.

It is a dictum of psychiatry that a "man's fate, his nobility and all his degradation"10 are molded by decisions he has already made by the age of five. Experience only elaborates on a script settled in childhood. In the words of Eric Berne,

> The child has a picture of the world which is quite different from the way it appears to his parents. It is a fairy-tale world, full of monsters and magic, and it persists all through his life and forms the archaic background to his script.11

Perceptions become experience only when put into a proper frame. The child gathers his awareness of the great outside into a frame of the simplest dimensions; and its value is for the most part emotive. Life on this level of fantasy is lived with the utmost intensity. The child is particularly alert to the violent and destructive, is even thrilled by them. They conform to the primary categories of childhood experience. The young can train themselves to live dangerously. They are not surprised by the clash of steel or the roar of cannons. And they have always known how the battle lines are drawn; that in a struggle between Evil and Good, between Caliban and Ariel, Caliban must triumph in the end. The child has seen the sights, heard the bugles cry. He can discount a great deal of adult claims for goodness as sheer nonsense. For the young boy and girl has wandered through to the other side of day, and here no angel choir stood whispering music to the "sleeping bosom." Those were crafty hands that watched the night; and they lay in wait for the innocent intruder. The very darkness snarled everytime the child strayed into its realm. Not angels but Sykes and Fagins ruled the dark.

His adolescence confirmed Greene's early perceptions. In *The Lawless Roads* he tells us of the sort of anxieties that kept plaguing him. The "school chatter and the disciplinary bell" only added to the tension. "The great Victorian buildings"[12] were a constant reminder to him of cruelty, hate and boredom. Thinly divided from the school by a green baize door was home, and next to the home was the mournful solitude of the croquet lawn. Greene risked an occasional foray into "the small countryside;" but there was no lasting peace in it either. For he could never forget that danger crouched across the door. The baize door would be his symbol of the "borderland" which was to be his proper mental territory. The door stood for divided loyalties, for emotional vacillation, and for a tortured mind. The "Victorian buildings of garish brick" represented a world view, even a philosophy. They spoke for the diseased prosperity of a technological society. For Greene, both the skyscraper and the slum were equally symbols of evil. He recognized in them a great danger to humanity; they constrained the spirit, and stifled the urge to create. The "chromium world,"[13] built on the debris of a nature violated and defiled, was a cage—not a home to live in.

On the other side of the door was "the small countryside where the fruit trees grew and the rabbits munched."[14] Here nature was quiet, fertile and in harmony, and one could rest with a measure of freedom.

> One escaped surreptitiously for an hour at a time [to hear] the rabbit restlessly cropping near the croquet hoops. It was an hour of release—and also an hour of prayer. One became aware of God with an intensity—time hung suspended—music lay on the air; anything might happen before it became necessary to join the crowd across the border.[15]

Here we already have the strains of melodrama which Greene would work into his dramatic scheme. "Across the border" meant

the pitchpine partitions of dormitories where everybody was

never quiet at the same time, lavatories without locks, . . .
walks in pairs up the suburban roads; no solitude, at any time.

The constraint was just too much for his taste, and young Graham
fled it.

Greene could not have realized at this time that the lack of solitude was as much a private mental condition as it was objective.
After all in every age there have been those who have triumphed
over every sort of violence, on the body and on the spirit. Greene's
first thought was of flight. On being successfully prevented in his
several attempts to run away from home, he took to playing risky
games with his life. At the age of 16, he was playing Russian roulette,
a most dangerous game, even if he stood a five-to-one chance in favor
of life. It is unlikely that death charmed him, but the thrill of the ultimate risk surely appealed to his imagination. Eventually he was
discovered in his mad venture and that landed him with a
psychoanalyst.

Fortunately for Greene, the analyst was a man of keen perceptions and of deep human sympathies. Greene recalls his six months
of analysis as being of the happiest in his life. They would have far-
reaching consequences not only for his life, but also for his career as
a novelist. The analysis trained him in habits of introspection. He
was taught how to get in touch with his own emotions, how to enter
in and stay with them. Henceforward he would be comfortable with
the desires and motivations that stir and tremble in the dark recesses
of the soul. He learned to direct his feelings in a manner that was
consonant with the rhythms of his total being. He saw that boredom
was not always to be fled, that it may be but one of the shifting
moods of the soul, a primary emotion:

> That agonizing (sense) of 'apartness' which comes before one
> had learnt the fatal trick of transferring emotion, of flashing
> back enchantingly all day long one's own image, a period when
> other people were . . . distinct from oneself. . . .[16]

Surely childhood boredom was authentic, equal to ecstasy. It was an
elemental experience to counterpoint the pure joy of infancy. One

had best come to terms with it. Besides, flight could never be final. Greene also learned that release comes with acceptance through a deeper awareness, and not by ignoring what appeared painful. The analysis made him want to "relearn the way to live without transference, with a lost objectivity."[17]

The analysis calmed his nerves but could not erase those early impressions he had of life. Indeed, he had perceived his "world once and for all in his childhood and adolescence," and no further experience could reverse or wipe off those primeval memories. Nothing he might learn or do in the future could cancel their influence on his life. That certain restlessness would remain, ingrained as it were in his personality. Neither change nor novelty, nor the vast continental spaces—between Liberia and Tabasco, Congo, Haiti and Vietnam—would cure him of that. He could now appreciate his need for something more lasting to guide and soothe his way. He had need for a Polaris to steer by, particularly when the seas were rough. And only some sort of a faith could answer this need.

Greene has recorded that belief came to him even as a boy, but "shapelessly, without a dogma, a presence above a croquet lawn."[18] It was more an ache, a dream, to withstand the pressures of life. It was too much like the self-projections of a tortured soul. One needed "to believe in heaven because one believed in hell, but for a long while it was only hell one could picture with a certain intimacy."[19] The Anglican church was no solace for Greene because it "could not supply the same intimate symbols for heaven" as it did for the fires of hell. Heaven was somewhat vague, sketched faintly by "a brass eagle, an organ voluntary, 'Lord, Dismiss Us With Thy Blessing,' the quiet croquet lawn where one had no business, the rabbit, and the distant music."[20] It was but an echo, the weak rumblings of a desire, too inadequate to complete the fierce polarities of primary experience. And so what Greene sought in the Catholic Church was other symbols, ardent and more archetypal, and absolute enough to rely on for a lifetime.

Greene's literary career divides roughly into three periods. The first begins with *Orient Express* and includes such important volumes as *It's a Battlefield, England Made Me*, and *This Gun For*

Hire. There is an acute social awareness in these books; even a Marxist inclination is discernible now and again. The dominant motifs are: boredom, a sense of betrayal, and an almost hopeless bid for a just ordering of society. There is a note of earnest pleading, and the tone is of desperate urgency. At a later stage Greene would return to these themes, though on a lower key. *The Quiet American* may be thought to inaugurate this latter phase. *The Comedians, The Honorary Consul* and *The Human Factor* are other significant works belonging to the third period. The tone grows steadily mellower with each book until, in the last mentioned, there is nothing shrill, not even a note of criticism. There is a deep acceptance of life, and a tolerance of those maladies that cannot be overcome. These are the fruit of ripe age which, knowing all, is capable of forgiving all.

However, the novels of the middle phase are Greene's signal achievement. He was a young man of thirty-four when the first of these, *Brighton Rock*, came out. The last in the series, *The End of the Affair*, was published in 1951, his forty-seventh year. Other works of this second phase, and among Greene's best, are *The Power and the Glory* and *The Heart of the Matter*. Each deals with matters of great moment and are important artistic creations. After a ten-year lapse, *A Burnt-Out Case* was added as a postscript to this most important period. All five books are discussed in detail further on. Introducing *The Confidential Agent* the author had confessed to "a certain vague ambition to create something legendary out of a contemporary thriller." How successfully his novels have realized his ambition is for us to assess. In order to appreciate his work properly it will be well to trace in brief the stages of Greene's artistic growth. To which task we presently address ourselves.

SOME DATES, BOOKS AND EVENTS

1904, Oct. 2	Born at Berkhamsted, Hertfordshire, son of Charles H. Greene, history and classics teacher and later headmaster of Berkhamsted School	Boer War in progress
1912-1922	Berkhamsted School	1914-1918 World War I
1922-1925	Balliol College, Oxford University	
1927	Marries Vivien Dayrell-Browning	
1926-1930	Sub-editor on *The Times*	1930 world-wide economic depression begins
1932	Begins book reviewing for *The Spectator* *Orient Express* (*Stamboul Train*)	
1934	*It's A Battlefield*	Rise of Hitler and the Nazis in Germany
1935	Travels in Liberia. Film Critic for *The Spectator* *England Made Me*	
1936	*This Gun for Hire* (*A Gun for Sale*)	
1938	Travels in Mexico, *Brighton Rock*	
1939		Germany and Russia invade Poland; England and France declare war on Germany; World War II begins.
1940-1941	Drama critic and literary editor for *The Spectator*; Ministry of Information, London.	
1941-1943	Sierra Leone, Department of Foreign Office *The Ministry of Fear* (1943)	The United States and Japan enter World War II
1943-1944	London: Department of Foreign Office	
1945		World War II ends

1944-1948	Director of Eyre and Spottiswoode *The Heart of the Matter* (1948)	
1948		Terrorist warfare underway in Malaya; guerrilla warfare against the French in Indochina
1951	Travel in Indochina; in Malaya for *Life* magazine *The End of the Affair*	
1952	Travel in Indochina for *Paris-Match*	
1954	Travel in Cuba; Haiti; Indochina for *The Sunday Times* *The Quiet American*	Division of Vietnam and French withdrawal
1956	Travel in Haiti	
1957	Travel in Cuba; China; Russia *The Potting Shed* (play)	Guerrilla warfare begins in South Vietnam
1958-1968	Director, *The Bodley Head*	
1961	*A Burnt-Out Case*	
1965		United States Armed Forces enter South Vietnam
1966	Settles in France *The Comedians*	
1969	Travel in Argentina; Paraguay; Czechoslovakia	
1971	Travel in Chile, Argentina *A Sort of Life* (autobiography)	
1973		United States withdraws from South Vietnam; Arab-Israeli War
1974	*The Honorary Counsel*	
1977	*Loser Takes All*	
1978	*The Human Factor*	
1979		Revolt in Iran
1980	*Doc Fischer of Geneva* or *The Bomb Party*	

THE MAKING OF AN ARTIST

Our interest's on the dangerous edge of things.
The honest thief, the tender murderer,
The superstitious atheist, demi-rep
That loves and saves her soul in new French books—
We watch while these in equilibrium keep
The giddy line midway.

> —Browning, *Bishop Bloughram's Apology*

If he "were to choose an epigraph for all the novels" he has written, Greene says, it would be the above passage from *Bishop Bloughram's Apology*.[1] indeed, these lines sum up the primary insights of his art. Whatever is most characteristic in Greene is stated here: eminently the melodramatic motifs with the tones heightened—an almost surrealistic impression. As with Bishop Bloughram's, Greene's world is out of joint and, quite rightly, the interest is held sharply "on the dangerous edge." His characters—frenetic in their fears, doubts, and despairs—strain precariously between the contraries of honesty and thievery, tenderness and brutality, hate and love.

An early influence on Greene was Robert Louis Stevenson, his mother's cousin. The young author's regard for his distinguished relative is well evidenced by the romatic vein in his own beginnings. Reading Conrad and Henry James further quickened his imagination and added depth to his insights. He also gathered from them important clues on organizing material and on the craft and style of narration. But it was Marjorie Bowen who set his creativity ablaze. Bowen was his boyhood find. Of her works, *The Viper of Milan* had the most telling impact on young Greene. It spoke of "perfect evil

13

walking the world where perfect good can never walk again, and only the pendulum ensures that after all in the end justice is done."[2] The truth of that saying staggered him. Bowen was being honest in a way most adults never are. The profundity of her insight did more than rouse an echo in Greene's soul.

Betrayal is the prize motif in Greene. The earliest and most persistent theme, it rings a recurring note throughout his work. Betrayed love, broken promises, double-crossing agents, and the manifold ways in which the life experience cheats one's expectations—all this is grist to his imagination. He even makes betrayals work for his plot; and this he does with true genius. In his stories they are often a trick to bring together the forces in conflict. They serve what Karpman[3] calls the role of the Connection. Karpman had come upon similar devices in fairy tales. On further scrutiny, he found that every story and drama uses some strategy to engage forces which, left to themselves, would tend to travel divergently. In Greene's scheme of things betrayals play an important part. Not infrequently they even guide the story to its climax.

But betrayals do more than serve the interests of the plot. Greene uses them to make weighty comments on the contemporary experience of life. The poignancy of the drama in *Brighton Rock* is greatly enhanced by Pinkie's betrayal of Rose, and Rose is his counterpart, representing the finer impulses concealed within himself. Similarly, in *The Heart of the Matter*, Scobie's tragedy does in fact begin at the quay where, from pity for the Portuguese captain, he connives at a grave offense. The very earliest of his victims is his own position as a government official. Later on, in his liaison with Helen, he would betray his fourteen years of married life. This liaison is itself a gross violation of the principles of life inasmuch as it is guided by pity alone. No other attraction is allowed—no consideration either of beauty or of goodness has any weight with Scobie. Helen is loved apparently because she is utterly unlovable. In *The Power and the Glory* the whiskey priest is faced with the possibility of a betrayal on an even grander scale. It is the insistent possibility of his betraying his sacred profession that gives point to the story of the whiskey priest.

The Man Within (1929) is the first novel Greene published and its theme is betrayal. Andrews, a cowardly member of a smuggling gang, springs a surprise on his comrades by informing on them. The police immediately crash down on the gang. Everyone of the culprits is rounded up, except Carlyon, the boss. But with Carlyon still at large no place is safe for the Judas, and Andrews takes to flight. On the outskirts of the town, by the woods, he comes upon a small cottage where Elizabeth, a young woman, sits guarding the corpse of her step-father. The girl shows sympathy, and gives him refuge; but she tries to arouse a sense of manly pride in him. She insists that if he believes he did right in informing on his colleagues, he must also go and testify at the Assizes. With much coaxing he goes. But while in town he sleeps with a prostitute—betraying the affection Elizabeth has shown him. Meanwhile the jury has found his testimony inadequate and orders the prisoners to be set free. Delayed at the prostitute's house, Andrews arrives too late to save Elizabeth from his enemies.

Greene's second novel, *The Name of Action* (1931), again has betrayal for its motif. Set in Trier it has for background the dictatorial rule of Demassener and the popular uprising against him. Demassener is a hard core puritan. He has closed down all the bars and brothels, and even has forbidden the playing of music. It is suggested he was never able to consummate his marriage. At any rate, Oliver Chant, the young British recruit to the freedom struggle, has a strong ally in Madame Demassener. Her love, however, is no great support for the cause; and in the denouement Chant bungles the revolution betraying the trust all Trier had placed in him.

Neither this book nor *Rumor at Nightfall* that followed in the next year was a publishing success. Both are derivative in theme and treatment, and lack the grip and authenticity that comes from original creation. These two books, as also *The Man Within*, suffer from a vaguely realized romanticism. Not that any one attitude is more appropriate to fiction than any other but the attitude taken ought to be pursued uniformly and with deliberation. This was not done in Greene's early work. His romantic tendencies are less than confident. They conflict with his primary outlook which is skeptical in tone. Perhaps the conflict is rooted in the author's sensibility. Impulsive by nature, he felt oppressed by a puritan ethos. It was a massive external restraint which, being internalized, made the oppression even worse. The conflict within upset his perspective. His art, in consequence, is wanting in force as well as in clarity.

The year 1932 started a new fashion with Greene. In despair over his failures he turned out a potboiler. *Orient Express* (printed in England as *Stamboul Train*) was composed in a hurry, Greene said, because money was short. Indeed, as a work of art it does not stand up to scrutiny. Still, the book was a success. The reception accorded it was a lucky break, not only because this was his first try with the techniques and style of the thriller—and Greene was quick to see how well his temperament responded to them—but more important, because of the standing it gave him with the leading literary lights of his day. Suddenly he was drawing a good deal of attention. Although not everyone approved of his portrayals of the contemporary scene, he roused a lively curiosity in most readers, and the reaction in general was benign.

Orient Express marks an important stage in Greene's development. It shows him as having shaken off the last traces of romanticism. We see him in a new mood, and Zola is his model. Greene's realism is no less stark than the master's. It is the realism of a keen observer of life and manners. Nothing seems to escape him, no detail of experience, however ugly, however prurient it may seem to another. Indeed, he implies a marked preference for the uglier side of life. The glamor of the "picture postcard" revolted him; he thought it too indecent a posture to be an option. The rough living of the primitives appeared ever so superior to the comforts of civilization. Preferable to the soulless gaiety of the cultivated West was

> even the seediness of civilization; of the sky signs in Leicester Square, the 'tarts' in Bond Street, the smell of cooking greens off Tottenham Court Road, the motor salesmen in Great Portland Street. . . It seems to satisfy temporarily, the sense of nostalgia for something lost: it seems to represent a stage further back.[4]

The farther removed civilization is from its roots, the more appalling is its response to life. Degenerate civilization is less unkind to humanity than "the smart, the new, the chic and the cerebral."⁵ At any rate, it was never unwise to contemplate decadence: for *pralaya*, the floods, presage enhanced fertility and a new creation. Indeed, who can say what splendor will not take wing from even the ashes of a civilization? Death was forgiving of one's weaknesses, and the death of a civilization allowed one some scope for new expressions. And it brought the individual closer to one's sources.

The response to *Orient Express* was not a little encouraging. The book addressed itself to an audience who had lived through one of the worst wars in the world's history. Still more immediate and frightening were memories of the Great Depression. The hunger and despair, the dread of unemployment—all this added up to form a mood. These events went to prove that all was not well with the advanced culture that produced them, that there was something radically inadequate. The average person was willing to be shown what was wrong, to be taught a better way. Greene's book found England in the sort of reflective mood it needed to start a cultural revaluation.

Quite early in his career, Greene perceived melodrama to be an apt "working tool" for the portrayal of social and moral degeneracy. A melodramatic note is already struck in *The Name of Action*, and this suited well its subject of political anarchy. Greene rarely had to 'invent' a plot; for the life he saw about had the quality of a thriller; he only had to uncover the details and organize them anew in a scheme of his own. The sense of "moral desperation" that we notice in his work is only a reflection of "the crises and confusion" of those days when the novels were written.

If their expert contrivance often seems to descend to sleight of hand; if the surrealism of their action and settings can result in efflorescences of sheer conjuring; if the mechanics of the thriller—chases, coincidences, strokes of accident, and exploding surprises—can at times collapse into a kind of demented catastrophe, these were not too remotely at odds with the possibilities of modern terrorism, police action, international intrigue and violence.⁶

"Spies, and murders, and violence, and wild motor-car chases" — all this is real life now. It is a world "remade by William Le Queux."[7]

Greene gives his thrillers added poignancy by relating them to the more ancient form of allegory. They are most successful when allegory and the immediate dramatic context are blended into a unity. Where this is done it is not unconvincing for an action to project itself generally, and as the very type of those struggles going on "unendingly in every mind and heart." Auden suggests "maybe this is why we like reading thrillers because each of us is a creature at war with himself. Further he is a self-deceptive creature who thinks he is feeling one thing or acting from one motive when his real feeling and motive are quite different."[8] Greene had his very first novel epigraphed with an adaptation of St. Paul: "There is another man within me that's angry with me." (Sir Thomas Browne). The words might well have belonged to a St. Augustine or John of the Cross, to Mahavir, Buddha or Jerome. The conflict between the higher self and the lower—St. Paul's "law of the members"—is after all a universal human experience; and being so central it is fine material for drama. And Greene has been quite explicit about his allegorical intentions.

Although Evelyn Waugh, his contemporary, scorns the use of topical interest in novels, Greene shrewdly exploits it. Indeed, few novelists of note have used so much material from the daily newspaper, and with such happy results, as does Greene. *Rumor at Nightfall* is set in a Spain torn by Carlist wars. *Orient Express* has the Depression for background. Other novels are similarly worked against contemporary events: international capitalist monopolies in *England Made Me*, racecourse murders in *Brighton Rock*, war scare in *This Gun For Hire*, diamond smuggling by neutrals and torpedoed ships in *The Heart of the Matter*. *The End of the Affair* uses war as a lived, day-to-day experience. In *The Power and the Glory*, the story of the Mexican religious persecutions is told with delicate skill. *The Quiet American* paints a vivid picture of the tragedy of Vietnam. In *It's a Battlefield* the focus is on the social unrest of the thirties at home.

It's a Battlefield takes as background the new interest in Marxism especially among the young intellectuals. The Russian experiment was still youthful in the thirties. Few had yet heard of repressions, of labor camps, witch hunts and liquidations. Capitalism lay buried under Wall Street, and what could be a more likely successor than socialism. Slogans of progress rent the skies, evoking dreams of a new age. Revolution was on every tongue. It seemed the "Glorious Millennium" was within a hand's reach. Even Greene shared in the enthusiasm and for a spell was a probationary member of the Communist party. The brief connection with the party left him gravely dissatisfied with its actual working.

The disillusion with social utopias, with politics and governments, comes through powerfully in *It's a Battlefield*. Its action begins with the death of a policeman, stabbed during a political riot. The assailant, a communist bus driver, had struck him only to protect his wife. But the incident is made out to be a case of homicide. The driver is convicted and sentenced to death. By the time the book opens even his appeal has failed. For the most part, our perspective is that of the bus driver's brother. As we follow him from office to office with faint hopes of winning a reprieve, we have a chilling vision of the sort of political bureaucracy that runs our world.

It's a Battlefield takes its title from Kinglake's *Eothen*. Kinglake wrote:

> In so far as the battlefield presented itself to the bare eyesight of men, it had no entirety, no length, no breadth, no depth, no size, no shape, and was made up of nothing except small numberless circlets commensurate with such ranges of vision as the mist might allow at each spot. . . . In such conditions, each separate gathering of English soldiery went on fighting its own little battle in happy and advantageous ignorance of the general state of the action; nay, even very often in ignorance that any great conflict was raging.

Greene's characters are not quite unaware of the "general state of the action," but they go on fighting their "little battles" as though they were. Each of them is preoccupied with private concerns. It is the fear of retirement for one, the insult of his ineffectuality for another. We note the utter helplessness of the journalist on the one hand; and we register the complacency of the Marxist leader, the hypocrisy in his speech and sentiments. We, too, sympathize with the convict's wife in her inconsolable misery.

This, his second thriller, shows Greene with sufficient control of the craft of narration. He now has a style of his own of which he is pretty confident. Although his beginnings showed some influence of Joyce, the latter's artistic creed is not for him. He certainly has little sympathy for the dogma of narrative realism. He claims it as every author's inalienable right to guide his reader in any manner he may choose. No doctrine, no aesthetic theory can interfere with a novelist's freedom. Greene does not regard art as an end in itself, but as a medium of creative expression. The rules of art serve where, and only insofar as, they answer a definite purpose. It is the needs of a specific occasion, the requirements of a particular effect that must guide the type and degree of authorial intervention. Principles of aesthetics have never made art; it is art that gives validity to the principles. In much of his early work Greene does not even make an effort to disguise his presence. He not only accompanies us to the arena and introduces us to the champions, but lest we should miss out on the nuances of the action, he stays around to guide us with a brief explanation, a philosophical aside or a reflection.

In *It's a Battlefield* there is a thorough grasp of the action. The environment is sketched incisively with swift strokes and, arrayed against this, the characters do convince. The careful attention given to the management of the milieu works to an over-all advantage, and particularly regarding characterization. Greene invests little in direct portrayal of his characters. Rather, they are studied through the camera eye, the narrative equivalent of the "medium shot", what Atkins has termed "the mass observer's vision."[9] "Both character and atmosphere are evoked by a cross sample of manipulating imagery." The key word is "manipulating." Greene is a perceptive student of people and events; but it is more than just plain observation we notice in his art. Indeed, each detail of imagery, every association is scanned with the utmost care, and directed to obtain a specific effect. There is never anything indefinite about Greene's mature art. No word or passage is superfluous, and nothing is really out of place. Economy and precision are incontestably his virtues.

An example of his style of characterization is the portraiture of the policeman's widow. The wife of the convict is our perspective. Greene speaks for her.

> Milly noticed everywhere the signs of a fussing and incompetent woman, a woman who drives the dust from one room to settle in another, who buys Danish eggs for economy and leaves the gas burning.

Similarly, the Private Secretary is covered by a quick sweep of the lens:

> One could see very clearly and to the best effect, a few selected objects: a silver casket, a volume of Voltaire exquisitely bound, a self-portrait by an advanced and fashionable Czechoslovakian.

Again, Greene shows us the vibrant London streets in a state of nervous excitement by fitting together carefully selected snapshots. Environment, in each of these cases, would appear to serve as an extension of a character's personality. Indeed, we may debate if, in reality, character and temperament are so dependent upon the accidents of an environment. But we cannot doubt that the close and organic relation Greene has established between his characters and their milieu adds noticeably to their depth and dimension.

In a well-argued essay, Austin Warren has defended this particular mode of characterization. Warren insists that setting may not only describe an individual's personality; it may be an active expression of one's will—hates, loves, desires, and ambitions. In this sense, the setting is a projection, in terms of the outside world, of a person's inner states, attitudes and emotions. A sunny disposition naturally tends towards the sunlight—but not so King Lear in his mad rage. Lear's mental state is well enough expressed by the wild storm in which he rushes about. Quoting "the self-analyst Amiel," Warren urges on us that "A landscape is a state of mind." He concedes that often it is understood simply as "the massive determinant—environment viewed as physical or social causation, something over which the individual has little individual control."[10] However, writers have proved conclusively that it may also serve, and precisely, as 'setting' for the play of individuality. Says Warren:

> environments, especially domestic interiors, may be viewed as metonymic, or metaphoric, expressions of character. A man's house is an extension of himself. Describe it and you have described him. Balzac's detailed specifications for the house of the miser Grandet or the Pension Vauquer are neither irrelevant nor wasteful. These houses express their owners; they affect, as atmosphere, those others who must live in them.[11]

Greene not only makes environment control his characters, he employs it to build their personalities. Unaided by setting, it would have been quite impossible to bring out such complexities of attitudes and behavior as his novels in fact do.

The cinematic vision—or "the mass observation"—is well suited to the sort of effects attempted in his books. *England Made Me* (1935) shows further improvement in craft. There is a remarkable mastery in the manipulation of tone and point of view. Suspense holds well. He has come to recognize his weakness for metaphysical conceits—the tendency to "wrap up" action "in thoughts, similes and metaphors"[12]—as a damper to movement. Pace consists in simple action: "a subject, a verb and an object" is its scope. Anything beyond, even an adjective, is likely to slow down pace and divert the attention. In *England Made Me* there is smooth progression, and the command over pace is good.

Its opening is a model of skillful narration. "She might have been waiting for her lover," it begins, evoking at the same time a mood of expectation and a foreboding of betrayal: maybe the loved one may never turn up. All this said in the brief space of less than a line. This novel is a favorite with the author. And indeed, its merits are many and various. Still, as a work of art it does not quite satisfy. We are presented with a gallery of portraits: Anthony, Kate, Minty and Krogh, each a slightly varied representation of Tiresias. And the landscape is that of the wasteland. Although the images are vivid, and the characters each separately convincing, the book does not quite impress. Perhaps there is a lack of depth. Because the images are familiar to us from Eliot and others, we tend to ask for more—a new insight, a larger vision. But no groundswell rises from below to give body to the (deliberate, we suspect) sense of diffuseness.

About this time Greene, along with a cousin, went on a tour through Liberia, a Black republic on Africa's west coast. This was just the impetus needed to clarify his world view. His account of the trip in *Journey Without Maps* (1936) reads fascinatingly. The unguided trek through the interior was what anyone could have wished for. It allowed him all the freedom he required to roam about and see life at firsthand. This live contact with a tribal culture was his road to Damascus. It struck him with the force of a revelation. Such supreme simplicity was a new experience to Greene. The tribal member accepted life complexly—in its power and beauty, but also in its horror. Everything had its proper place, gradation, and meaning. Nothing was rejected offhand. Indeed, whatever belonged to life was invested with a sacred significance. In Africa one had no need to transfer one's emotions; and there was never a moment of boredom. Unsophisticated and poor, this country allowed anyone greater freedom than did the civilized West.

Africa did not offer freedom from bodily want—he had not seen worse poverty anywhere. What struck Greene was the freedom of spirit which, in the face of poverty, could afford to be magnanimous. The bounty was almost godly. Variegated in its rhythms—loving, gentle, and awesome—life here excluded nothing from its purview. No social code constrained its natural flow. Flamboyant gestures did not replace its sense of mystery. One lived here at the level of instincts—not raging, nor wild, but governed with a humane wisdom. Life was unvitiated by the complex, was more authentic and intuitive, and was lived with a passion unknown to the West. Greene felt that here were "hints of an explanation." If one were to recapture passion, it must be by a return to Africa. One must come to terms with this darkness which was primitive yet ageless, innocent but no less wise.

This Gun For Hire (1936) is the first novel to come after his trip to Liberia. It does show the advantage. Africa has, as it were, brought about a sea-change in Greene's perspective. There is a new depth about him, a dimension that was missing before. Whereas he had seemed somewhat bewildered and uncertain about his goals, now there is a clear sense of direction. The characters, too, share in the quality of the dark, the simplicity and the terror, and are further enriched by this suggestion of an elemental gentleness about them. Raven, the protagonist, moves us in a way no earlier character had done.

Raven is unusually deprived, with a scarred childhood and a harelip. Generally Greene's protagonists are all anti-heroes; Raven is no exception. Society is never fair to its victims, often too ashamed of them to lend a helping hand in their struggle for existence. Raven's deformity is his manacle. His face elicits not trust, only suspicion. Even he has internalized this feeling of revulsion. The injury is no mere cicatrix on his soul: it is an open wound, livid and loathsome. Raven has drifted easily into a shady career.

"Murder didn't mean much to Raven, it was just a new job." And so he is hired by the armaments production interests to kill the head of a European state. The crime almost starts a war. It would have, if Raven, double-crossed and on the run, had not met a young girl. Although he is naturally suspicious of people, and particularly of women, Raven trusts her and he cannot resist confiding in her. The girl however persuades herself that to avert a war she ought to report the murder. Raven goes to his death doubly confirmed in his cynicism.

The book, a great success, was still no more than a trial run for the ones that followed. Many discerning critics credit *Brighton Rock* as being one of Greene's best; and with this novel we enter upon a phase of deep psychological and religious explorations. The other volumes to come under this definition are *The Power and the Glory, The Heart of the Matter, The End of the Affair* and *A*

Burnt-Out Case. We shall have occasion to discuss them individually and in detail. By 1954 Greene's interest had swung back to social and political motifs.

The Quiet American (1955) has the Indo-China war for background. The protagonist is Pyle, a quiet but impulsive American youngster. His mission is to set up a puppet government in Vietnam under American tutelage. Fowler, an Englishman, is the narrator and the reader's point of view. Degenerate in his ways and worldly wise, he is a proper representative of the milieu in which he had his origin. But Fowler has a cultural maturity which Pyle lacks. By making Fowler our perspective, Greene successfully registers his impatience with the sort of innocence that can countenance the unmitigated agony of a whole nation. The narrator remarks of Pyle: "I never knew a man who had better motives for all the trouble he caused." That remark we may safely take as Greene's own comment on the American intervention in Vietnam.

"You can't blame the innocent, . . ." Fowler says. "All you can do is to control them or eliminate them. Innocence is a kind of insanity." That tone is struck again in *A Burnt-Out Case*: innocence may not be the good it seems; at times it may be a cover for the worst egotism. Such is the case of Marie Rycker. Mme Rycker's immaturity results in a man shot dead and an African mission set in turmoil. To Mother Agnes' remark "She's a poor innocent thing, . . ." Querry responds; "Oh, innocent . . . I dare say you are right. God preserve us from all innocence. At least the guilty know what they are about."[13] Indeed, Fowler knows what he is about; Pyle only thinks he does. Fowler has seen how impossible it is to curb the latter in his zeal. He now persuades himself that in order to save Vietnam from a bloodbath, Pyle must go. He becomes a party to the American's murder. A political journalist by profession, and a shrewd man, Fowler has always prided himself on his objectivity. To keep clear of partisan affiliations has been nearly an obsession with him. But Pyle's murder has unmasked his pose of detachment. At the end, and thus the book closes, Fowler is heard wishing he could say, "sorry" to someone.

Our Man in Havana (1958), "an entertainment," is a comedy satirizing the British Secret Service. With its complex ironies, it is one of the most delightful works of Greene. The narrative style fittingly is of the simplest kind. The prose is assured; the pace, light and quiet.

The Comedians (1966) takes up its thematic note from *The Quiet American*. Here, again, the author is seen arguing in favor of some commitment, whatever the cause. A life not committed to some value is not worth living. *The Comedians* goes further still. It sees indifference as the very ultimate in egotism. Even violence may be an expression of love: "One is an imperfection of charity, the other the perfection of egoism." Compassion may prove inconvenient, may even land the individual in painful situations. But the alternative—to play safe—is to sell one's soul. Greene's comedians illustrate the condition of "The Hollow Men":

> Shape without form, shade without color
> Paralysed force, gesture without motion.

Neither alive nor quite dead, they play at life as if at a charade. There is no passion to give significance to their doings. Even sex yields no ecstasy. As with Brown, the protagonist, no enthusiasm is quite engaging in the absence of belief. No conviction has any power to inspire; neither love nor hate moves them. There are no heights, nor abysses, to their world. Brown is heard reminiscing towards the end: "I saw myself on a great plain, walking and walking on the interminable flats."

Comedy, once again, is the dominant motif in *Travels With my Aunt* (1969). Henry Pulling, a retired banker, is stuck with an elderly aunt. Henry swears by the norms of respectability, whereas Aunt Augusta follows a different code. An assiduous traveller, she supposedly has had a tumultuous life. What it was like is not stated. When Henry agrees to travel with his aunt, he has the best opportunity to find out. True to type, she guides him through a shiftless twilight society, mixing with hippies, war criminals and CIA men. We see the respectable Henry smoking pot, and breaking currency regulations. He even connives at murder. The climax comes with his belated discovery that Augusta is none other than his own mother. The travels have made him anew: now, like his mother, he is able to enjoy life, even the risk of it.

The Honorary Consul (1973) deals with a political kidnapping and its sad aftermath. The story is set in an Argentinian town, and the protagonists are Father Rivas and Dr. Plaar. A radical group, egged on by rampant poverty, injustice and bureaucratic corruption, has decided upon violent revolt. They plan to kidnap the visiting American ambassador and bargain for the release of their comrades from prison. The ambush however ends in a fiasco. For the man taken is not only not the American ambassador but actually is the British "honorary consul."

This novel brings to the fore some recurrent notes, such as the failure of institutional religion in the face of injustice and violation of human dignity. To an oppressed nation, the Argentinian church has no more consolation to offer than some pious platitudes. The character of the priest is powerfully drawn. Particularly convincing is his introspective mood and anguish when confronted with starved faces to whom he must promise an elusive spiritual reward. Frustrated, Father Rivas has given up his priesthood to join the revolutionaries. With delicate sympathy, Greene here outlines the priest's dilemma and his efforts at authenticating his vocation. But the revolutionaries are all amateurs, with hardly any experience in political action. The blunder with the kidnapping has sealed the doom not only of the cause but even of their lives.

The Human Factor (1978) is Greene's Jubilee number. It marked fifty years of novel writing. It is also his fiftieth book, of which twenty-two are novels. Like *Our Man in Havana*, this book also has espionage as its primary motif. The spy story appears to have a special fascination for the Anglo-Saxon reader. In its framework Greene's tale is reminiscent of Kim Philby and the treason he engineered in the sixties. The spy accepts no principles as valid except those of his own profession. No value, no reasons of the heart can stand up to those others. Greene's protagonist however is not a professional.

The epigraph is from Conrad: "I only know that he who forms a tie is lost. The germ of corruption has entered into his soul." Maurice Castle has formed a tie. It is Sarah, his South African wife and her son. He is also beholden to the Communists, for it is they who helped her escape from her country and its racial laws. Now that he is heading the Secret Service bureau for South Africa, Castle has vowed to inhibit the repressive policies of that government. Not that there is much he can do. But he has no doubt about where his allegiance is due. His way is leaking out useful information to the Russians. "Uncle Remus" is a particularly sensitive plan involving a collusion of Western interests with South Africa against Russia. With the leakage of this document Castle senses the enemy forces upon him. He signals the alarm and is spirited away to Moscow. Sarah however is left behind with her child. Castle's last conversation with her on the phone trails off on a weak note. "When the spring comes—" are the very last words, before the line goes dead. And we are left to surmise it will be a long time indeed before the winter thaws and the lovers are reunited.

Failure, indecision, and betrayal—all these are recurring themes. Greene's characters are all disillusioned. And they are often frightened. Caught within the tangles life ingeniously weaves around human destinies, they can think of no strategem by which to free themselves. Indeed, to what purpose a strategem? For defeat is certain. One cannot change that, at most one may delay the blow for a while. This is a distressing picture, gloomy and dark. Yet we are not sure it is not true to our experience of life. Greene does not paint his world in black and white, but in black and gray. He is a master in somber shades, and these seem to quiver on the edge of sadness. There is an echo of the *nada*, the eternal Nothing, in him. Symbols of death are on rooftops and on the roads. Mosquitoes, beetles, and bugs swarm in his world—all degenerate forms marking sterility. This is a world of dead ends. And the characters rush about hither and thither. Only in death is there any relief.

This is a vision to frighten us. But do we not recognize this smog of fear? It is the same that hovers over our own lives. Greene has simply caught and cast it in a new form. He has formed it "in terms of the great public world we all share." But his world is not at all very different from what we live in day after day. We all know the bonhomie and the adolescent brashness of the "middleclass." We have wondered what lay beneath the layers of make-up and plucked eyebrows. We are not always taken in by the mask of a meaningless smile. But we see in snatches, and we forget. Greene remembers and fits the pieces together. And his vision is larger and more comprehensive. What we see, and what he has caught in his fiction, are the varying faces of a frightful boredom. Edwin Muir was not far wrong to say that in Greene "everything is shown up in a harsh light and casts fantastic colors." "But, such is life," we can imagine Greene replying; "life is seldom more kind, or gentle." For his perceptions, melodrama was a most apt medium. He calls it his "working tool." It has enabled him "to obtain effects that would be unobtainable otherwise." What these effects are we shall presently inquire.

BRIGHTON ROCK

It is true to say that the glory of man is his capacity for salvation; it is also true to say that his glory is his capacity for damnation. The most that can be said of most of our malefactors, from statesmen to thieves, is that they are not men enough to be damned.

— T.S. Eliot[1]

There are plenty of thrillers in contemporary fiction but *Brighton Rock*, with all the features of a common potboiler, commands a rare distinction. There is pace in it, and high-grade suspense; the inevitable sexual motif is worked casually into the plot. The action is about delinquency and gang wars; it treats of violence and poverty in the city slums. The crisis occurs when society stakes out its claims and, to protect its forms, hunts the challenger to his death. There is grim realism in the telling, but realism of a type that is compatible with the thriller scheme. Contemporary life, it would seem, lends itself naturally to the requirements of melodrama.

Apparently the book was conceived as a story of murder and detection; the interest was to be on the chase, something exciting in its own right. The original plan would have allowed a larger and more kindly emphasis on Ida Arnold, the portly society girl who functions as the sleuth. But Ida does not move us very much, and she does not seem to enjoy the author's sympathy. It is Pinkie, the haunted murderer, who steals the show. For the most part he becomes our perspective. As though unnoticed by the author,

---

All quotes from *Brighton Rock* (Penquin Books, 1975).

Pinkie has dealt the coup to his rival and taken control. The outcome is a tragedy with Pinkie as hero.

As with the Elizabethan tragi-comedies, in *Brighton Rock* everyone has his pick. Being a thriller the action makes a direct appeal to popular taste, but the 'high brow' and the connoisseur are not left in the cold. There is a strong emphasis on pace and suspense; but these effects do not supplant character. Pinkie is well developed to bear the weight of a tragedy. The tragic and the melodramatic elements are well balanced and harmonized in a complex pattern. The result is a work of unique beauty.

The tragic note appears early in the novel. It is associated with the very air of Brighton. The holiday crowds, jostling through the streets to the pier, are not exuberant; nor are they free from care. On the contrary they are described as "cramped" and "closed" and "bewildered." They seem "determined" about something, but in a "weary" sort of way. We cannot trust their laughter either; it shows the strain. By a clever manipulation of descriptive detail, Greene guides us along. Our expectations are aroused in the right direction, and to the right degree. Indeed, he has announced his theme in the epigraph: "This were a fine reign/ To do ill and not hear of it again," from *The Witch of Edmonton* by Dekker, Ford, *et al*.

But not to hear of evil done is not real life. Only melodrama allows for happenstances. There is room there for contingency, for coincidences; not in tragedy. In tragedy, evil is fertile and breeds its own kind. Thus Pinkie, our protagonist, is condemned by the forces acting within him. Every move of his complicates the situation and leads him into something even worse. The murder of Hale has profited him in no way; it has only set the tone to his future career. For there is always the need to cover up a first crime—by murder or even worse. And at the end Pinkie's position is no more secure than at first. Indeed, it is immeasurably worse. Pinkie, like Macbeth, is urged on by a limitless ambition; and like Macbeth he, too, draws upon himself the hounds of retribution.

Brighton Rock might well have been a disaster. The attempt to blend tragedy and melodrama is not without its risks. The work might have ended up as two different books, within the same cover only by mistake. Instead, we are offered an integral experience. There is rare ability in the telling; and the elements of the two genres are well apportioned and fused. In consequence, the novel emerges in a manner both fresh and exciting. It is indeed a tribute to Greene's aesthetic ingenuity that what might have been a flaw, a hesitation, a serious failure of invention, has been so transformed. For what accounts for the peculiar charm of this book is precisely the tension built by the action of tragedy upon melodrama.

Pinkie and Ida represent the hostile forces, and a confrontation between them cannot but be dynamic. Their interaction is also the basis on which the two genres are linked. They speak for opposing world-views. Greene seems to take a naughty delight in exposing the tavern girl. With her "monumental legs," her "blown-up charms" and her "air of ribald luxury," she is the social aesthete. It is cliches that govern her life—"Right and Wrong," vengeance, and "a bit of fun." Hers is a vaguely realized moral sense. She hardly sets any store by the individual and his uniquely personal claims. Pinkie, at the opposite extreme, cares nothing for society and its rights. He is the embodiment of an unqualified egotism. His "slatey eyes [are] touched with the annihilating eternity." (p. 21)   Still, he has ample energy. It is only because his vitality has been repressed that he has grown dangerous

The two worlds are naturally incompatible. Hers, the world of unregarding morality, is challenged and destroyed by his primitive dynamism, even as she hounds him to his death. But strangely it is his egotism that wins out in the end. For it opens a door to him, allows him an entry into the realm of transcendental realities. He is insistently drawn to the finest experiences open to man. And Ida never is.

Ida is allowed very little background. It is Pinkie who shares most of the author's awareness. She does not enjoy the author's knowledge that Right and Wrong are cliches, and without absolute value. And so she cannot realize that they have no binding force, that as Greene says in *Orient Express* they are simply slogans "mouthed by politicians on innumerable platforms, printed in bad type on bad paper in endless newspapers."[2] Often they serve as machines of torture to whet the sadistic impulses of a corrupt bureaucracy. The little thief they clamp in jail, but the smarter ones are encouraged to climb up to power and even greater influence. Pompously, almost, Ida is built up as a keeper of the social conscience.

> Vengeance was Ida's. . . . If Fred had killed himself, she'd find it out, the papers would print the news, someone would suffer. Ida was going to begin at the beginning and work right on. She was a sticker.(p. 37)

A little later, digging down "into her deepest mind, the plane of memories, instincts, hopes," she comes up with a statement of her creed. " 'I like fair play,' she said. She felt better when she'd said that and added with terrible lightheartedness: 'An eye for an eye, Phil. . .' " (p. 77)

There is a subtle sense of irony here. Ida has the makings of a Eumenides, but her "terrible lightheartedness" gives her away. The author indeed shows a cunning control of his material—"like a film director who makes his personal comment with a camera angle" (to use his own words about Mauriac).[3] Ida's loud claims to moral guardianship are tried on the touchstone of experience and found wanting. She does not come off well at all. "Vengeance was Ida's just as much as reward was Ida's." And what reward does she lay claim to? "The soft gluey mouth affixed in taxis, the warm hand-clasp in cinemas, the only reward there was." If that is all there is, surely it is not much to boast of. Still, Ida has her own motives: "vengeance and reward—they both were fun." (p. 37)

"Right and wrong," she declares on another occasion; "I believe in right and wrong. . ."

> and delving a little deeper, with a sigh of happy satiety, she said, "it's going to be exciting, it's going to be fun, it's going to be a bit of life, Old Crowe," giving the highest praise she could give to anything. . . . (p. 44)

There is not much ambiguity about this character. Of Ida's extreme vulgarity there is no doubt. Her sentiments are cheap and, if

they are at times played up to the tone of the sublime, it is only for
the pleasure of seeing them deflated further on. Her favorite haunts
are the race-course, the cinema and the airless Brighton pubs. The
setting describes the character.

"Poor old Fred" is but a casual acquaintance; she can hardly
even recall his features. Yet in death he has apparently grown in
importance. The "cheap drama and pathos" of his last frightened
hours appeal to her. She would follow up on the death in real
earnest.

Ida is decidedly sentimental. We are told "she was of the
people," but not one genuine sentiment is evident in her. The
people she belonged to are rather products of mass media. She is
most at home with cheaply popular fiction. "She cried in cinemas
at 'David Copperfield'." When drunk, old songs came easily to her
lips. "Her homely heart was touched by the word 'tragedy'."(p. 32)

There is yet another side to her character, and this is shown up in
her frigid fascination with funerals. "Death shocked her." Yet her
obsession is such she cannot quite keep herself from a funeral. She
is there at Fred's wake. The body lay wrapped in a wreath of
flowers—but what an insult! Surely, "that wasn't life."

> Life was sunlight on brass bedposts, Ruby port, the leap of
> the heart when the outsider you have backed passes the post
> and the colors go bobbing up. Life was poor Fred's mouth
> pressed down on hers in the taxi, vibrating with the engine
> along the parade. (p. 36)

Life then is a parade of enjoyments, even small ones. Not for her
the great desire, not the spasm, nor the fire. Her yearnings never
billow up; they only smolder on.

She dreads the annihilation of death. It is so frightening she
dares not even indulge the thought. "That one day she too, like
Fred, would be where the worms . . . her mind couldn't take that
track."(p. 144)   The justification for life was to enjoy it. She has
aphorisms ready to dull ordinary disappoinments. A broken leg or
a lover lost were nothing much to cry over. "Broken hearts. . .
always mend." Always? At any rate, it did no good to sulk over it

and "life was so important." (p. 36)   At Henekey's, soaked in Guinness, she is quite happy. She was "having a good time." (p. 29)   And she felt kindly to all the world. "Have a fine time . . . a bit of fun. . ."—she was enjoying life to the hilt.

Whenever we meet Ida, she is "out for a bit of fun." (p. 18)   At a restaurant she comes upon Phil Corkery, an acquaintance. "You wouldn't mind a bit of fun here?" Phil suggests. And pat comes the reply, "Why should I? It doesn't do anyone any harm that I know of." It would be quite irrelevant to suggest that it might do no good either. It is the moment that matters and the ritual before her. "It's human nature," she said. "She bit at her eclair and repeated the familiar password. 'It's only fun after all'." (p. 145)

That "after all" is devastating. It puts her view of life in a poor light. Like second-rate wares, her life is all a gloss. Sex is only "fun after all." There is not an overtone of tenderness, no affirmation of another person. It is not "the awful daring of a moment's surrender,[4]" that T.S. Eliot speaks of in *The Waste Land*; it is only a moment's indulgence. "Fun" is the habit, justified as "human nature" and defined by a negative: "does no one any harm." That is why she disturbs us. She is a phony, and we sense danger even in her optimism, "whether she was laughing in Henekey's or weeping at a funeral or a marriage." (p. 36)

The surrender of self is at the core of love and, this being quite out of bounds for Ida, she has little satisfaction from the act. She goes through the motions all right but is denied the ecstasy. "Men always failed you when it came to the act," she broods."She might just as well have been to the pictures." (p. 151)   Only habits stick. And so to lull her unease she has recourse to her aphorisms, again: "a bit free-and-easy perhaps, a bit Bohemian."

> It wasn't as if she got anything out of it, as if like some people she sucked a man dry and cast him aside. . . . God didn't mind a bit of human nature.(p. 151)

Still, this is a terrible admission—not to have "got anything out of it." It comes through as an indictment of her way of life. After all the frenzied efforts, after a lifetime in pursuit of pleasure, there is apparently nothing for her but sterility. The author could not have implied a stronger condemnation.

Pinkie offers a picture in contrast. No liquor for him to dull the senses. He scorns all forms of sensuality and is deeply suspicious of the pose of cheeriness. He never feels at one with the holiday crowds. On the floors of the Cosmopolitan, the "two-backed beasts" reeling to rhythm only nauseate him. Sex is taboo.

Pinkie's attitude to life, like Ida's, is defined in relation to sex. But he spurns even the word. That word expresses a relationship that his system cannot tolerate. That relationship is too outrageous for him even to want to discuss it. It was an affront to his ego, a temptation and, at one time, he had even contemplated becoming a priest so he could escape the urge.

"A priest? You a priest? That's good," Dallow said. He laughed without conviction, uneasily shifted his foot so that it trod in a dog's ordure.

"What's wrong with being a priest?" the Boy asked. "They know what's what. They keep away —" his whole mouth and jaw loosened: he might have been going to weep: he beat out wildly with his hands towards the window: Woman Found Drowned, two-valve, *Married Passion,* the horror — "from this."

"What's wrong with a bit of fun?" Dallow took him up, scraping his shoe against the pavement edge. (p. 164)

"This" is the newspaper headlines stuck to his windowpane and the cheap sex manuals Dallow had bought at the pennystore. To most of his gang sex is just "fun." At least on this score, they were on Ida's side. Pinkie must fight his battle alone. "The word 'fun' shook the Boy like malaria." Only the author has sympathy for him.

Pinkie is understood to be a victim of childhood trauma. Childhood is an important stage in everyone's life; for Greene's hero it is significantly so. Greene likes to quote from the poem, *Germinal,* composed by George William Russell ("AE"):

> In ancient shadows and twilights
> Where childhood has strayed
> The world's great sorrows were born
> And its heroes were made.
> In the lost boyhood of Judas
> Christ was betrayed.

"The Saturday night exercise" of his parents rings a recurrent note in the Boy's mind. As a child he often lay awake watching them from his single bed, quite forlorn. The "stealthy movement . . . in the other bed" was no reassurance. In the Boy's imagination it was early established as something wildly ignoble, a baffling and horrid ritual.

> His father panted like a man at the end of a race and his mother made a horrifying sound of pleasurable pain. He was filled with hatred, disgust, loneliness: he was completely abandoned; he had no share in their thoughts—. . . a soul in purgatory watching the shameless act of a beloved person. (p. 186)

Pinkie never got over the memory, and so for him sex is not a type of the ecstatic, but an index to the world's evil. Never again would he trust it.

Thus Pinkie's relationship with Rose is vitiated from the start. "When he looked at the girl who admired him, the poison oozed out again."(p. 88)   He too is roused to a passion, but not of the usual sort. With him it is a sullen disgust, as if she might defile him or deprive him of something very precious and his own.

> He watched her with his soured virginity, as one might watch a draught of medicine offered that one would never, never take: one would die first—or let others die. (p. 88)

Nevertheless he goes with her. He is compelled to because she knew about the murder and he had to keep her mouth locked. If he married her the law could not force her anymore to testify against him. But "it wouldn't be for long." It would only be a last resort, and a ploy to give him time. "He didn't want *that* relationship with anyone: the double bed, the intimacy, it sickened him like the idea of age. . . To marry—it was like ordure on the hands." (pp. 100-101)

He is scared both of sex and of the thought of having to endure the company of another for perhaps a lifetime. He has seen what twenty-five years of marriage have done to Prewitt and his spouse. He has watched her creeping about in her basement, hair tousled and with the mark of weariness and hatred etched on her face. Incredible, how anyone could look forward to such a relationship. Worse still, that people should want to qualify "a dirty act" with fine words such as "love, beauty . . ." (p. 92) They indeed knew nothing. But Pinkie is not one to be taken in by lovely words. "There was nothing to be excited about, no gain to recompense you for what you lost."(pp. 92-93)

Pinkie is irremediably egotistic. Consequently even his asceticism is tainted: evil is his *raison d'etre*. Granted this, he is still a more weighty character than Ida. In Greene one learns the use of *epoche*, the art of suspending one's beliefs. Hatred and love appear intermittently as varied expressions of the same experience. The lieutenant of police in *The Power and the Glory* is described as "a little dapper figure of hate carrying his secret of love." Yet he is the first to recognize in his much slandered opponent "a good man," and a hero. He even jeopardizes his good reputation to be of service to him. Bendrix, the narrator of *The End of the Affair*, similarly, confuses his passion for hatred. In Greene's fictional world, love and hate are not antithetic. Strangely they appear even as bed fellows. True, being elemental impulses they are somewhat similar, too; and they are expressed with an intensity unusual with other emotions. At any rate, the author is decidedly on Pinkie's side. The Boy's egotism is preferable to him to the sterile charm of a gadabout like Ida. And Pinkie has all the vitality.

Brighton treats Pinkie as an outcast, which compliment he returns to it. Ida on the other hand is no alien to this society. She belongs to it—and not only to Brighton.

> There was no place in the world where she felt a stranger. . . .
> There was nothing with which she didn't claim kinship: the
> advertising mirror behind the barman's back flashed her own
> image at her: the beach girls went giggling across the parade:
> the gong beat on the steamer for Boulogne: it was a good life.
> (p. 72)

Not so good about the dark regions where Pinkie held his sway.
Everywhere else she was quite at home for she had her friends
everywhere.

> She had only to appeal to any of them, for Ida Arnold was on
> the right side. She was cheery, she was healthy, she could get a
> bit lit with the best of them. She liked a good time, her big
> breasts bore their carnality frankly down the Old Steyne, but
> you had only to look at her to know that you could rely on
> her. She wouldn't tell tales to your wife, she wouldn't remind
> you next morning of what you wanted to forget, she was
> honest, she was kindly, she belonged to the great middle law-
> abiding class, her amusements were their amusements, her
> superstitions their superstitions . . . she had no more love for
> anyone than they had. (p. 80)

Ida is civilized and she is liberal; she is clean and sterilized in her
habits. In her seem incarnate the whole of contemporary social
ethos.

In a later scene the antagonists are made to confront each other.
The timing of it could not be improved upon. The setting is Rose's
room. Ida is already there as the scene begins, trying to persuade
her to testify against the murderer. Pinkie enters the room, and is
suddenly aware of how much common ground he and Rose
covered between them. He felt no antagonism now. There was only
"a faint nostalgia": "She belonged to his life, like a room or a chair:
she was something which completed him. . . ."

> What was most evil in him needed her: it couldn't get along
> without goodness. . . . She was good, he'd discovered that,
> and he was damned: they were made for each other. (p. 126-28)

An unusual aligning of forces, this. The very good and the very evil fight on the same side, but there is no fraternizing between either and the mediocre. Ida protests weakly to Pinkie: "You leave her alone . . . I know all about you." But her tone is defensive—as if she knew soon she herself must leave. She did not belong here.

> It was as if she were in a strange country: the typical English-woman abroad. She hadn't even got a phrase book. She was as far from either of them as she was from Hell—or Heaven. (pp. 126-27)

Heaven and Hell were locked in the strangest of alliances. What business was it of hers to interfere?

The rhetoric enlarges upon Ida's inconsequence. "She doesn't know what mortal sin is," laughs Rose with scorn. Apparently not even Hell would have her. "Right and wrong. That's what she talks about. . . . As if she knew." The girl dismisses her with contempt: "Oh, she won't burn. She couldn't burn if she tried."(p. 113).   And this is what differentiates her from the older woman: she could burn. She was worthy of hell, and so was Pinkie. They had the power to choose between heaven and hell, although there is never a doubt about what Rose's choice is to be. She would share his lot, even pain unending. "I'd rather burn with you than be like her." (p. 114)

In the denouement Rose questions Pinkie: "Is *she* good?" " 'She?' The Boy laughed. 'She's just nothing.' " (p. 127)   And the author nods his approval. Pinkie's egotistic energy is preferred to Ida's smug moralism. It is true she achieves a sort of success inasmuch as she drives the boy to his death, but even in triumph she comes through as a paltry figure. Greene is incontestably with the hell-bound pair.

However, it is not enough for an author to indicate his private sympathies, he must also persuade us and carry us along. Greene effects this transvaluation by means of a manipulating rhetoric. R.W.B. Lewis points out how this is done. "The conventional values of right and wrong," he says, "are lured into prominence and then annihilated." Greene does this, as Lewis observes, "by a

series of seeming contradictions that sometimes appear strained
. . ., but often make arresting similes."[5]

Oxymorons are powerful weapons in his hands. He uses them to
deflate the familiarly ascribed dignity of conventional ideas. Ida's
optimism is said to be "remorseless." Her compassion is "merci-
less." By a collusion of apparently antithetic notions, a point of
view emerges which is Greene's very own. He implies that an opti-
mistic attitude is not enough. Nor is optimism always right. It may
yield nothing unless it is nurtured in humility. Similarly,
compassion is not genuine unless it is sensitive to the concerns and
feelings of the other.

Pinkie's union with Rose is not very "happy" but at least it is
fruitful. There is somewhat of passion and ecstasy in it. So far as it
goes it is satisfying, although it does not go very far. "Good or evil
lived in the same country, spoke the same language, came together
like old friends, feeling the same completion." (p. 127) Ida's
numerous liaisons, we have seen, failed to mediate this sense of
completion for her. This fact in her life explodes familiar valu-
ations of morality. But Greene is not just an iconoclast. He has a
very clear purpose in challenging tradition.

This authorial attitude towards Pinkie merits some further remarks. It is not as if he has discovered in his protagonist new veins
of virtue. On the contrary, he is neither noble nor handsome. He is
not even decent to deal with. The only good he could ever boast of
is his energy and even that is of a twisted kind. He is a brute and
destructive; does he deserve the sympathy the author lavishes upon
him? On one consideration alone: he is himself a victim. Every
victim moves us, however momentarily.

It does not take much perception to see Pinkie as emotionally inadequate. He is mentally deformed and subject to many an
obsession. Francis Kunkel offers the insight that it may even be
that Pinkie "finds sexual release and relief from the horror inside
him in the practice of torments."[6] So some critics opine. The root
of his evil then is a sexual problem. His energies are not
channelled. Instead, they are "repressed" and "perverted" into
sadistic enjoyments. His "abstention from liquor, chocolates,
cigarettes, dancing, gambling and girls," then, are varied ex-

pressions of a psychic condition. They are ways of an "escape," and are a "sign that he is afraid to get entangled with life."[7]

Other opinions hold that Pinkie is a character meant to suggest a critique of social injustice. Greene had done the same with Raven in *This Gun for Hire*. According to this line of thought, both Pinkie and Raven "are pathetic reminders of the existence of the 'submerged tenth' . . ." In them, as Gilbert Thomas says, is implied "a necessary warning that such men do exist in our midst with very little to hinder their headlong course of moral and physical destruction."[8]

Pinkie himself seems to support this argument as, for instance, when he makes ("with dreary pride") this fantastic claim: " 'I suppose I'm real Brighton,' as if his heart contained all the cheap amusements, the Pullman cars, the unloving weekends in gaudy hotels, and the sadness after coition." (p. 220) The book's title reinforces the claim. Perhaps not many readers are aware that the "rock" of the title is a stick of hard candy with the word "Brighton" etched indelibly across its length. Hence the punch in Ida's cynical observation with reference to Pinkie: "Bite it all the way down, you'll still read Brighton." (p. 198)

Obviously Pinkie's character owes much of its horror and darkness to his early upbringing. Both his childhood and the town where he grew up went to shape him, both played a part in fashioning his sensibility. The repressions of childhood evidently shut him off from a good deal of experience, particularly those that might have enhanced his life. The incipient cruelty of his environs further hardened his heart. All this combined to make him hostile to the rest of the world. He had not had even an imperfect vague romantic conception of Good. "Heaven was a word," a state or place unknown and undreamt. (p. 228) It was but something on the other side of death.

All this then gives to the character a sense of depth and history. The twin theories only prove how convincing the portrayal really is. But to regard the Boy as merely a stunted child or "a victim of the slums" is to miss a dimension. Surely *Brighton Rock* is not "a sociological invective against the causes of juvenile delinquency." This is only a part of the rhetoric. Indeed, Brighton has contributed to the viciousness; but we must never forget that the same soil has also nurtured a goodness, Rose. As H.R. Haber notes, "The boy's compulsion to commit evil is thus as much spiritual as it is environmental."[9] Rose's character is the exact antithesis to Pinkie's evil. She is the book's symbol of creative innocence. His compulsion then may not be explained away; nor can he disown all responsibility. It is much too complex. His evil is truly a spiritual condition.

Pinkie is somewhat of a spoilt priest. There is a suggestion of thwarted spiritual ambitions. There was a time when he had strained after the Transcendent, he had sought after redemption, had yearned for peace. He "was in a choir once," he tells Rose. It must have been a passion with him at that time, for the prayers and the music of the liturgy keep haunting him. "*Agnus dei, qui tollis peccata mundi, dona nobis pacem.*" The invocation for peace, addressed to Christ whose lamb-like innocence and forbearance must mediate peace for mankind. On earth "a glimpse of Heaven," it is solely the gift of the divine spirit. And we suspect even Pinkie had once enjoyed such a glimpse. For his voice now is broken with a touch of regret."In his voice a whole lost world moved—the lighted corner below the organ, the smell of incense and laundered surplices, and the music."(p. 52)

All that is past. It is only a memory now, and Pinkie has given up the habit of hope forever. His instincts have been poisoned. His innocence corrupted. And corruption in humans is a willed act. It is a decision in knowledge. This is all perhaps that the old priest implies in the epilogue. "*Corruptio optimi pessima,*" he exclaims. The worst is the good corrupted. The suggestion is that Pinkie has not been always so evil.

But the boy we meet in the novel is marked with signs of "the annihilating eternity." He is not only cruel, he revels in his cruelty. He enjoys tormenting his victims. Nails, splinters—anything at all is a weapon in his hands. But in the touch of razor blades he takes a particular pleasure. He has an itch to tear a strip of sticking plaster from Spicer's cheek so he might see the skin break. Rose lifts her face for a kiss, and all he wants is to "strike her and make her scream." (p. 167)

At least on one occasion the demonic in him comes out into fuller view. Pinkie and Rose have decided to get married. They are now at the registrar's office to solemnize their vows. Rose is a bit aflutter with thoughts of the coming event, the enormous significance of what they are about to do. "We're going to do a mortal sin," she murmurs. The act of signing the marriage contract was like signing away their two souls to the devil. It was even worse: it was a desecration of the sacrament, a mockery of God. But Pinkie's response to her is a sneer. "It'll be no good going to confession ever again," he tells her "with bitter and unhappy relish." "As long as we're both alive." (p. 167)

He watches her with a sort of pride. He has already won her over to himself. The contagion has taken effect.

> He had graduated in pain: first the school dividers had been left behind. Next the razor. He had a sense now that the murders of Hale and Spicer were trivial acts, a boy's game, and he had put away childish things. Murder had only led up to this—this corruption. He was filled with awe at his own powers. (p. 167)

With the marriage he has bought "his temporal safety in return for two immortalities of pain." He has no doubt that he is doomed forever, that this is a mortal sin. "And he was filled with a kind of gloomy hilarity and pride." (p. 169)

Pinkie believes himself damned once and for all, and he has come to reconcile himself to the fact. "He saw himself now as a full grown man for whom the angels wept." (p. 169) He has reached the dead end; there is no escape from here. But the "here," the prison, is himself—a room haunted by the demons of thwarted desires, ambitions, pride. But he is resolved to survive here, and even to excel. This is his portion; he will triumph in it. He scarcely can conceive of an experience except in terms of pain.

The author, however, does not agree that the decision is anything so final. He makes goodness pursue and attack Pinkie's evil, not only in the person of Rose but also directly. Even as he is driving her to the place set for her suicide, he has "a sense that somewhere, like a beggar outside a shuttered house, tenderness stirred." But the beggar belonged out in the cold, and Pinkie would not let love in. "He was bound in a habit of hate." (p. 231)   He has no use for "human contacts, other people's emotions washing at the brain." To be left alone—this was his need. And to have "nothing to think about but himself. Myself: the word echoed hygienically on among the porcelain basins, the taps and plugs and wastes." (p. 231)

His egotism is so extreme, and alarmingly entrenched, that Pinkie reminds us of someone possessed. No less a critic than R.W.B. Lewis has called him a type of the anti-Christ.[10] Another critic, H.R. Haber, describes him as a pollutor of the sacraments.[11] Whether or not Greene meant to emphasize Pinkie's actions as a ritual of evil is not certain. But his hell worthiness is never really questioned. The urge is there: demonic, and powerfully insistent. A small provocation is all it takes to spill the venom that is dammed up within. "It's not what you do," he boasts ingenuously to Rose. "It's what you think. . . . It's in the blood. Perhaps when they christened me, the holy water didn't take. I never howled the devil out." (p. 127)

Naturally he no longer takes "any stock in religion." However, he is fully possessed of the polarities of religious experience. He has definite convictions regarding them, particularly regarding Hell. "Hell—it's just there," he exhorts Rose. "You don't need to think of it—not before you die." (p. 91)   Yet nothing occupies him so much as this. "The Boy couldn't picture any eternity except in terms of pain." (p. 97)

"Life's not so bad," Rose says imploringly but a while before her planned suicide. But the boy screams at her:

> "Don't believe it. . . I'll tell you what it is. It's a jail; it's not knowing where to get some money. Worms and cataract, cancer. You hear 'em shrieking from the upper windows—children being born. It's dying slowly." (p. 226)

Not entirely untrue—only his vision does not span wide enough. He proceeds to make of his fragmentary insights an absolute creed.

"*Credo in unum Satanam*," he mocks, inverting the Christian testament of faith. It is then that we are suddenly made aware of "the slatey eyes . . . touched with the annihilating eternity."

In Pinkie's character maybe Greene meant to present "the conscience of his graceless historical world." Haber thinks so. But the boy is only "an attribute of Greene's spiritual sphere." He cannot contain the whole of it by himself. He must need to be supplemented by his opposite, the polarity of the Good.

Rose is a perfect foil to Pinkie's evil genius. If Pinkie is conditioned by his environment, Rose's situation is never any better. They both have very unhappy associations of childhood. Both have the same moody parents. The cold stove, the unwashed floors, and the table strewn with crumbs of stale bread—none of this is peculiar to Pinkie alone. Dirt and ugliness are the common heritage between them. Yet all this had such diverse effects upon the two. It confirmed Pinkie in his cynicism and he has become a sadist. Rose on the other hand has only grown in compassion.

The narrative discredits Pinkie's scornful remark that Rose is "just green." She has never been ignorant about Pinkie. From the start she has known about the murder. She is not quite unaware that he may be courting her only to stop her from testifying. "She knew by tests as clear as mathematics that Pinkie was evil." But she has the audacity of the very young and of one very much in love. She believes love must conquer all. Her love, the unconditional surrender of it, cannot fail to draw an echo within his soul. And she is prepared to wait even a lifetime to see it flower.

> She was like a child who crosses her fingers and swears her private oath. She said gently: "I don't care what you've done" as she might have denied interest in a broken window pane . . . (p. 113)

And Pinkie *is* moved. "Some knowledge of the astuteness of her simplicity, the long experience of her sixteen years, the possible depths of her fidelity touched him." He is awed by such trust. The magnanimity of her promise renders him "speechless". He had learned he could buy fidelity by force, perhaps by threats. But this which Rose was offering him was purely gratuitous. It beat him.

Thus Pinkie and Rose together represent the spiritual sphere. He is the symbol for a supreme egotism. Nothing and nobody is too dear or sacred to sacrifice to his own interest. She on the other hand is distressed by even the crying of a child. But it is in agreeing to a suicide pact with Pinkie that she proves the magnitude of her love. Sensitized to spiritual realities, they are very much alive to the awesome dignity of deciding their own destiny. Before the clear diamond of their deeper perception, Ida's moralism is but a bauble. A total stranger to their world, she has not the slightest conception of the sort of worries that torment the pair of lovers. "Right and Wrong," honor, and "fun"—these were her diet. But for Pinkie and Rose "their taste was extinguished by stronger foods—Good and Evil." (pp. 199-202) Even to acknowledge the spiritual absolutes is to come a step nearer to freedom.

Discussing Baudelaire, T.S. Eliot observed that "it is better . . . to do evil than to do nothing," that his "capacity for damnation" is as much "the glory of man" as his capacity for salvation.[12] In *Brighton Rock* the two extremes are never wholly at variance. They meet and acknowledge each other. Inasmuch as he has established a relationship with Rose, the implication is that Pinkie's viciousness is not the final word.

But neither tragedy nor melodrama could support this additional meaning. The focus of melodrama is Ida; tragedy is realized in the treatment of Pinkie's character. Pinkie's potential for salvation, the subtle movement of the divine within the soul, is ordinarily beyond the scope of tragedy. This had to be indicated by other means, by structures of a different nature. Greene's way is to work a frame of allusions into the narrative.

Brighton Rock, then, is worked on at least three different levels. They cross and recross each other, and it is a tribute to Greene's skill that the experience is one of unity and enrichment. The third level, of allegory, is woven neatly into the texture of the action. Often it is placed in Pinkie's consciousness. As the story gathers momentum, the stress within Pinkie is enhanced. A case in point occurs during the drive to complete the suicide pact. The "sin" of the nights before is rather on Rose's mind. She wonders if perhaps

Pinkie repented their coming together be-cause of the sanction of eternal punishment. But he assures her to the contrary.

> It was quite true—he hadn't hated her; he hadn't even hated the act. There had been a kind of pleasure, a kind of pride, a kind of—something else. . . . An enormous emotion beat on him; it was like something trying to get in, the pressure of gigantic wings against the glass. *Dona nobis pacem.* (p. 239)

The sexual union mediated for the boy something so fine he cannot name it. Obviously he has never known anything like that before. Even the memory of it affects him in a peculiar way. "An enormous emotion beat on him." It is clearly something beyond him and overpowering in its effects. Whatever it be, it has found out the weak and brittle spot in him and is applying the pressure. Wings suggest open skies, a limitless freedom. He himself is the object of gigantic efforts.

Transcendence is a frightening possibility. It signifies new demands made on his person. He must break once and for all from all that he has hitherto been, break from habits of thought and behavior, and even from memory. He must acquire new habits. Although his soul hankers after peace, the price is just too high. It may well be that the cry from within him called up the Wings, but he has no will to meet the demands.

> He withstood it, with all the bitter force of the school bench, the cement playground, the St. Pancras waiting room, Dallow's and Judy's secret lust, and the cold unhappy moment on the pier. If the glass broke, if the beast—whatever it was—got in, God knows what it would do. He had a sense of a huge havoc—the confession, the penance, and the sacrament—and awful distraction, and he drove blind into the rain. (pp. 239-40)

Still his heart cries, "Peace"; still the Wings beat on his door; but his spirit is still locked in habits of hate. This is conflict of the first order and promises to be solid drama.

However, the action of the Divine upon the human soul does not ordinarily come within the purview of a narrative scheme. It is a subtle pressure, a still small voice speaking to the heart, a gentle throbbing at the depths of our self. And yet, remarkably, Greene, *has* given it a scheme. Framed within the network of reiterating allusions, the quiet pursuit is a thing alive. It operates through snatches of music, through remembered fragments of the liturgy, and through symbols of gull and water.

Allegory is perhaps the freest of narrative schemes inasmuch as its progress is unhampered by rules of time and space. It may both range back in time and reach out to the future, and no law prevents its jumping the arbitrary barriers of space. And this, maybe, is what Robert O. Evans has in mind when he speaks of "a sense of tremendous historical perspective and spatial extension. "[13] The allegorist enjoys a much wider latitude than the conventional storyteller, perhaps because his art operates at the deeper levels of the Subconscious where the disparate areas of our experience are fused into "an organic meaningful unity."[14] Ezra Pound, T.S. Eliot, and Joyce were all aware of this, and made ample and creative use of the advantage. Often in their work the "here-now" becomes extended in meaning to the "always and everywhere." And this effects, in the reader, a sense of "sudden liberation." Even an instant of charged perception can thus illumine thought that complex meanings are rendered easy and a whole new world lights up before us.

Greene makes effective uses of allegory in the interweaving of motifs in the minds of his characters. In a passage noted above, Pinkie's sudden impulse towards freedom is supported by a liturgical theme. With Ida urging her to testify against Pinkie, Rose is haunted by a Biblical motif: treachery and a god-like love. "A God wept in a garden and cried out upon a cross."

> "You're crazy," the woman said. "I don't believe you'd lift a finger if he was killing you."
> Rose came slowly back to the outer world, greater love hath no man than this. She said, "Maybe I wouldn't." (p. 199)

The scheme of allusions is the more remarkable for being

worked into the base of the melodramatic structure. It is a montage and, like Eliot's in *The Waste Land*, carries great powers of
conviction. Greene takes pains, as Evans points out, to ensure that
we are moved by his story of "ageless religious conflict within the
human soul." [15] To this end the dove-tailing of allegory and melodrama works greatly to his advantage.

The liturgical motifs are stated, and repeated over and again, in
the form of truncated phrases from the Ordinary of the Mass. At
every major turn of his life's story such phrases come to Pinkie's
lips: "*Agnus dei, qui tollis peccata mundi . . . dona nobis pacem.*"
It is an invocation to Christ, "the Lamb of God, who takes away
the world's sins." It is a prayer for mercy, for forgiveness, and for
peace that hopefully would ensue from remis sion of sins. The
prayer is on Pinkie's lips as he decides to betray Rose into
marriage. It follows him on his decision to do Spicer in. It pursues him even more urgently on the long final drive which was to
dispose of Rose on a suicide pact. Sin is said to be an act of
rebellion against the Spirit. The stronger resistance Pinkie puts up,
the greater the determination of the divine Hound.

The prayer beats out a rhythm of haunting intensity in Pinkie's
soul. The more diabolical he gets, the more insistent its call. It is
Pinkie's tragedy that much as he yearns for it, he is not capable of
the works that bring about peace.

> His imagination wilted at the word. He tried in a half-hearted
> was to picture "peace"—his eyes closed and behind the lids he
> saw a gray darkness going on and on without end, a country
> of which he hadn't seen as much as a picture postcard. . . .
> (p. 150)

It is so much outside of his experience that his mind is inadequate
even to conceive it.

Just as the liturgical fragments, so music too serves the purpose
of allegory. Pinkie is as much disturbed by music as by the idea of
peace.

> The orchestra began to play: he felt the music as a movement

in his belly: the violins wailed in his guts. He looked neither right nor left but went on. (p. 21)

It moaned in his head . . . it was the nearest he knew to sorrow. (p. 46)

Music makes him uneasy like a promise one is reluctant to accept—one did not know what claims it might make on him: change, repentance—an awful distraction. Pinkie is threatened.

Life held the vitriol bottle and warned him: I'll spoil your looks. It spoke to him in the music, and when he protested that he for one would never get mixed up, the music had its own retort at hand: "You can't always help it. It sort of comes that way." (p. 50)

Shortly after, his defenses are in fact broken down by means of music. Responding to a popular number, he is recalled to an experience of years ago when life had appeared more simple. Then the horizons had not become so narrow. There was promise in the future, and in music was the symbol of freewhen life had appeared more simple. Then the horizons had not become so narrow. There was promise in the future, and in music was the symbol of freedom. "Why, I was in a choir once," the Boy confides to Rose.

. . .and suddenly he began to sing softly in his spoilt boy's voice: "*Agnus Dei, qui tollis peccata mundi, dona nobis pacem.*" In his voice a whole lost world moved—the lighted corner below the organ, the smell of incense and laundered surplices, and the music. Music—it didn't matter what music—"*Agnus Dei,*" "lovely to look at, beautiful to hold," "the starling on our walks," "*Credo in unum Dominum*"— any music moved him, speaking of things he didn't understand. (p. 52)

The things he does not understand are those of peace. He cannot trust these just as he would not believe in the possibility of ecstasy or transcendence.

Hell is his one overweening concern. "Of course, there's Hell," he rasps out at Rose.

> "Flames and damnation," he said with his eyes on the dark shifting water and the lightning and the lamps going out above the black struts of the Palace Pier, "torments" (p. 52)

When Rose interposes anxiously that there must be "Heaven too," he merely shrugs off the suggestion: "Oh, maybe . . . maybe."

Music pursues him, just as did the prayer for peace, particularly at the crucial episodes in the novel. When the two are combined the effect is a rhythmic experience of unusual intensity. When he decides to murder Spicer, music and prayer work up to a frightening crescendo. It is like voices in the dark:

> "the nightingale singing, the postman ringing" but as his thoughts circled closer to the dark, dangerous and deathly centre the tune changed: "Agnus Dei qui tollis peccata mundi . . ."; he walked softly, the jacket sagging across his immature shoulders . . . — "dona nobis pacem". . . (p. 98)

Having registered their marriage, the couple are watching a cinema. With the actor singing "under the restless stars in a wash of incredible moonshine," his emotions surge up in an explosion of anguish.

> Suddenly, inexplicably, the Boy began to weep. He shut his eyes to hold in his tears, but the music went on—it was like a vision of release to an imprisoned man. He felt constriction and saw—hopelessly out of reach—a limitless freedom: no fear, no hatred, no envy. It was as if he were dead and were remembering the effect of a good confession, the words of absolution. (p. 179)

But, the author adds, "being dead it was a memory only. . . ."

Visual images further reinforce the allegory. The more prominent among them are water and the gull. These symbols support and further define the religious motifs delineated through music and liturgy. The gull is a symbol for Pinkie himself. "The gulls swooped up to the top promenade, screaming and twisting in the sunlight. . . . It was so clear a day you looked for France." (p. 140)

The gulls screaming on a clear sunny day and "the pale sea curdled on the shingle"—this is no mere scenic detail. The collusion of images here is striking. What are the gulls screaming for on a sunny day? And why indeed the "curdled" sea. The scene is done from Pinkie's perspective, and uppermost in his mind is his crime. He is alone and frightened, "walking . . . towards the territory he had left—oh, years ago."

It is by the seaside lane where they strangled Hale with a piece of rock candy that both Spicer and Pinkie are drawn together. Spicer's haunted look has even attracted some curiosity, and the gulls are about him too. As he walked on mesmerized, "a seagull flew straight towards him between the pillars," and "like a scared bird caught in the cathedral, then swerved out into the sunlight from the dark iron nave." Robert O. Evans offers a good discussion of this gull motif in his "The Satanist Fallacy."

Allegory is an extended metaphor. By relating Pinkie (and Spicer) to a gull the author may have meant to indicate their un-realized potential. Pinkie's ambitions are as vast and limitless as the sky, but he feels himself unequal to realizing his inmost desires. He is only "a scared bird." To emerge fearless into the sunlight, he has need to be purified, and to gather strength. But this is possible only if he would allow himself to be "caught in the dark iron nave" of a cathedral.

The reference to the cathedral is significant especially insofar as it is unlit. Several of Greene's protagonists are fascinated by the dark interiors of churches. Sarah Miles seeks peace inside a church which is gray and stacked with ugly statues. The church is no less grim and imposing in *The Power and the Glory*. The Indian cemetery is indeed a most weird place, but to the whiskey priest this is a truer representation of his faith than the neat, well-lighted churches of his prosperous reign. Greene seems to suggest that the cloud of darkness is also the cloud of glory; one must be brave enough to enter it before one can partake of the glorious Presence.

For Pinkie and Spicer, that cloud is their essential selves, composed of their drives and most primitive impulses. It is through the
mysterious play of the elements that one reaches out into the
sunlight.

The gull motif is repeated in a more direct reference to Pinkie
himself. There is but the slightest change in the imagery.

> The gulls which had stood like candles down the beach rose
> and cried under the promenade . . . a gull dropped from the
> parade and swept through the iron nave of the Palace Pier,
> white and purposeful in the obscurity: half vulture and half
> dove. (p. 131)

The slight alteration concerns the description of the gull. The bird
is purposeful and is credited with possessing qualities of a contradictory nature. It is both gentle and ferocious and between the
contraries is an intolerable tension. What imagery could better
describe Pinkie's character? What could convey so well whatever is
significant about this haunted soul, its anguish as well as its need
for freedom, and the chasm that separates desire from achievement? Pinkie is vulture-like in his furious hatred, but a dove in his
yearning for peace: "half vulture, half dove."

However the vulture in him is more tenacious than the dove. His
egocentric impulses are just too deeply entrenched for the gentler
aspect to emerge. Hate is in his blood stream. He is driven by it.
His betrayal of Rose's self-effacing loyalty is just about as far as
egotism can go. His dastardly scheme to do away with her presents
an image of evil incarnate. Its symbol is the bottle of vitriol he
carries about his person. The acid burns only to destroy. It cannot
generate either light or warmth; here we have a telling figure of
hell. But the bottle breaks in his hand, engulfing his person in
fumes. Screaming he rushes into the sea. Only the fathomless can
quench his agony, and it takes him to itself.

This further association with the waters supports the allegorical
intent. Water is commonly used in religious rituals as a symbol of
purification. It is through an immersion in water that a neophyte is

initiated into the mysteries of religion. This ritual circumstance is used to advantage in T.S. Eliot. In the first section of "The Waste Land," Madame Sosostris instructs the reader to "Fear death by water." We have echoes of this in *Brighton Rock* where Pinkie confesses his fear of death by drowning. In spite of this fear, Pinkie's favorite haunts often have the sea as a background. It is as if the author were saying that, though stricken and in flight, the boy is never very far away from the waters of redemption.

Following the comparison with Eliot a step further, Madame Sosostris' ironic caution to fear death develops in a later stage into the actual drowning of the Phoenician merchant. He

> passed the stages of his age and youth
> Entering the whirlpool

For all his fear of water, Pinkie is driven to leap into the sea. And the image of the sea, as A.A. DeVitis notes, is "the traditional symbol of changeless change, of continuity." [16]

> 'Stop him', Dallow cried: it wasn't any good: he was at the edge, he was over: they couldn't even hear a splash. It was as if he'd been withdrawn suddenly by a hand out of any existence—past or present, whipped away into zero— nothing. (p. 245)

In the sea, life does not end, it is transformed. Pinkie is cleansed by it and, now redeemed, he is snatched up by a life that goes on and on, to eternity. Like the Phoenician sailor, he is swept into the whirlpool. Without a thought or a concern he may now dwell in peace and in the "deep sea swell," "A current under the sea/Picked his bones in whispers."

There is an interesting episode in Georges Bernanos' *The Diary of a Country Priest*. Mlle Chantal is an intelligent girl who is very exasperated with adult hypocrisies and is resolved to take her vengeance on her parents and their world. In this scene we meet her in anguished discourse with the priest-protagonist. "What do I care if life lets me down," she dares him. "I'll get my own back. I'll just do evil out of spite." To which the priest replies:

> "And when you do, you'll discover God. Oh, no doubt I'm putting it very clumsily. And besides, you're no more than a child. But at least I can tell you this: you are setting off with your back on the world, for the world does not stand for revolt, but for submission, submission to lies, first and foremost. Go ahead for all you're worth, the walls are bound to fall in the end, and every breach shows a patch of sky."
>
> "Are you saying all this for the sake of talking—or are you—"
>
> "It is true the meek shall inherit the earth. And your sort won't try and get it from them because they wouldn't know what to do with it. Snatchers can only snatch at heaven." [17]

Indeed, Pinkie is a snatcher. And he is on the warpath. Like Mlle Chantal he cares nothing for hypocrisy and sham or for the sort of "reward" that was Ida's. He wants more, and ever more than what the world can offer. His character, passionate and energetic, quivers with this larger potential. In reading about Pinkie, we feel the walls may collapse any moment and show "a patch of sky." Indeed the novel is insistent on "the pervasive potentiality" [18] of his repentence and eventual regeneration. Pinkie cannot easily submit to it. At least he would postpone the surrender to the very last. Through his fevered brain runs insistently this refrain: "Between the stirrup and the ground, he mercy sought and mercy found." (p. 91) There is a strong suggestion that in the end he did indeed find both mercy and peace. This is what the old priest implies when trying to console Rose he says: "You can't conceive, my child, nor can I or anyone—the . . . appalling . . . strangeness of the mercy of God." (p. 246)

"The most vicious men have sometimes narrowly evaded sanctity," Greene declared once. It is as much his contention that "the greatest saints have been men with more than a normal capacity for evil." [19] The statement sums up the rationale of a character like Pinkie. It is also an apt introduction to Greene's next important work, *The Power and the Glory*.

THE POWER AND THE GLORY

Does it matter? Grace is. . . everywhere.

—Georges Bernanos

The Power and the Glory (1940) is the story of a Catholic priest in Mexico, and its dramatic context is the religious persecutions of the thirties. Several Mexican states at about that time went Communist. Although as a political doctrine Marxism was yet in its infancy, the winds did favor change. At the time, revolution was most of the content and the main slogan of Communism. But the new was not to be built on the rubble of the old; all that belonged to what was must be cleared away, even ruthlessly. And this was the first task of the Marxist government. Atop the agenda was elimination of religion.

Before persecution began in Mexico, the protagonist was a gentleman in every sense. He was cultivated in speech and manners and much sought after. He was smart and ambitious, and presided like a god over the parish committees. He was a guest of honor in the houses of the rich. With the widows and the housewives he had his winsome ways. A local celebrity then, he had not tasted of privation—when, suddenly, everything was changed. Religion now was an offense, proscribed by an ordinance. The priests who would not apostatize were either shot or forced to go on the run. To be found with even a sacred relic was to court arrest and worse. And

---

All quotes from *The Power and the Glory* (Penguin Books, 1979).

our protagonist is the only priest to stay behind. A heavy price is placed on his head, and he is forced underground. Not that he is pining after the glory of martyrdom. But there is the vast parish— the entire state now is his parish—that depends solely on his ministrations. The sick need to be consoled, the sinner helped back to God. He is needed to nurse the waning faith. So he stays seeking safety in the dark, resting briefly by the junk heap or the hedge.

He traveled light, jettisoning piece by piece the trappings of priesthood that were too burdensome in flight. The heavy altar stone was the first to be left behind. Then the breviary. Now he only carried on him a little wine for the Mass—and some brandy for himself. The alcohol helped to drown the misery and had become a habit. Drunk, he even begot a child. Still, he goes the rounds of his priestly tasks; and this is how we meet him—broken, dishevelled, but urged, nevertheless, with a sense of mission.

The epigraph is from Dryden: "Th' inclosure narrow'd; the sagacious power/ Of hounds and death drew nearer every hour." Thus we are warned from the outset to expect a scheme of melodrama. At the center is a picaresque hero, the whiskey priest. The humor implied in his character somewhat lightens the tragic intensity.

In *Brighton Rock* melodrama was a means to confront two disparate world-views. It serves a similar purpose in the present work—but there is a difference. Pinkie's antagonist has few saving graces: Ida is vulgar, crude and sentimental; she has no understanding at all. The priest's pursuer is quite the opposite to all this. Ida is mediocre and a woman of easy virtue. The lieutenant is a rebel; there is passion in him and ample energy. Even his hatred is graced by virtue of his idealism. He is a character that creates drama.

The author is initially kind, even partial, towards the lieutenant. Although the whiskey priest is to play the hero, it is the other who wins the first rounds. As the priest staggers on-stage—filthy, unshaved, drunk—he cuts only a figure for ridicule. His habit of giggling to himself does not make him any more appealing to our sense of the rational. It is as though the author were debating with himself who might better play the hero. The one is a rogue; the other, the lieutenant, an ascetic.The scales are weighted fairly on either side. If eventually the die is cast in favor of the whiskey priest, it is for no lack of admiration for his opponent. We suspect the priest has the lead only because the material at hand demanded it.

The action is initiated with the priest defying the law. Law proscribed worship as treason. It stipulated that priests should get "rehabilitated": marry and live on government pension. Few of the clergy could agree to such conditions. Many fled to neighboring states. Many more were hunted down by the troops. Only the whiskey priest remained to practice his profession and he is in hiding. We first see him through the eyes of the lieutenant—a clever strategem of the novelist. By keeping the perspective uninterruptedly the opponent's, the tone is set exactly right. The lieutenant is poring over a faded newspaper photograph—a Church service, a First Communion party.

A youngish man in a Roman collar sat among the women. You could imagine him petted with small delicacies, preserved for their use in the stifling atmosphere of intimacy and respect. He sat there, plump, with protuberant eyes, bubbling with harmless feminine jokes. . . .

"He looks like all the rest," the lieutenant said. It was obscure, but you could read into the smudgy photograph a well-shaved, well-powdered jowl much too developed for his age. The good things of life had come to him too early—the respect of his contemporaries, a safe livelihood. The trite religious word upon the tongue, the joke to ease the way, the ready acceptance of other people's homage. . . a happy man. A natural hatred as between dog and dog stirred in the lieutenant's bowels. (pp. 21-22)[1]

Indeed, the lieutenant is himself no stranger to the forms of Catholic worship. He is a "lapsed Catholic," and his characteristic sentiment is that of disillusion. He is angry at the "white muslin dresses," "the candles and the laciness." Years ago he might have

reposed a great deal of faith in the institution of the Church. Now both the Church and worship are symbols of a betrayal. They recall to his mind the "immense demands made from the altar steps by men who didn't know the meaning of sacrifice." (p. 22) The priests spoke for a piety that was uniformly unenlightened, stiflingly emotional, and often very unjust. They appeared grossly insensitive to human suffering. Indeed, how could the well-fed, well-tended clergy feel with the poor and the very deprived?
(pp. 22-3)

The lieutenant's response is conditioned by his childhood. He was poor and unhappy and, to his mind, unhappy because he was poor. And the priests, plump and powdered, went on preaching the virtues of poverty. Surely, they could not have known what it really meant, who devalued the importance of man's lot in the world. "It is only a question of time," he assures his superior, and he would catch him.

The lieutenant is an idealist of a caliber one meets but rarely. He is entirely dedicated to an idea, his devotion touching on the attitude of worship. Indeed, we do notice "something disinterested in his ambition: a kind of virtue in his desire to catch the sleek respected guest of the first communion party." (p. 23) The priest had to be destroyed because his kind poisoned young minds with the potion of inaction. He is a type of heretic.

The Mexican youth are very much in the officer's thoughts. It is a commonplace of his idealogy that salvation lay with the young. Often on the roadside he would stop, watching children at play. They moved him with "an insecure happiness." "The brown intent patient eyes" held him in a spell. It gave him much satisfaction that "it was for these he was fighting." And he would fight on until he has "[eliminated] from their childhood everything which had made him miserable, all that was poor, superstitious, and corrupt." No lying myths for them; no gods, no rituals. No "insubstantial hope" to gloss over their own and others' failures. "They deserved nothing less than the truth—a vacant universe and a cooling world, the right to be happy in any way they chose."(p. 58) Truth must make them free.

The lieutenant feels outraged that anyone should any more

believe in the legend of a loving God.One's own experience must determine the scope of one's emotions. The lieutenant has himself never known love. Nor has he yet loved anybody. The children only stir him to an "insecure" feeling. He feels inadequate and uneasy with them. He does not know the language of love and he cannot realize that affection is not only expressed by acts of great consequence but often by "the faintest of contacts."[2] After all, it is rarely that a love is as dramatic as Mark Anthony's, or as lavish or rhetorical as Shah Jahan's. Often it is a gesture, the pressure of a "hand on a hand,"[3] of "an arm round the neck."[4] To all of this, the territory of the heart, the lieutenant is a stranger. He fancies that if he loved the youth of Mexico as much as he professed he must do something to redeem that love.

Something in the lieutenant is wildly intolerant of humanity's saner impulses. For himself he has given up expecting anything positive from life.

What he had experienced was vacancy—a complete certainty in the existence of a dying, cooling world, of human beings who had evolved from animals for no purpose at all. He knew. (pp. 24-5)

It was no use feigning otherwise. No fiction could negate the absolute certainty of his experience. Momentary thrills do not engage him. Sex is but an "unimportant motion of the body": he could well afford to do without it. A strain of music is wafted on the wind, and it throws him into a spasm of impatience. If only to keep it out, "he would have walled in [his room] with steel." He would, if he could, have "eradicated from it everything which reminded him of how it had once appeared to a miserable child." (p. 25) He compares well with Pinkie in his drive. He is as much a nihilist. "To destroy everything: to be alone without any memories at all"—this is the limit of his ambition.

Pinkie however was merely egoistic; no well-defined ideology supported his anarchic drives. The lieutenant, on the other hand, is a servant of an ideology. His energies are well tended, his passions channeled. His nihilistic impulses are aimed at a definite goal.

There is about him a grim purposefulness, the look of a prophet—or of one used to staring at a dying world and "cold empty ether spaces."

He is also a stern pedagogue. We are asked to notice "something of a priest in his intent observant walk—a theologian going back over the errors of the past to destroy them again." His room is shown to be austere—"as comfortless as a prison or a monastic cell." He is in earnest pursuit of the cold light he has seen in the west. By juxtaposing the wavering whiskey priest with the prophet of socialism, Greene presents before us a major debate of our times.

The priest is a most unlikely choice for the protagonist. He typifies none of the conventional virtues of a hero. None of the ordinary emotions is embodied in him. He excites neither our admiration nor pity. Ragged, unwashed, he is quite reduced to the seediness of his surroundings. He appears unworthy of our trust; he has few claims to our affection. He seems as much a traitor to the Church as he is to the State. He is an anomaly of a priest and a scandal to the pious. A weakling and a brandy-bibber, corrupted with an ill-begotten child, he is by his own admission a coward. Nothing about him seems to measure up to the dignity we normally associate with the figure of a protagonist. He appears like a rogue, a *picaro*; as much unpredictable as he is ridiculous.

On further acquaintance, however, the character gains in depth. With the focus falling sharply on the priest's seedy mien we recognize another man within. Beneath the mask of a rogue we notice a rugged kind of heroism. In the very first scene we have seen him let slip his last chance at escape because he is called to minister to the needs of a sick woman.

> He was like the King of a West African tribe, the slave of his people, who may not even lie down in case the winds should fail. (p. 19)

It is the author who tells us this, but the thought is the priest's—the *raison* for his carrying on, braving the heat and the rain and the police who may surprise him any day.

Still, there is much to compare between the hunted and the hunter. The antagonists of *Brighton Rock* are drawn in sharp contrast to each other. There is little to connect Ida with Pinkie. The distinctions between the priest and lieutenant are more subtle. No Dives and Lazarus chasm separates the two. While the protagonist is shown as very unpriestly, about the lieutenant there are distinct marks of traditional priesthood. He is intent, austere, and with a strong sense of mission. His habitat is monastic. Just as the whiskey priest feels himself like a slave of his parish community, so does the lieutenant feel toward the police squad. "He might have been chained to them unwillingly." (p. 20)   Each is an ideologue, each scornful of the smug and the compromising in his ranks. Both are evangelists, but of different creeds. Both make overtures to the young. The priest wins over Coral Fellows, the daughter of a plantation owner, but is cruelly disowned by his own daughter. The lieutenant has his admirers among the more radical youth. The prize is the boy Luis, and on him the opposing forces converge, demanding allegiance. His vacillation and final commitment trace the meandering course of the author's sympathy for the rival claimants—Church and Marxist Socialism.

The lieutenant is a fascinating character. His energies, though seemingly ruthless, are well directed in the service of a cause. The cause is the new world that must need be built up for the young. He is committed heart and soul to the vision. For their sakes he would stop short of nothing, even "a massacre."

> First the Church and then the foreigner and then the politician—even his own chief would one day have to go. He wanted to begin the world again with them, in a desert. (p. 58)

This is a thrilling conception, heroic in its ambition. "The new children would have new memories: nothing would ever be as it was." (p. 24)

Nothing might be wrong with this, except that the vision rests almost wholly on negatives. The urge to destroy is immeasurably strong. Even his compassion is defined in terms of what must be removed. But when it comes to expressing his concern for his protégés, the Mexican youth for whom he labored, the lieutenant is rediculously at a loss. He knows none of their names. Pointing to Brigitta he exclaims that she "is worth more than the Pope in Rome." (p. 75) But of course the Pope meant nothing to him— would the girl matter any more if, at a future date, she should be temerarious enough to question his vision or his doctrine? We are not satisfied that she would.

In order to track down the whiskey priest faster, the lieutenant proposes that innocent people be taken as hostage and shot.

> "I will tell you what I'd do. I would take a man from every village in the state as a hostage. If the villagers didn't report the man when he came, the hostage would be shot and then we'd take another.
>
> "A lot of them would die, of course."
>
> "Wouldn't it be worth it?" the lieutenant demanded. "To be rid of those people forever." (p. 24)

Yet, "those people" are the same ones he is avowedly fighting for. But a while ago he was even willing to stage a massacre for their sakes. Apparently they are important only insofar as they support his plans for them. Resisting, they are better done away with.

The lieutenant is committed to a faceless generality. If he is in the service of the masses, the masses are very much of an idol for him. He cares little for the individuals that the mass is composed of. The priest, on the other hand, is only concerned for individuals. It is always somebody in dire need of his ministrations that frustrates his attempts at escape. The sick person has special claims on his attention.

Brigitta, his daughter, is an object of his special care. He has contributed to her deformity; he has brought her forth into a loveless world. And she already knew such a lot, prematurely grown old. An important motive for his staying back in the godless terrain is to protect her: "If he left the state, he would be leaving her too, abandoned." (p. 67) Indeed, he is preoccupied with thoughts of her. He feels a great affection for her, but is apprehensive of the awful forces of corruption he sees converging upon her.

If only he knew how he could drag her away even by force from the evil that lurks all around. "He was aware of an immense load of responsibility; it was indistinguishable from love." (p. 66)   His heart pounding "in his breast unevenly, like an old donkey engine," he thought out ways "to save her from—everything." (pp. 66-8)

Brigitta has given a purpose and a new urgency to his life. His priestly cares had never affected him so intensely. "For years, of course, he had been responsible for souls, but that was different a lighter thing. You could trust God to make allowances." (p. 66) But she was the fruit of his corruption, and it was his responsibility to protect her. "You couldn't trust small-pox, starvation, men . . ." He feels inadequate to the task. "This, he thought, must be what all parents feel: ordinary men go through life like this crossing their fingers praying against pain, afraid. . ." (p. 66)

He seeks her out by the rubbish-heap where she sat "with an effect of abandonment. The world was in her heart already, like the small spot of decay in a fruit. She was without protection—she had no grace, no charm, to plead for her." (p. 81)   It was the contours of his sin that he saw in watching her. There is nothing to be proud of, no virtue he might boast about. She is just as ugly as the despair that gave her being. And suddenly his heart is shaken "by the conviction of loss."

> He came a little nearer: he thought—a man may kiss his own daughter, but she started away from him. "Don't you touch me," she screeched at him in her ancient voice, and giggled. Every child was born with some kind of knowledge of love, he thought; they took it with the milk at the breast: but on parents and friends depended the kind of love they knew— the saving or the damning kind. Lust too was a kind of love. He saw her fixed in her life like a fly in amber—Maria's hand raised to strike: Pedro talking prematurely in the dusk: and the police beating the forest—violence everywhere. He prayed silently, "O God, give me any kind of death—without contrition, in a state of sin—only save this child." . . .
>
> He went down on his knees and pulled her to him, while she giggled and struggled to be free: "I love you. I am your father

and I love you. Try to understand that." He held her tightly
by the wrist and suddently she stayed still, looking up at him.
He said, "I would give my life, that's nothing, my soul . . .
my dear, my dear, try to understand that you are—so
important." (pp. 81-2)

The sense of loss pursues him through his haunted existence in
the state. This is what had kept him from any serious effort at
escape. Blundering into safety later he is ashamed and guilty
thinking of "his daughter left to her knowledge and her ignorance
by the rubbish-dump. He had no right to such luxury." (p. 164)

Such concern, such total absorption with another's destiny
indeed is rare. And this concern is what raises the priest in our
esteem. Neither the lieutenant's energy nor his efficiency are really
questioned. His theories are perhaps more scientific, his doctrines
more enlightened than the priest's. But it is the priest who elicits
our sympathy—this despite his many weaknesses, his seedy looks
and apparent cowardice. Maybe we are awed by the depth of his
compassion. His love does not count the cost.

That was the difference, he had always known, between his
faith and theirs, the political leaders of the people who cared
only for things like the state, the republic: this child was more
important than a whole continent. (p. 82)

The lieutenant would approve of this last statement. What is
remarkable about the priest is that he demonstrates the truth of it
in his own life. "He would stay another month, another year . . .
jogging up and down on the mule he tried to bribe God with
promises of firmness." (p. 83)

The conflict is absorbing. The forces are chosen with care and
are well balanced. Suspense holds. Part of the interest is also the
expert management of the narrative. The action is enhanced by the
use of "parallel montage," adapted from the screen. The cross-
cutting sequence was a major innovation to the art of story telling.
It allows maximum scope to the dimension of space, while keeping
suspense at a high pitch. The focus shifts from the harried

protagonist to his pursuer, but is soon back on the protagonist. The spatial and the temporal structures are thus harmonized into a single complex pattern. Neither one is compromised to give an advantage to the other. On the contrary both are enriched to the highest degree. At one moment we are watching the priest ineptly performing his duties. And suddenly before our eyes are the lieutenant and the police squad. We see the priest crouched in the darkness of a banana godown. There is a knock and the police demand to search the house. He is even caught once—but on the charge of carrying liquor and comes out unrecognized. Their paths keep crossing and re-crossing without effecting the relief of discovery. The tension is such one begins to want to expedite the crisis and the resolution. But these do not come until the priest decides of his own to give himself up.

The idea of offering oneself as price-money for the life of another is no new concept in Christian mythology. Jesus nailed to a cross is the leitmotif in all Christian experience. His self-oblation is deemed the more meritorious for being voluntary. The deciding factor was not political but the will to redeem mankind; and the decision was Jesus' own. Not rarely Catholic authors have moved in to exploit the theme.

Several of Georges Bernanos's novels have priests as protagonists; often their role is to serve as scapegoats. In *Journal d'un Cure de la Campagne* the hero cries impulsively to Mlle Chantal: "I'll answer for your soul with mine." [5] In *Sous le Soleil de Satan,* the young Pere Donissan assumes to himself the sin of Mouchette. Possessed and miserable, she has to be redeemed by the priest's own life. He also feels it his duty to answer for the sins left to his care in the confessional. A crushing burden, this, but his calling is to carry it.

Several of Green's heroes and heroines show the same motivation. Thus Rose in *Brighton Rock* yields up her life, even her eternal happiness, or love of Pinkie. [6] Scobie renders up his claims to peace so that the delirious victim of a torpedoed ship may be spared her death-agony. [7] Sarah Miles makes herself a victim in *The End of the Affair.* [8]

Thus the whiskey priest is in no way peculiar in giving his life, even his soul, to ransom his child. As often happens in Greene the priest is taken up on his word. He is given an opportunity to prove himself when, from across the safety of the border, he is lured back to the territory of danger. The bait is that an American criminal lies dying on the other side and is asking for the priest. The priest is "quite certain that this was a trap."

> But it was a fact that the American was here, dying. . . . There was no question at all that he was needed. A man with all that on his soul. . . (p. 180)

This would be the end. He "had come to the very edge of time: soon there would be no tomorrow and no yesterday, just existence going on forever. . ." (p. 186) But their souls were "so important," the criminal's and Brigitta's, that he dares not grudge them his life. The whiskey priest is Greene's conception of "the appalling mysteries of love moving through a ravaged world."[9]

Green's interest is not only in telling a good story. He has other purposes and these are of a philosophical nature. It is part of the book's design to confront the positions held by the two men: one, a resolute follower of Marx and the other, a wavering, incompetent priest. The long, tedious march to the capital is their opportunity. "Tell me this," said the lieutenant,

> "what have you ever done in Mexico for *us*? Have you ever told a landlord he shouldn't beat his peon—oh yes, I know, in the confessional perhaps, and it's your duty, isn't it, to forget it at once. You come out and have dinner with him and it's your duty not to know that he has murdered a peasant. That's all finished. He's left it behind in your box."
> "Well, we have ideas too," the lieutenant was saying. "No more money for saying prayers, no more money for building places to say prayers in. We'll give people food instead, teach them to read, give them books. We'll see they don't suffer." (p. 194)

The argument is well framed. It has force and, so far as it goes, it is convincing. Indeed, nothing could be less ambiguous. It reads almost like a theorem.

The trouble is, human life is never that simple, even the most ordinary life of a peasant. No algebraic equation can do justice to it. "But if they want to suffer. . ." the priest replies. There is eloquence in that ellipsis. Any other punctuation would imply greater completion and commitment on the speaker's side—whether as a statement or a question. But human response to suffering is not a matter that may be decided upon with any finality. The priest acknowledges it as a mystery to ponder on. It is a datum of experience, has been, and is likely to remain to the end. No amount of discussion can unveil its meaning for individual human beings. And no effort, neither art nor science nor philosophy, has ever put an end to its occurrence. Thus the priest's reply suggests a deeper level of perception.

" 'A man may want to rape a woman,' insists the lieutenant. 'Are we to allow it because he wants to? Suffering is wrong.' "

"And you suffer all the time," the priest commented, watching the sour Indian face behind the candle-flame. He said. "It sounds fine, doesn't it? . . . And what happens afterwards? I mean after everybody has got enough to eat and can read the right books—the books you let them read?"

"Nothing, Death's a fact. We don't try to alter facts."

"We agree about a lot of things," the priest said, idly dealing out his cards. (p. 194)

The lieutenant has laid his cards down on the board too. His trump is a concern with suffering. He is genuinely occupied with the problem and would do anything to efface it altogether.

Ironically, the priest is not concerned. It is his conviction that suffering cannot be removed once and for all. It would remain to the end of time—a fact, like death.

"We have facts, too, we don't try to alter that the world's unhappy whether you are rich or poor—unless you are a saint, and there aren't many of those. It's not worth bothering too much about a little pain here. There's one belief we both

of us have—that we'll all be dead in a hundred years."
(pp. 194-5)

The argument goes back and forth. It is like a fugue. A theme is
introduced, repeated with modifications, summed up. Although
the matter dealt with is weighty, the tone is light and the dialogue
moves easily and with energy. The summing up is done by the
priest.

"Listen," the priest said earnestly, leaning forward in the
dark, pressing on a cramped foot, "I'm not as dishonest as
you think I am. Why do you think I tell people out of the
pulpit that they are in danger of damnation if death catches
them unawares? I'm not telling them fairy stories I don't
believe myself. I don't know a thing about the mercy of God: I
don't know how awful the human heart looks to Him. But I
do know this—that if there's ever been a single man in this
state damned, then I'll be damned too." He said slowly, "I
wouldn't want it to be any different. I just want justice, that's
all." (p. 200)

There is such conviction, so much sincerity in the words, that the
other is silenced.

The lieutenant had set out on the trail of "the sleek respected
guest of a First Communion Party." Instead he discovered first a
"picaro," and then a saint. "'You aren't a bad fellow,'" he
concedes. "'If there's anything I can do for you . . .'"
(p. 201) Thus the last word is the priest's. Struck suddenly by the
other's quiet heroism, the lieutenant volunteers to persuade padre
José to come and shrive the prisoner. But Padre José is too much
of a coward to rise to the challenge. He proves Greene's thesis that
it is better to be evil than mediocre. The lieutenant who dared
damnation is more likely to receive grace than the cowardly Padre
José.

With the last priest in custody, the lieutenant's months of
frenzied search are over. But there is no triumph in it. What he
experiences is a sense of absurdity. "He felt without a purpose, as if

life had drained out of the world." (p. 207)   That night his sleep is disturbed with extraordinary dreams. Yet he cannot "remember afterwards anything of his dreams, except laughter, laughter all the time, and a long passage in which he could find no door." (p. 207)   The laugh is on him. The dream reflects his new mood— the sense of vacancy and irony.

Part of the irony is that he has lost his venom. It is as if the priest had drained out all his anger. Hatred does not move him any longer. "The dynamic love which used to move his trigger finger felt flat and dead." (p. 220)   Walking home from the execution he meets Luis, the Mexican youngster. He greets the boy but smiles "painfully" hinting at a sense of apology. On a previous occasion the boy had been thrilled at the sight of his revolver. Now he "crinkled up his face and spat through the window bars, accurately, so that a little blob of spittle lay on the revolver-butt." (p. 220)

Faith often has what it takes to survive the harshest persecutions. Dead, the priest is a martyr; his heroism is firmly established. Within hours of the execution, a stranger calls at Luis's home. He sports "an odd frightened smile"—just like the whiskey priest's. " 'I have only just landed. . .' he said gently. 'My name is Father—' But the boy had already swung the door open and put his lips to his hand before the other could give himself a name." (p. 222)   Heroism of whatever sort wins admiration. The priest's heroism has won yet another generation to God and to the Church.

The priest's character is built up by an extraordinary process. When we meet him first at the dentist's his aspect is such he does not even inspire trust. But by the end he has become a martyr and a hero. The metamorphosis is effected with an ease that is remarkable even for a seasoned writer. Greene packs ample information as background to the early scenes, but he does so quietly, without in any manner calling attention to it. The portrait is drawn spatially.

Edwin Muir was early in recognizing the uses of a spatial dimension to a plot. Ordinarily we only associate plot with a time scheme. Indeed, plot is defined as an arrangement of scenes in a particular sequence. Where is room for space in it? And to build it up spatially—would that not interfere with movement and hamper suspense? Edwin Muir thinks not.

> To say that a plot is spatial does not deny a temporal move-
> ment to it, any more, indeed, than to say, that a plot is
> temporal means that it has no setting in space. . . . The main
> object of the one plot is to proceed by widening strokes, and
> to agree that it does so is to imply space as its dimension. The
> main object of the other is to trace a development, and a de-
> velopment equally implies time. The construction of both
> plots will be inevitably determined by their aim. In one we
> shall find a loosely woven pattern, in the other, the logic of
> causality.[10]

The plot, then, may have either a simple movement or a complex one. The earth does not spin round the sun in a simple straight-forward motion. So with a plot. Its forward thrust is somewhat hampered as other forces cut it at a tangent such as the need to define character, to establish the setting, and all the other rhetorical devices employed to guide the reader. True, all this may be done minimally. If the tangential, wave-like, "widening" strokes are weak, then the action will bound off at a very quick pace. But no story depends on pace alone, and no great story can overlook the importance of developing character. It is here that a spatial scheme becomes handy.

The whiskey priest is a complexly drawn character. He is spatially related to many others in the book. The British expatriate Dr. Tench, the turn-coat priest living in perennial contumely, the irresponsible Captain Fellows, and the mestizo—each of them brings out through association particular aspects of the priest's character. Of Mauriac's work Greene said that events do not quite modify character; they rather reveal it. In Greene this is also true. But it is not merely the episodes that reveal the whiskey priest, but also his symbolic alignment with his fellows in the cast. Nor does he simply stand at the center. He is dynamically related to each of those others "as the spokes of a wheel relate to the hub.[11] He is caught as in a snapshot, flanked by representative humanity.

In the whiskey priest one notes not only strains of saintliness but also those of sinfulness. Every shade of intermediate virtue is referred to him by his central place in the radial design. *The Life of Juan* read out by the Catholic mother is the popular idea of a saint, but this model of sanctity Greene dismisses as unrealistic and a poor gauge of true religious heroism. The life of the whiskey priest does not "stir us with the spiritual passion" usual with an hagiology,[12] perhaps, but it does strike us as recognizably human, and because it is least idealized it also persuades us.

Dr. Tench and his reactions to his milieu help to accentuate the priest's sense of total abandonment. The dentist would have fled the country long since if only he had the courage. Only ennui keeps him. The priest's condition is somewhat like this as we meet him in the first scene. He simply does not have the will to begin all over again. And when he blunders into safety, he is easily persuaded to go back to the zone of danger.

Captain Fellows is a kind of Peter Pan, the boy who never grows up. This is suggestive of the priest's temptation. Fellows is narcissistic, in love with his own voice and his own accomplishments; even "happily at home with nature" so long as it does not make any claims on him. With his responsibilities as husband and father he is scarcely at ease. He has left it to his little daughter to run their home. Coral thinks of her parents simply as "a boy you couldn't trust and a ghost you could almost puff away." (p. 33) For the priest to shirk his sacred duties would be just as inexcusable and mark a regression. The thought of Captain Fellows is a reason for his resolutely keeping to the road.

Even in the half-caste the priest marks a resemblance; was he not also a Judas? The half-caste tagged after him for the money, but he himself had betrayed his solemn vows—and to what profit? He can hardly claim to have lived up to the nobility of his vocation. Even on the eve of his execution he is wracked with the thought that he has "to go to God empty-handed, with nothing done at all." (p. 210)

The priest is also to some extent identified with the American gangster. Before the law he is no less a criminal than Calver. Significantly, their "wanted" pictures face each other on the walls of the police-station. The priest even experiences a sense of brotherhood with Calver and rushes into a known trap so that he may be with the homicide in his last hours.

The defrocked Padre José is the priest's idea of an alternative to his situation. As Coral Fellows suggests, by renouncing his vows he could buy his safety. They might even provide him with a substantial allowance. But the ex-priest's life is framed in eternal mockery. It is the very picture of misery and nothing in the book can equal it. The Padre is "in the grip of the unforgivable sin, despair." Not that despair is a stranger to the whiskey priest, but he has been saved from making a habit of it. He too has committed grievous mistakes, but he put them away—"out of sight and mind." "Somewhere they accumulated in secret—the rubble of his failures. One day they would choke up, he supposed, altogether the source of grace. Until then he carried on, with spells of fear, weariness, with a shamefaced lightness of heart." What saves him is his sense of the mystery of redemption: "a damned man putting God into the mouths of men: an sort of servant, that, for the devil." (p. 60) He is very quick to the little ironies of life..

He was a different man in times of peace. He was ambitious then, whether running a parish, directing a plethora of activities, or presiding over guilds and pious associations. He had a sense of his own importance. He was also less soiled by experience. There had been no serious sin, and in his naivete he had believed it a small matter to save souls—"as easy as saving money." But no longer. "Now it was a mystery. He was aware of his own desperate inadequacy." (p. 82) Guilt may be a burdensome thing, but it may on occasion give valuable insights into the mystery of an individual's being. "What an unbearable creature he must have been in those days," he muses. "That was another mystery: it sometimes seemed to him that venial sins—impatience, an unimportant lie, a neglected opportunity—cut you off from grace more completely than the worst sins of all." Innocent, he had not cared much for anyone. "Now in his corruption he had learnt . . ." (p. 139)

Thus his sin was an occasion for a spiritual awakening.It shook him out of lethargy. He might no longer defend himself with the fine mutations of theology. Save the most "simplified mythology" (p. 60) everything was thrown over by the roadside. Only "the simple ideas of hell and heaven moved in his brain." He can retain nothing more sophisticated—only "the simplest outline of the mystery." (p. 65)   Reduced to the status of the "unaccommodated man" he must learn to find his way through the primeval regions of darkness and terror, of ecstasy beyond thought. It is a world of insolvable mysteries; but now in his awakening he is simply content with inhabiting them.

It is not all mere negatives either that define the priest in his new awareness. Neither theology nor the lack of it could save Padre José from despair. The whiskey priest is redeemed by his enhanced capacity for love. His sin has aroused in him greater understanding of other people, and compassion for them. Although Brigitta is often in his thoughts, she is not the only object of his love. It broadens out to all the world, including the turn-coat priest, the Judas mestizo, the criminal—even his sworn enemy, the lieutenant.

The priest owns an altogether new vision. It is the flowering in him of a religious consciousness whose roots lay in the mythical past. The vision is realized significantly in a weird Indian cemetery, ". . . an odd grove of crosses stood up blackly against the sky, leaning at different angles." It is not even kept. Nothing about it of "the tidy vestments . . . and the elaborately worked out symbols of the liturgy." Nothing calculated to enthrall and to edify. "It was like a short cut to the dark and magical heart of the faith—to the night when the graves opened and the dead walked." (p. 154)

Though somewhat crude, though dark and magical, his faith now is strangely responsive to the paradoxes of the Gospel. Jesus appears to have revelled in these. Pain and pleasure, loss and gain, death and life—Jesus liked to pair the opposites together in equations of cause and effect. So does the priest. He even exhorts the rugged peasantry to seek out what is painful. "Joy always depends on pain," he tells them. "Pain is part of joy. We are hungry and then think how we enjoy our food at last . . . We deny ourselves so that we can enjoy." As if they needed to be told, for whom self-denial was a way of life. Still, he cries out at them:

"I tell you that heaven is here: this is a part of heaven just as pain is a part of pleasure." He said, "Pray that you will suffer more and more and more. Never get tired of suffering. The police watching you, the soldiers gathering taxes, the beating you always get from the jefe because you are too poor to pay, smallpox and fever, hunger . . . that is all part of heaven— the preparation. Perhaps without them, who can tell, you wouldn't enjoy heaven so much. Heaven would not be complete. (p. 69)

Not much sublime thought here, perhaps. There are no pregnant expressions, no niceties of speech or phrasing. What redeems the priest's exhortation is the ring of sincerity and his utter conviction.

An effect of the new awareness is his extraordinary resilience. One could think up nothing less exhilarating than his present situation. Yet, he is happy. He can even laugh. "It is one of the strange discoveries a man makes that life, however you lead it, contains moments of exhilaration; there are always comparisons which can be made with worse times—even in danger and misery the pendulum swings." (p. 59)   Watching his congregation of half-clad peasants he feels "an absurd happiness."

It was as if he had been permitted to look in from outside at the population of heaven. Heaven must contain just such scared and dutiful and hunger-lined faces. (p. 71)

Momentarily he enjoys "an immense satisfaction that he could talk of suffering to them now without hypocrisy—it is hard for the sleek and well-fed priest to praise poverty." (p. 71)

The joyful bounce is a token of the priest's enlarged humanity. To sulk is as much an expression of a failure of imagination as to boast. The mestizo who brandishes his sins with an "immense self-importance" does not share the priest's knowledge at the confessional. "Man was so limited: he hadn't even the ingenuity to invent a new vice: the animals knew as much." (p. 97)   But the mestizo is "unable to picture a world of which he was only a typical part—a world of treachery, violence, and lust in which his shame was altogether insignificant." (p. 97)   Humanity's failures, however grave they may seem, are of no lasting consequence: so the priest's experience has taught him. This bespeaks quickened perceptions.

In the prison cell his sensibilities are put to the ultimate test. He is detained for carrying contraband liquor. There surely are others in the overcrowded cell accused of similar offenses. But there are also hardened criminals. Dirt and stench are everywhere. From a corner by the fence come whimpering cries of pleasure. A madman mutters something about a daughter somebody has carried away. It is stiflingly hot. And amidst the heat, the darkness and the stench, the priest is happy. He is feeling quite at home. "He had a sense of companionship which he had never received in the old days when pious people came kissing his black cotton glove." He is touched by "an extraordinary affection. He was just one criminal among a herd of criminals." (p. 128)

The prison scene is among the most sccessful in the book. It is powerfully drawn and comes up for special note here for the way it recapitulates the dominant strains of the spatial design. In the space of a short scene, and simultaneously, the priest is confronted with every shade of the human tendency. The cell contains, among others, a pious Catholic woman and an atheist. Possibly some dark corner hid a Judas. The scene happens at the very geometric center of the book. Its crucial importance must justify a detailed exposition.

The room is so overcrowded it is not even possible for an individual to shift to a more comfortable position. But somehow a woman has edged her way to the priest and is demanding that he hear her confession. He points out how little privacy there is, that an Act of Contrition would do in the circumstances. Suddenly there is movement in the far corner, stealthy and breathless. Then, again, the cries of pleasure, to which the pious woman reacts violently: "'Why don't they stop it? The brutes, the animals!'" The priest advises forebearance.

What is the good of your saying an Act of Contrition now in this state of mind?"

"But the ugliness . . ."

"Don't believe that. It's dangerous. Because suddenly we

discover that our sins have so much beauty—"

"Beauty," she said with disgust. "Here. In this cell. With strangers all round."

"Such a lot of beauty. Saints talk about the beauty of suffering. Well, we are not saints, you and I. Suffering to us is just ugly. Stench and crowding and pain. *That* is beautiful in that corner—to them. It needs a lot of learning to see things with a saint's eye: a saint gets a subtle taste for beauty and can look down on poor ignorant palates like theirs. But we can't afford to."

"It's mortal sin."

"We don't know. It may be. But I'm a bad priest, you see . . ." (p. 130)

On the one side there is a stiff intolerence; on the other, a godly understanding. As for the woman, her piety is only a mask. She is consumed with jealousy, and her indignation is self-righteous. Her reaction is self-regarding, his generous. The priest's compassion is founded on his correct appraisal of his position among his fellow mortals. "He was just one criminal among a herd of criminals." (p. 128) He would not arrogate to himself the role of God. He would not sit in judgment over others' behavior.

Again the cry came, an expression of intolerable pleasure. The woman said, "Stop them. It's a scandal." He felt fingers on his knee, grasping, digging. He said, "We're all fellow prisoners. I want drink at this moment, more than anything, more than God. That's a sin too."

"Now," the woman said, "I can see you're a bad priest. I wouldn't believe it before. I do now. You sympathize with these animals. If your bishop heard you . . ." (p. 131)

"'When I get out of here,'" she threatens him, "'I shall write . . .'" The priest laughed. A silly remark that one. She had no sense of her surroundings, no sense of change at all. "But again he became serious. It was more difficult to feel pity for her than for the half-caste who a week ago tagged him through the forest; but her case might be worse. . . . He said, 'Try not to be angry. Pray for me instead.'" She takes a Parthian shot at him: "'The sooner you are dead the better.'" (p. 131)

Thus the movement is brought skillfully to completion. The dialogue is masterful, and the scene done from a multiple point of view. The woman is allowed just enough time to propose her point of view, when the priest takes over. She began on a note of heroism: "I wouldn't mind suffering"; had fancied in the priest a kindred soul: "Think. We have a martyr here . . ." It is her despair to find him just another mortal who cannot deny consanguinity with sinners.

The scene is crucial to the novel. It shows the leap of understanding the priest has lately achieved. While he decries the woman's complacency, he is actually censoring his early self. In the old days he had known what to say to her type, "feeling no pity," "speaking with half a mind a platitude or two"—"quite harmless ones," to be sure, calculated to reassure her. Now, at the threshold of death, such civilities appear to him wildly incongruous and of no use to anyone at all. His duty in compassion was to show up to her the pride that lurked under the gloss of her righteousness. If he could break through her complacency, perhaps there was still hope. But her mind is crammed with generalities. The point of such parables as the Lost Coin and the Prodigal Son is lost on her. She may never understand the life of a St. Paul or a St. Augustine. Like the brother of the prodigal, she denies compassion to the sinner. She cannot appreciate the saying that with God everything is possible; that even sin may be the bed for sanctity's nurturing.

Dietrich Bonhoeffer offers a striking contrast between the ethical type and the Incarnate God. God's becoming man, he suggests, is a mystery with awesome consequences. It means God's unconditional pledge of friendship to everyone. It means further that even in its sinfulness humanity is acceptable to God.

Jesus is not concerned with the proclamation and realization of new ethical ideals; He is not concerned with Himself being good; He is concerned solely with love for the real man, and for that reason He is able to enter into the fellowship of the guilt of men and to take the burden of their guilt upon Himself.[13]

The "love for the real man" is thought of as unconditional. It does not demand innocence as a prerequisite. Instead it shares the human lot, and in so doing invites upon itself the verdict of guilty.

> Jesus does not desire . . . to look down on mankind as the only guiltless one while mankind goes to its ruin under the weight of its guilt; He does not wish that some idea of a new man should triumph amid the wreckage of a humanity whose guilt has destroyed it. He does not wish to acquit Himself of the guilt under which men die. A love which left man alone in his guilt would not be love for the real man. As one who acts responsibly in the historical existence of man Jesus becomes guilty.[14]

The Gospels are not concerned with spelling out a system of ethical absolutes. Jesus never interested himself with being thought of as good. The burden of his teaching is something other than innocence. The emphasis is on surrender, on one's willingness to receive mercy and grace. And grace is only his who owns up to his own inadequacy. There is no escaping "the guilt in responsibility" except by denying the essential "reality of human existence." "And what is more he cuts himself off from the redeeming mystery of Christ's bearing guilt without sin and he has no share in the divine justification which lies upon this event."[15]

The pious woman is guilty of the most intolerable pride. By seeking to set her "own personal innocence above [her] responsibility for men," she falls a prey to "the more irredeemable guilt" which was the sin of the Pharisee. She does not realize that it is "precisely in a man's entering into the fellowship of guilt for the sake of other men" that true innocence proves itself. In the person of Jesus even God took to Himself the "sinful" nature of man. What claims has any man to sit judging his fellows? For Bonhoeffer it is a consequence and "an essential part" of incarnational mystery "that the man who is without sin loves selflessly and for that reason incurs guilt."[16]

The prison scene is an allegory on the human condition in the world. The cell is said to be "very like the world: overcrowded with lust and crime and unhappy love: it stank to heaven." This is yet only a statement on the nature of things. The position the priest takes to this prison-world is quite the opposite of the pious woman's. He is exhilarated to find himself in proper company— the company of criminals. The priest "realized after all it was possible to find peace there." (p. 125) Not "also there", nor "even there." "There" is used as an absolute condition, the human situation the world over. This was the sole motive of Christ's dying: to save this world. And who was he, the priest, to condemn the least of men, even the fang-toothed mestizo? "How could he pretend with his pride and lust and cowardice to be any more worthy of that death than this half-caste?" (p. 99)

He is kind even to the pious hypocrite. Who could say what wounds festered beneath the veneer of her pride, what disappointments lay buried under the cover of moral indignation. It is too dark yet to study her face, but the voice has a familiar ring. And,

> When you visualized a man or a woman carefully, you could
> always begin to feel pity—that was a quality God's image
> carried with it. When you saw the lines at the corners of the
> eyes, the shape of the mouth, how the hair grew, it was
> impossible to hate. Hate was just a failure of imagination.
> (p. 131)

He feels "an enormous responsibility" even for the pious woman.

Watching his fellow prisoners he is still more humbled. Many of them had committed no crime except that of loyalty; they were hostages for his sake. They had chosen to suffer rather than betray his identity. Indeed, what was he to deserve such heroism? "He prayed silently: Oh, God, send them someone more worthwhile to suffer for. It seemed to him a damnable mockery that they should sacrifice themselves for a whiskey priest with a bastard child." (p. 135)

There is little dispute regarding either the significance of this scene or the power of its delineation. A great deal is said in a minimum of space. A major achievement is the unfolding in depth of the priest's character. By unveiling a deeper, spiritual reality in

him the author defends his allotting a central role to the protagonist. All power, it is true, belongs to the lieutenant and he exercises
his power without hesitation or doubt, even ruthlessly. But he is
denied fulfilment, and he finds no glory whatever in exercising his
authority. His lot is dramatized in the dream he has on the night of
the priest's martyrdom. In this dream he wanders mindlessly in the
labyrinths of his own soul with the laughter echoing on all sides.
The priest's life is fruitful even in death.

The Power and the Glory delights us most of all by its humanism. It does not take a great deal of perception to see that life is
rarely simple as it is lived out; but only a person of exceptional
compassion can accept the complexity. Greene's hero has this
compassion. He is not fighting any cause, he is not a crusader. Although he is concerned with what people make of themselves and
their potential for freedom, he does not force himself upon their
attention. His humanism is deep and encompassing. It is suffused
with an awareness of the mysterious workings of grace. His God is
a Father to the just and the unjust alike. His arms are open at all
times to receive the sinner.

Evil does not frighten the priest nor is he quite repelled by it. It
simply enhances his faith regarding the bounty of God. To sacrifice
oneself for the good or the beautiful is no great matter. It calls for
no overriding love. Nor is there great heroism in offering one's life
for a pet idea—for home, children or country. But "it needed a
God to die for the halfhearted and the corrupt." (p. 97) Christ is
the priest's ideal, his exemplar. His task is to repeat the role of a
victim-God; he is *alter Christus*, another Christ. He is driven by the
force of this conviction.

The rationale of the sacrifice on the Cross is that every person,
whatever his or her peculiarities, his or her corruption, is made in
the image of God. In every individual there is a manifestation of
the divine.

> God was the parent, but He was also the policeman, the crim-
> inal, the priest, the maniac and the judge. Something resem-
> bling God dangled from the gibbet or went into odd attitudes
> before the bullets in a prison-yard or contorted itself like a
> camel in the attitude of sex. (p. 101)

In Christ's catalogue of the saved, there are no exceptions, no hopeless cases, no irredeemables. He had died as much for Judas Iscariot as for Simon Peter. He had died to redeem the God-image in everyone—the multifarious Face of God.

The priest has an unusual vision of Christ. Into a grassy arena lined with statues of saints suddenly come alive, Christ descends dancing and reeling to the tinkly rhythm of a marimba. He "danced and postured with a bleeding painted face, up and down, up and down, grimacing like a prostitute, smiling and suggestive." (p. 176) Criminals, prostitutes and madmen—all this constituted the Body of Christ. The priest wakes up "with a sense of despair that a man might feel finding the only money he possessed was counterfeit." (p. 176) But soon after, mercifully, the gory face fades and its place is taken by another, one that reflected "the glory as of the only-begotten of the Father, full of grace and truth." (p. 176) This image completes the picture of Man as a creature who simultaneously both the criminal and the child of God.

This complex apprehension of man's estate is the basis of the priest's compassion. It helps to sustain him amidst the hardships of a godless state. If everyone were potentially the repository of God's likeness, there was surely much to hope for. Desecrated, the temple does not cease to hold the divine presence. This knowledge accounts for the priest's sense of humor, the lightheartedness. He is fully at home with the criminals. Trailed by the mestizo he giggles to himself, thinking how clownish the other might seem if looked at from the right angle. " 'Thieves, murderers,' " he admonishes the pious woman, " 'Oh well, my child, if you had more experience you would know there are worse things to be.' " (p. 129)

R.W.B. Lewis has voiced a complaint against this book. Although here "the divine image for once irradiates and redeems the human," he says, "it is seen doing so only to the most squalid, repellent and pain-wracked of human conditions—just as the omens of sanctity are seen only in an unshaven brandy-biber." [17] This may be so. But even the sinner deserves mercy, and none would surely grudge it if the Father should lavish his love on the prodigal who has returned. Perhaps God does entertain special affection towards the sinner. Lewis's complaint is not that; it goes deeper, to the roots. In *The Power and the Glory*, he says, "Natural beauty is not enhanced, but natural ugliness is touched by grace; for what nauseated Minty in *England Made Me*—the notion of God incarnate—is just what most exhilarates the priest." [18]

There are several positions that may be taken towards human nature; and everyone does in fact take a position. Minty's logic has for its major the contention that human nature is essentially ugly. Lewis evidently does not support this. He might contend, on the contrary, that there is much that is good and naturally beautiful in human kind; and natural beauty, in his opinion, must deserve divine approbation. Greene does not debate the point. Nor does he take a position against natural beauty, provided it is genuine. It is the pretensions of culture that he is against, and much in contemporary western civilization, he thinks, went to distort genuine human impulses.

It was in 1935 that Greene paid a visit to Africa. He was instantly impressed with what he saw there, and, a few years later, he also visited Mexico. In both places he encountered a life style that was by every account different from what he knew. Decadent it appeared at first, but he found it immensely more satisfying than the civilized way of the West. Here was no flamboyance. Life was at the simplest, the most elemental; gentle, yet it was also ecstatic. It is against this vision of a primitive excellence, an aboriginal paradise, that Greene's characters are drawn.

In Greene the word "beauty" has interesting overtones. Louise Scobie is charming to a "fresh" youngster like Wilson, but to Scobie, her husband, she is a neurotic and a bully. It is not that the author denies her the tribute of her physical charm. But in the absence of a "spiritually" creative awareness, her natural attributes do not interest him very much. Physically, the whiskey priest has little appeal. It is his inner bounty that transforms him. His character is lit by the aura of a divine compassion.

The workings of grace are often hidden and rarely amenable to the hand of the novelist. An author must work with that strata of human experience which is readily available to every man and woman, and yet is fresh and dramatic. The divinity rarely intervenes in our life in such a dramatic fashion. Sudden conversions may be apt subjects of drama; gradual growth is scarcely so. Still, *The Power and the Glory* moves us in a way novels rarely do. Part of the explanation is the inner dynamism symbolized in the priest. Though the protagonist does nothing that may be termed overtly dramatic, still in the ambiguity of his character is a plausible ground for the play of melodrama. He represents within him the cross-currents of human impulses. We notice in him the ebb and flow of weakness and renewed fervor, of resolution and fall. His conflicts are by their nature rather unusual, and a good deal more interesting than in melodrama of the common run.

Perhaps even God is partial "to the most squalid, repellent and pain-wracked of human conditions." So believed many of the greatest literary authors. Such Dostoevskian heroes as Alyosha and Smerdyakov have to pass through the purgatory of suffering and humiliation before they achieve true liberation. So with King Lear. From Shakespeare to Bernanos, Peguy and Greene, through Tolstoi and Pasternak runs an uninterrupted line of predilection for the "pain-wracked of human conditions." Greene is in no way peculiar but is at the heart of the great Western tradition when he weights the scales to give an extra significance to suffering. For indeed, it was a death that bought redemption. Through deaths sprout new forms of life. Greene would seem to consider suffering the true baptism; and it is a baptism of fire, through which his heroes are ushered into the paradisiacal way. But his is no Lawrentian way of heightened sensual delights. The ecstasy that Greene's characters work for is more spiritual and existential. It is "the finer taste" and the "finer pleasure" of authentic human existence.

The priest's dignity is further enhanced by the comparison drawn between him and Christ in His passion. The parallel is compelling—and apt, as every priest has a mandate to be "another Christ." A Priest is ordained to repeat and continue Christ's mission to the world, and this is the basis for his dignity. Despite his weaknesses, the whiskey priest does try to live up to his vocation. Daring persecution, he stays on to preach to the poor, to console the sick. And he himself is consoled by the vacant, famished faces that mill around him on the barren hillside. He is tempted in the wilderness. He is denied by everyone, and betrayed, and finally, after a prolonged period of trial, is executed for his faith.

Initially the resemblance is not very clear. But as the story picks up momentum, the parallel becomes striking. Christ died crucified between two criminals. On the wall of the prison-office, the priest's picture is also pinned against that of a common criminal.[19] Christ's death was a voluntary decision. So is the priest's. Returning to the socialist state, the priest is quite certain he is walking into a trap. But the American gangster, Calver, lies dying across the border, and his eternal salvation may depend on the priest's ministrations. Somewhere in that godless state also is "the sullen unhappy knowledgable face," his Brigitta. The memory is a shot of pain. "'O God, help her. Damn me, I deserve it, but let her live for ever,'" he prays. (p. 208)   His redemptive role is ever before his eyes. Submission was the core of Christ's mission—submission of all, even His very young life, to the Father. The priest too may hold back nothing, even his soul. He must surrender all.

The Holy Mass is a commemoration of the Last Supper. The Mass in Maria's hut, too, may be the priest's last. For even as he is concluding the service, his enemies overtake him—but they do not recognize him. Called up before the lieutenant, the priest feels "an enormous temptation to throw himself in front of the lieutenant and declare himself—'I am the one you want.'"—echoing Gethsemene: "I have told you that I am he. . . . If I am the one you are looking for, let these others go." (p. 76)[20]   In the six pages that follow the cock crows twice. Another six pages, and the priest is disowned by his people, even by Maria, the mother of his child. Subsequently he is arrested, but only for carrying contraband. There follows the great desolation.

This is a lengthy period of spiritual distress and evoked with great feeling. The priest comes out of the prison disappointed that God had not thought him worthy of martyrdom. Wearily, he trudges off in search of Coral Fellows—"how could he live through the rains with nobody daring to give him food or shelter?" (p. 141)   Coral was a brave girl; he could count on her daring. But coming to the Fellows' bungalow, he finds it deserted. The Fellows have moved, and the only sign of life there is the faint whimpering of a mongrel bitch trailing a piece of bone. Scraps of note paper are scattered all about. From them a child's familiar handwriting peers out at him. The vultures keep their unblinking vigil from the rooftops. His hunger and loneliness have a demeaning effect on the priest. His misery is such that he wrests the bone from the bitch, and puts it into his own mouth. He was "furious—that a mongrel bitch with a broken back should steal the only food." (p. 144)

The priest's is a "desert-experience," and he must do it alone. He is in the region of desolations where there is "only rock/ Rock and no water and the sandy road/ The road winding above among the mountains . . ."[21] The road winds endlessly into a horizonless future. There is no end in view to his travails, to the anguish, to the hopelessness. Spiritual writers call this "the dark night of the soul." Greene must consider it of some importance in the scheme of his story, for he does not spare space in developing it to maximum advantage.

> . . . ever since that hot and crowded night in the cell he had passed into a region of abandonment—almost as if he had died there with the old man's head on his shoulder and now wandered in a kind of limbo, because he wasn't good or bad enough. . . . Life didn't exist anymore; it wasn't merely a matter of the banana station. Now as the storm broke and he scurried for shelter he knew quite well what he would find—nothing. (p. 147)

Page after page bring out the same experience—that of the limbo. The row of deserted huts, the flop-flop of vultures, and the darkness broken only by a stray shaft of lightning—every detail accentuates the desolation. "The huts leapt up in the lightning and stood there shaking, then disappeared again in the rumbling darkness." (p. 147)

The rain sweeping up from the Campache Bay, he runs for shelter. He reaches for the first hut. The door is open, but there is no one in there at all—"Just a pile of maize and the indistinct gray movement of—perhaps—a rat."

> He dashed for the next hut, but it was the same as ever (the
> maize and nothing else) just as if . . . Somebody had
> determined that from now on he was to be left alone—
> altogether alone. (p. 147-48)

The narrative crawls, is heavy and burdened. There is a delirium-
like quality about the style. In fact the priest is moving along in a
delirium. At the Indian cemetery, he tries to quench his thirst by
sucking at his own trousers. On the cross, Christ was offered a
sponge soaked in vinegar.

The desolation grows on the protagonist until his last hours in
the prison. He is now awaiting execution, set for the morrow. He is
overcome—not with fear of damnation. But he feels "an immense
disappointment because he had to go to God empty-handed, with
nothing done at all." "It seemed to him, at that moment, that it
would have been quite easy to have been a saint. It would only
have needed a little self-restraint and a little courage."
(p. 210) There is under-tug of despair here. It reminds us, again,
of the ninth hour on the cross, and the cry: "My God, my God, why
hast thou forsaken me?" The priest feels as though he "carried the
visible marks of the dying" on his body. (p. 154)

These allegorical readings are supported by the lieutenant.
Having ordered the execution, the lieutenant walks home, and our
attention is called to "something brisk and stubborn about his
walk, as if he were saying at every step, 'I have done what I have
done.'" (p. 220) But this is straight from the Roman Consul,
Pontius Pilate. Asked to rephrase Jesus's charge and title, he had
retorted to the high priests and the pharisees: "Scripsi quod
scripsi," what I have written, I have written. The lieutenant's
identification of himself with Pilate who gave Jesus away to death
clinches the parallel with particular force.

This identification with Christ is climaxed with the revised
judgment of Luis's mother. A piously Catholic woman, she has had
only scorn for the brandy-bibber so long as he lived. She was even
anxious lest his example should corrupt her children. Now there is
no longer any anxiety, not the faintest of doubts about the priest's
credentials for the crown of sanctity. She declares him without

qualification "one of the martyrs of the Church . . . one of the heroes of the faith." (p. 219)   We may smile at the irony. Still, even this supports the allegory. This is how Mark records the events subsequent on Jesus's death: when "the centurion who was standing in front of [Jesus's cross] had seen how he had died, [he said:] 'in truth this man was a son of God.'"[22] The man and woman of good will cannot but recognize heroism, however and in whatever guise they may find it.

R.W.B. Lewis has a study of Greene titled "Between the Horror and the Glory."[23] If we change it to read "*Through* Horror *to* Glory," it would register more correctly the meanings in *The Power and the Glory*. The "horror" is the priest's knowledge, gathered through sin. With a single sexual lapse, he has been forced out of "the sinless empty graceless chromium world" of his former days, and flung at the very heart of evil. Here he learns, by slow degrees, the merits of being poor and unworthy—the lesson of the Magnificat. This awareness is the source of his salvation.

In sin, it would seem, is the priest's heroism nurtured. This is not a doctrine on which everyone agrees. Is not evil at the opposite pole from virtue? And if so, how is the one said to support and nourish the other? Could vice ever be "the manure in which salvation flowers"?[24] This is a problem, even an enigma. However, an enigma is the soul of Christian experience. Believers call it the mystery of redemption. And on this mystery is founded the whole of the faith. The Gospels express this sense of mystery by means of paradoxes. The grain of wheat, so long as it remains whole, is unproductive; dying, it yields fruit a hundredfold. So with human life. When life is outwardly full, rich and exciting, it is likely to inhibit the deeper awareness. Let the walls crash upon the senses, and a whole inner world is likely to open up. Death, Jesus warned, is a precondition for rebirth. Even the producing branch is subjected to the test of the knife. Through his sin, the priest is cauterized of the virulent effects of his egotism. Thus cleansed, he is made ready for the final laying down of his life. The new growth from his death is the rekindling of faith among the youth of Mexico.

Grace never really destroys anything of the human. On the

contrary it builds on it, and for this purpose it sometimes finds it necessary to check the unbridled sweep and flow of human nature's impulses. But the aim of this channeling is to free the finer potentialities of the human spirit, to enrich and to transform them. Pain operates as a door to an intense creative effort, to an inner awakening, and here on the frontier between the visible and the invisible does one meet his Maker. And "on the frontier of the invisible world," every Christian author must recognize "*angoisse* is a sixth sense, and pain and perception are identified."[25] In *The Heart of the Matter* Greene explores further into the nature and possibilities of this anguish.

THE HEART OF THE MATTER

What are the roots that clutch, what branches grow
Out of this stony rubbish? Son of man,
You cannot say, or guess, for you know only
a heap of broken images, where the sun beats,
And the dead tree gives no shelter.

—T. S. Eliot, *The Waste Land*

"But sin, sin also serves," is a keynote in Paul Claudel's *The Satin Slipper*. And Claudel is not alone in this rather unorthodox doctrine. Other writers—Charles Peguy, Leon Bloy and Georges Bernanos, for instance—have voiced similar opinions. It is as if, with their religious upbringing, they cannot quite dismiss sin from the total view of things. A realistic appraisal of life would seem to demand that even sin has a place in the economy of salvation. Greene shows it may in certain circumstances quicken the spirit and aid the process of freedom. This, surely, has happened to the whiskey priest. Through a transgression, strains of heroism are released within him that had long lain in an enervating darkness. Sin then enhances life—but only given a climate of faith. Cut off from the reach of grace, it is more likely to poison life. And this is what we notice in *The Heart of the Matter* (1948).

This novel has nothing in it of the thriller, although the thriller had long been Greene's forte. For over a decade he had worked at fashioning it into an apt medium for the sublimest and the most delicate effects. But now he turned to a different manner of narrative. The scheme of *The Heart of the Matter* is traditional Victorian; perhaps his need to probe character weighed with him to favor this older arrangement. For the thriller does not allow for

---

All quotes from *The Heart of the Matter*, (Penguin Books, 1978).

such a need: to linger over character would dampen pace; suspense would suffer. The thriller is equally wary of deep authorial involvement with characters and their world-view. It does not look kindly on authors using it as a forum for discussing their attitudes on life. But perhaps Greene did mean *The Heart of the Matter* as a personal comment. The spotlight is held unwinking to some selected facts of contemporary experience. It focuses on the fears, the anxieties, and the conflicts that fluster the human spirit in our day. To this purpose, a tragic manner is best suited.

The action takes place in Sierra Leone. This is a small British colony on the west coast of Africa. Greene had served there during the war on a Secret Service mission. Unbearably hot, wet and infested, the climate was reminder enough of the terrible pathos of human life. "Swamps, rain and a mad cook," Greene said, were his excuse for *The Heart of the Matter*. The war aggravated the sense of tragedy. Mosquitoes, beetles, dead pye-dogs and vultures—vultures pre-eminently—are strewn around in good measure. These are prominent background motifs in the novel. A seedy setting, to be sure—but something about it appealed to Greene. And it is he who informs us: "Those days a love of Africa deepened there, in particular, a love for what is called the world over 'the Coast.'"

The protagonist, Henry Scobie, is a middle-aged man, the deputy police commissioner of a small district. Major Scobie has very few ambitions. Neither power allures him nor the prospects of a promotion. Loyal and honest, he is content to do his job as well as he may; and as the novel opens he is among the least corrupted on the scene. However, his wife Louise is far from happy. It is not only that the climate is somewhat harsh; her snobbish disposition has kept her very lonely. She wants terribly to get away from it all. Scobie must arrange a holiday for her in South Africa. But he can ill afford this with his scanty resources. In order to oblige her, he has to borrow from a very corrupt merchant, thus compromising both his dignity and his responsible position as a government official.

While Louise is away on her holiday, the victims of a torpedoed ship are brought ashore. Among them is a nineteen-year-old,

Helen Rolt. The shipwreck took her husband. She is not very pretty. And the forty odd days in an open boat on the sea have not been kind on her features, either. Any victim moved Scobie: the girl's misery makes an instant appeal to his compassion. For him she is not simply one of the many victims of a torpedo. He fancies her as the prototype of the human spirit mocked and buffeted by the unregarding Fates. He can not just stand and watch her perish. A wondering Helen responds to his sentiments with the utmost gratitude. Their feelings grow steadily stronger, until one day they form a secret liaison. In a moment of weakness Scobie even pledges himself solemnly to the girl. Shortly afterwards Louise arrives home. Her return sets in motion a complex chain of action and reaction; and suddenly Scobie is made aware of broken pledges. He finds he has taken on more than he could really bear: he is answerable to two women, rivals for his love. Both have absolute claims on him. This is a situation of his own making, but he is not adequate to cope with it. Pity had urged him on; now it has him ensnared. In bare outline, this is the story.

The book opens in a specialized locale. On the physical plane it is only a small white colony in West Africa, but at a deeper level we recognize scars of violence and meanness and a lifetime of inhumanity. The decadence is everywhere felt. The sense of putrefaction and anesthetized sensibilities is powerfully evoked through association with the hospital.

Scobie turned up James Street past the Secretariat. With its long balconies it had always reminded him of a hospital. For fifteen years he had watched the arrival of a succession of patients; periodically at the end of eighteen months certain patients were sent home, yellow and nervy, and others took their place—Colonial Secretaries, Secretaties of Agriculture, Treasurers and Directors of Public Works. He watched their temperature charts every one—the first outbreak of unreasonable temper, the drink too many, the sudden stand for principle after a year of acquiescence. The black clerks carried their bedside manner like doctors down the corridors; cheerful and respectful they put up with any insult. The patient was always right.

Round the corner, in front of the old cotton tree, where the earliest settlers had gathered their first day on the unfriendly shore, stood the law courts and police station, a great stone building like the grandiloquent boast of weak men. Inside that massive frame the human being rattled in the corridors like a dry kernel. No one could have been adequate to so rhetorical a conception. But the idea in any case was only one room deep. In the dark narrow passage behind, in the charge-room and the cells, Scobie could always detect the odor of human meanness and injustice—it was the smell of a zoo, of sawdust, excrement, ammonia, and lack of liberty. The place was scrubbed daily, but you could never eliminate the smell. Prisoners and policemen carried it in their clothing like cigarette smoke. (p. 14-15)

The coastal town is a significant setting for Scobie, just as in *The Power and the Glory* the prison cell is for its protagonist and Brighton for its delinquent boy hero. The colonial town is Scobie's habitat. He is set here firmly as the lead in a nightmare scenario. He is bounded by its peculiar compulsions, and his destiny framed against its asphyxiating smallness. Here freedom is but a dream dreamt in the small hours of the night and dissolving into the morning air. This is no world for the innocent. Only the smart, the crafty, and the pervert may survive here. No ideal can contend with their force. Yet Scobie is deeply attached to the place.

Why, he wondered, swerving the car to avoid a dead pye-dog, do I love this place so much? Is it because here human nature hasn't had time to disguise itself? Nobody here could ever talk about a heaven on earth. Heaven remained rigidly in its proper place on the other side of death, and on this side flourished the injustices, the cruelties, the meanness that elsewhere people so cleverly hushed up. Here you could love human beings nearly as God loved them, knowing the worst: you didn't love a pose, a pretty dress, a sentiment artfully assumed. (p. 35-36)

The response and motive are both convincing.

Scobie's response convinces all the more for its depth and its well-tended background. For his sentiments echo those of his prototypes: of Pinkie who felt a stranger anywhere but the dark, dingy lanes of Brighton with their "cheap amusements, the Pullman cars, . . . the unloving weekends."[1] Scobie, likewise, is most at home in his colony. In his active liking for the ugly, he compares even better with the whiskey priest. He shares the priest's quaint insight that peace and joy may be more easily found amidst the stink of mean poverty than among the flamboyant rich. And Scobie concurs with the priest that, whatever one did, the world would go on being "overcrowded with lust and crime and unhappy love." It indeed "stank to heaven."[2] In refusing to take notice of the "magnificent gesture,"[3] the pose or the artful sentiment, Scobie is at one with the whole host of Greene's protagonists. Thus in a way he incorporates in himself the frightening insights into life tested and portrayed already in several of his prototypes. But it is as a representative figure that Scobie is doubtless most authentic. He is surely more sensitive and more completely realized than any other of Greene's characters.

The colony, we learn, is hostile to all that is genuine of life's impulses. Spontaneity is smothered, laughter here rings cracked and hollow, smiles are wan and easily turn into grimaces. The sexual impulse is so abused as to become a mere hollow routine. Yet, in a more supportive context, it might have stood for a harbinger of liberation and a symbol of vitality. Greene's young people are rarely shown in the simple absorption of love. Instead we see genuine emotions substituted for by a pose or gesture, a rehearsed and unmeaning act. We note "the plump slipshod haunches" posing among wild flowers, the "body arms thrown up in suburban ecstasy towards the sky."[4] And we recognize the grand financier entombed within his layers of glass, steel, and concrete.[5] These are the unchanging symbols of contemporary life that Greene has detailed for us. The portrayal is convincing; it also underscores an awful irony. For it seems to compare the helpless selfconsciousness of the materially endowed and the materially striving with the fullness and the freedom of a residual humanity. Old England had surely known the art of a gay, care-free existence; the contemporary individual reared on the commercial truths of duplicity and evasion, knows only anxiety and a soulraking sense of emptiness. Indeed he is riddled with it. "Behind the bright bonhomie of his glance, behind the firm handclasp and the easy joke,"[6] a discerning eye will see lurking a hopelessness vaster than he had ever envisioned. Skirting the purer taste of good and evil, modern humanity must enthuse itself with the dullness of mediocrity—the cardinal virtue of a "sinless graceless chromium world." Thus the African colony not only symptomizes a disease; it sketches in very stark colors a mentality, an attitude towards life: one, however, that Scobie cannot accept.

Scobie is afflicted with an awful sense of inconsequence. In fact it has not once occurred to him "that his life was important enough one way or another. . . . When he thought about it at all, he regarded himself as a man in the ranks, the member of an awkward squad, . . ." (p. 115). But his squad has no commander. Without one, corruption has spread everywhere and muckraking has become a pastime. Traders have their stocks sent underground, causing artificial shortages. Policemen trick the poorest of their scanty earnings. Protection is assured only to the rich or the very wicked. Apparently even governments are only "employed to bolster up an old world which is full of injustice and muddle."[7] The poor are indeed nobody's concern. "There was a retort in this colony to every accusation. There was always a blacker corruption elsewhere to be pointed at. The scandalmongers of the secretariat fulfilled a useful purpose—they kept alive the idea that no one was to be trusted. That was better than complacence." (p. 35). A murky vision indeed, this—though we expected nothing different. For we have surely been told of its smell of a zoo, of sawdust and excrement, and we have been warned of its lack of liberty. Still we are shocked at the sense of uninhibited debauchery which is evoked here in the first scene and sustained through to the end.

The emotional climate thus evoked is enhanced through further association with symbols of the wasteland. Besides the omnipresent vultures, dead pye-dogs, pimps, prostitutes and such other forms of degenerate life are used to build up the scenery. By a clever manipulation of such physical accidents, "a mood and a point of view" are generated, "whose main consciousness is Scobie."[8] Graham Martin has demonstrated in his essay how the prison's "lack of liberty" is, through metaphorical association with an actual smell, established as an irreducible fact of life."[9] Detached from the supporting imagery, Scobie's character would have somewhat lacked conviction. But as it stands, Greene's portrayal is compelling.

The background motifs in *The Heart of the Matter* are then a sense of bewilderment, emptiness and repressed guilt. These are all supported by the secondary characters. Harris and Wilson are representative. Asexed and with a convulsive shame over his corporeality, Harris symbolizes a diseased puritanism. Wilson is more secretive, vain, and even not trustworthy; there is something quite clownish about his responses to life. Wilson's uncomplimentary but true reflection on Harris is no less applicable to him and to the majority of the novel's characters: "the poor sprite is/ Imprisoned for some fault of his/ In a body like a grave." (p. 62)

Like the grave indeed! And the novel's rhetoric allows us no key to freedom. There is no oracle provided, no spiritual guide or custodian of unchanging truths. The Tarot pack is either lost or its charm forgotten; it cannot mediate a spiritual recovery. For even the priests in the novel have not escaped the blight of wasteland. They too are "the hollow men" like the rest: only "a paralysed force."[10] Father Clay, a pious neurotic, is obsessed with eternal damnation. His priestly impulse to heal and nurture the human spirit has atrophied from the very start. The only other priest we have in the book is Father Rank; and Father Rank is no great inspiration, either. Though quite sensitive to the demands of his call, he is equally helpless and painfully conscious of his own futility. His loud hollow laughter echoing through the vast dining hall at Tallit's counterpoints the cockroach hunt between Willson and Harris with the consequent recriminations, frayed tempers and remorseful nights. And together they aptly sum up the book's experiential milieu.

This milieu controls Scobie's attitude towards his world. In another context his responses may seem excessive; they may even have answered to the description of "perverted sentimentality." But in the setting of the novel the emotion is amply justified; indeed would seem the only correct one. For it is not simply Scobie who tells us that "here you could love human beings nearly as God loved them, knowing the worst." We know this is also the author's judgment. Our appreciation of the novel's world at this stage is, in fact, dependent on our accepting Scobie as a reliable guide. This is not to doubt that Scobie would quite naturally win our admiration; we are generally drawn to such a lofty figure of integrity and uncorrupted idealism. But we accept him as our point of view because we are confident of the author's concurrence.

All drama is germinally conflict. Tragedy, like other dramatic types, is a well reasoned elaboration of a major conflict, its crisis and resolution. Whatever particular scheme a conflict follows to its resolution, there is, in tragedy, a close aligning of the component parts. One conflict begets another, and that a third; and the whole is centered around a master conflict which signals the play's motif. Now, often, the dramatic element that links and holds together the various component parts is the protagonist. Sometimes he provokes the conflicts. Whether or not he does that, he is most responsible for their proper elaboration: hence his greater claims to our attention. He also engages our sympathies, guides them in the right direction and, in a successful work, holds them to the end. But to do this he must seem complex and yet consistent, and be convincing to our sense of realism. He may indeed surprise us, but should never give offense. Should he not engage us, the play or novel will have failed. Therefore it is a matter of some importance to inquire about how well our protagonist plays his role.

Scobie fascinates us first with his pessimism. It is not that such denial of life is unheard of. Still, rarely are we treated to so intimate an exposé of it. Scobie embodies an unqualified admission of defeat. He believes in no future and denies, quite rightly, that there is reason enough for celebration. He would not be talked into believing that there is a final solution, an ultimate meaning, to life. He takes misery as a fact of experience; it is a fact as happiness never is, but he can accept no justification for the misery he sees all about him. "What an absurd thing it was to expect happiness in a world so full of misery," he broods while investigating Pemberton's suicide. He is resolved that he will not be deceived by appearances.

Scobie's character gains significantly through a comparison with other Greenean types. With Pinkie he shares the sense of a world that is "dying slowly."[11] He agrees with the lieutenant of *The Power and the Glory* that to live is simply to endure the "cold empty ether spaces."[12] It is "a dying, cooling world" where "human beings had evolved from animals for no purpose at all."[13] But Scobie also differs somewhat from these others in his response to life. For unlike them he does not rebel. Nor does he cherish hopes of rebuilding the world on newer foundations. To build and to destroy are both equally futile to his way of thinking. Both point up a hopeless ambition, and his fifty year's experience has taught him to suspect this. He has learned beyond the possibility of a doubt that nothing is to be gained from engaging oneself in life. Life is rotten beyond repair; nothing on earth can ever quicken it.

Thus the hero we meet from the outset is a man of recognizable dimensions; and he is one who has come to terms with defeat. "Scobie built his home by a process of reduction," we are told. "He had cut down his own needs to a minimum." We learn further that he is the submissive type who would not even defend himself against the predatory instincts of others. Unresisting, he has been "out-maneuvered by a junior official in the interminable war over housing." Rather than sulk over it or plan to do better in the future, as other mortals might in similar conditions, Scobie only prides himself upon being "a good loser." There is thus a sense of Olympian detachment about him which we immediately recognize and grudgingly admire. It enables him to look on unmoved as lesser persons strain and struggle in the furtherance of their varied illusions.

Scobie's character is delineated in a uniquely impressionistic manner. The method, perfected over the years in a dozen novels, has become characteristic with Greene. It is a somewhat glossy manner of presentation and consists, largely, in intermeshing the portrait and environmental details. The technique has been described as "the mass-observer's vision." As one critic has put it, in Greene's novels "both character and atmosphere are evoked by a cross sample of manipulating imagery."[14] Some few selected articles set on a desk may be so worked as to describe the man who sits behind it. Similarly, a woman's character may be drawn convincingly with reference to her room. Setting here is taken almost as an extension of one's personality.

Thus Scobie's environment is sketched in a manner neither wasteful nor irrelevant. His room is described with precision and with great care for the specifying detail. Indeed, in his case the room defines its owner.

> Scobie climbed the great steps and turned to his right along the shaded outside corridor to his room: a table, two kitchen chairs, a cupboard, some rusty handcuffs hanging on a nail like an old hat, a filing cabinet: to a stranger it would have appeared a bare uncomfortable room but to Scobie it was home. Other men slowly build up the sense of home by accumulation—a new picture, more and more books, an odd-shaped paper-weight, the ash-tray bought for a forgotten reason on a forgotten holiday; Scobie built his home by a process of reduction. He had started out fifteen years ago with far more than this. There had been a photograph of his wife, bright leather cushions from the market, an easy-chair, a large colored map of the port on the wall. The map had been borrowed by younger men: it was of no more use to him; he carried the whole coastline of the colony in his mind's eye: from Kufa Bay to Medley was his beat. As for the cushions and the easy-chair, he had soon discovered how comfort of that kind down in the airless town meant heat. Where the body was touched or enclosed it sweated. Last of all his wife's photograph had been made unnecessary by her presence. She had joined him the first year of the phony war and now she couldn't get away: the danger of submarines had made her as much a fixture as the handcuffs on the nail. Besides, it had been a very early photograph, and he no longer cared to be reminded of the unformed face, the expression calm and gentle with lack of knowledge, the lips parted obediently in the smile the photographer had demanded. (pp. 15-16)

The portraiture here is vivid indeed; it is powerful and convincing. Besides defining the character of the protagonist, the scenic details also enforce on us a specific perspective which, consistently, is identified with Scobie's.

The portrait thus created is almost that of a recluse. Scobie's withdrawal from life, however, is not necessarily passive. In fact, it is expressed as a passionate urge: "He dreamed of peace by day and night." At Mass he is so overcome by the invocation for peace that he has to press his fingers "against his eyes to keep the tears of longing in." But the peace of his dreams is also quite different from what is invoked at the liturgy. In its religious context, the word has connotations of a sense of being full, of contentment; it implies a plenitude that satisfies an eternal longing. (And surely it is in this sense that Eliot used the Upanishadic invocation at the close of *The Waste Land*.) For Scobie, however, peace means not fulfillment but a negation; it is described by the image of "the great glowing shoulder of the moon heaving across his window like an iceberg, Arctic and destructive in the moment before the world was struck. . ." (p. 60)   It is but an objective correlative to his compulsive urge to escape. The society of men is too weird for his liking, far too complex for his comfort. It is only quietude, peace he is after: alone by himself he might yet enjoy a measure of rest.

With the later scenes the nature of his peace-loving becomes more clearly apparent. Scobie has just returned from an exhausting tour of Bamba. The scenes that meet him on the road are fascinating for their details. The houses stand

> white as bones in the moonlight; the quiet streets stretched out on either side like the arms of a skeleton, and the faint sweet smell of flowers lay on the air. If he had been returning to an empty house he knew he would have been contented. (p. 94)

The scene, grave and subdued, is wholly suggestive of death. The image of the houses standing out "white as bones in the moonlight" appears alongside other symbols, no less evocative of the graveyard. Together they give to Scobie's longing a body and a content and indeed a very distinct tone. The deserted streets, the eerily quiet night, the faint sweet aroma of flowers as at a wake, and the subconscious expectation of returning to an empty house—all this is meant to clarify the nature of Scobie's withdrawal.

After sending Louise off on her holiday, Scobie comes home listening sharply for "the deep tones of silence." He is momentarily afraid lest his newfound freedom should prove illusory and is much relieved to know that "now there was nothing to listen for." (p. 102)

> Except for the sound of the rain, on the road, on the roofs, on the umbrella, there was absolute silence: only the dying moan of the sirens continued for a moment or two to vibrate within the ear. It seemed to Scobie later that this was the ultimate border he had reached in happiness: being in darkness, alone, with the rain falling, without love or pity. (p. 135)

All except this silence is to him illusory.

Desire is the root-cause of suffering, decreed Buddha. Love and pity are both expressions of a desire, and desire robs a person of freedom. Desire is binding and Scobie would not be bound to a decrepit world. His distrust of the pleasurable, the ecstatic, and the thrilling therefore ought not to surprise us very much. He is only at home in a world that has recognized its essential seediness and has come to terms with this recognition. He takes the wise old man at his word that all is vanity and a chasing the wind, that everything is riddled with a weariness far too large for words, that neither youth nor wealth nor pleasure is worth one's while.[15] Of course he has missed the companion saying that it is best for a man "to eat and drink and enjoy what he has earned" and with a thankful heart, because "even this comes from God."[16] For him such indulgence smacked of heresy and, as a result, he is quite incapable of relating to his life as meaningful the very pleasurable hours he has with Helen Rolt. He returns from Mrs. Rolt's "feeling an extraordinary happiness, but this he would not remember as happiness, as he would remember setting out in the darkness, in the rain, alone."

(p. 140) Scornful of desire, denying all pleasure, Scobie must have his peace.

Peace then means to him a disavowal of certain associations and memories. According to his script, *peace* reads equal to *no emotion*. Consequently he dreads every occasion when another's needs or aspirations might make demands upon his compassion. Yet once the demands are actually made, he is unable to stand by uninvolved, as a mere onlooker. An obsessive pity and an urge to withdraw are, then, complementary strains in his character.

The dual tendency of Scobie's personality is brought out convincingly in his reaction to his daughter's death years ago. His wife, in England, had kept him informed of the child's progress, but two of her telegrams got mixed up so that her second message had already arrived and announced the daughter's death when the first message came tardily to convey hopes of recovery. Scobie recalls how disappointed he felt through his confusion, thinking that there was some mistake, that his child was still alive. "I thought 'now the anxiety begins, and the pain'." But when he realized the error: "it was all right, she was dead, I could begin to forget her." (p. 156) This is a complex portrayal of a real emotion. It surfaces, without analytical violence, the major facets of Scobie's character. We notice his anxious withdrawal from life's concerns, and yet poised against it is an intense responsiveness to suffering. The two drives are mutually exclusive and yet in Scobie's person they are united, and in no haphazard manner but compellingly. Their frenzied interaction within the protagonist's soul is, germinally, the dramatic action.

The prime object of Scobie's pity is his wife Louise. She is also the leading partner in the playing out of his tragedy. Her role is to support the dominant emotions delineated in Scobie's character, which she does admirably. As object of his pity her profile is surely convincing; and because her company is quite intolerable, she also justifies his urge for solitude. For all that, her character is drawn in a rather sketchy manner. The book indeed denies her all claims to individuality. She has no being independent of the limited role allotted her. She might as well be no more than a stage piece pulled and pushed around by the plot. Along with Helen and Scobie's legend of God, Louise suffers from the appearance of being stage-managed to suit Scobie's point of view. The result is a loss in dimension for these characters, and for the reader an astigmatic perspective. The undue advantage Scobie gains in the process inhibits the reader's judgment and blinds him to the truth that Scobie is incontestably a man in error. Here perhaps was an error of judgment on the side of the novelist.

We meet Louise for the first time, through Scobie's eyes, as he comes home from office to find her in bed, indisposed. "Under the mosquito net she reminded him of a dog or cat." His image of her but a moment later is that "of a joint under a meat cover." We learn that her eyes are closed, her hair matted, dark and stringy with sweat; her face has the sickly tinge of atabrine: she is "so completely 'out'." But the image has an immeasurable appeal to his sense of pity. "These were the times of ugliness when he loved her, when pity and responsibility reached the intensity of a passion." Pretty and graceful, Louise should have drawn no sympathy; but Scobie is "bound by the pathos of her unattractiveness." (pp. 21, 22, 23, 28)

Predictably Louise cannot answer any positive need in him. His own needs are few and, apparently, a woman's love is not among them. His disengagement from life is so nearly complete that he expects nothing of value from it. His wife is not a partner to him but a responsibility to be borne with patience. There is no personal charm about her, no mystery, nothing of the unique or the individual; and all this we accept on Scobie's word. Never, indeed, does her personality affect him with a sense of perplexity or doubt or incomprehension. For him she is merely somebody rather pathetic, ugly, and unimaginative. "Like an animal she gave way completely to the momentary sickness and recovered as suddenly." He is only aware of her dependence on him.

For his utter lack of regard for Louise, Scobie yet has an exaggerated sense of responsibility on her account. He blames himself for having failed her in life. "Women depended so much on pride, pride in themselves, their husbands, their surroundings." And Scobie has failed utterly in bolstering up his wife's vanity. He is aware that no one can ever guarantee another's happiness, that one can scarcely even hope to understand another completely. But Louise's misery has a massive impact on his sensibilities. He is borne down by "the tide of her melancholy and disappointment." He has "led the way" for her; he is responsible because he "formed her face." "'I've landed her here' he thought, with the odd premonitory sense of guilt he always felt as though he were responsible for something in the future he couldn't even foresee." He might have added, "And I have landed myself with her here"; for his own situation is no more enviable.

The newly inserted scene with Wilson and Louise Scobie on their evening walk helps to set her character in perspective.

> "Henry doesn't love me," she said gently, as though she were teaching a child, using the simplest words to explain a difficult subject, simplifying. . . She leant her head back against the guichet and smiled at him as much to say, it's quite easy really when you get the hang of it. "He'll be happier without me," she repeated. (p. 76)

An ant is moving up her neck and Wilson makes to flick it away but ends up kissing her. He is elated at his deed, his romantic sentiments fully aroused. "It seemed to him that an act had been committed which altered the whole world." Louise's response is typical: "'I hate him,' she said, carrying on the conversation exactly where it had been left."

This scene, deleted from the original and re-introduced in the Collected Edition of 1971, was a saving afterthought. For it corrects to a degree the imbalance in narration and somewhat redeems Louise's character. Indeed, it is not very hard to appreciate the anger of a neglected wife. We recognize as quite natural, and legitimate, Louise's scorn for her husband who, in her view, is a chronic failure. We readily sympathize with her need for some avocation, poetry or friendship, to fill her lonely hours. Nor are we surprised that her misery should now and again break and spill over in little spurts of hate. Louise does not forgive her husband for not upholding her pride. Scorning his pity, she still appeals to it whenever this should pay off. She delights in tormenting him with a nickname he detests. Unfeeling, she baits him into financing an exorbitant holiday for her. When Wilson ventures that Scobie could not possibly find the means, she only retorts: "That's man's business," as if his anxieties were no concern of hers. And with a devastating lightness she adds: "'He'll do anything for me.' . . . 'Oh,' she said, 'but he has a terrible sense of responsibility.'" (p. 79)

Though uninhibited in her egotism, Louise cannot be denied a measure of integrity. She at least does not pretend to a virtue she does not possess. She is conscious of her misery and her hatred. And indeed she herself suffers no less than what she inflicts. Although her hatred must necessarily affect the destiny of her husband, this can be overemphasized. On closer scrutiny one may even find that the harm she does him is less than what he does himself with his muddled compassion. That she successfully plays on his sense of responsibility is no less a commentary on his weakness than on her cynicism.

Considered psychoanalytically, Scobie's confusion may be traced to a vaguely diagnosed nihilism. He persists in viewing life through the colored filter of his fifty years. His perplexity is not altogether uncommon: at the root of most neuroses there is a deranged perspective. The imbalance in Scobie's mental perspective is shown by his unconscious denial of whole ranges of experiential data. His life clearly is blighted by the shadow of his own cynicism. The result is a misapprehension of realities and objective situations, and his response, in consequence, is miserably inadequate.

Scobie's self-befuddlement adds an extra dimension to his personality. It contributes to his tragic flaw, expressed as pity, an emotion both complex and wholly unauthentic. The author has rightly designated it as "the terrible promiscuous passion." Pity is an indulgence Scobie cannot resist, and his defense of it is not unconvincing. "It isn't beauty that we love," he says, "it's failure—failure to stay young for ever, the failure of the nerves, the failure of the body." Scobie is in the grip of an awful compulsion.

Pity smoldered like decay at his heart. He would never rid himself of it. He knew from experience how passion died away and how love went, but pity always stayed. Nothing ever diminished pity. The conditions of life nurtured it. (p. 178)

And so he would go through life driven by this "terrible desire to protect."

Although the novel's rhetoric is so geared as to support Scobie's reading of his situation, it does not thereby excuse his indulging in pity. If Scobie were right that life had no ultimate meaning whatever, then surely there was nothing worth saving either, for anyone; hence he ought to have known his efforts were altogether in vain. Also it should have seemed somewhat temerarious for him to usurp the redemptive role and to imply that he was the elect charged with salvaging what was already lost. "There was only a single person in the world who was unpitiable, oneself." This touches on idolatry.

No doubt, Scobie's emotion is a corruption of compassion.[17] The author says he meant to show it as a species of pride, since pity and pride are often closely aligned. Scobie errs in not taking into account his limitations. Pity may be all right for the gods, but what mortal has the means to satisfy it? Who but a god alone can read the human heart, or plumb its depts or assuage its pain? Compassion is noble, but pity is never truly human. We notice that even the "greatest of commandments" has stopped short at a "Love thy neighbor as thyself." Scobie, like the legendary Icarus, tries the impossible; and it is the fascinating account of his frenzied efforts that the action unfolds before us.

"Pity is cruel. Pity destroys. Love isn't safe when pity's prowling round."[18] So Greene wrote in his 'entertainment,' *The Ministry of Fear*. His objective in *The Heart of the Matter*, he has said, was "to enlarge on" that same theme: "the disastrous effect on human beings of pity as distinct from compassion."[19]

The "disastrous effect" shows very gradually. But it is already noted in the first chapter, in the scene with the Portuguese captain, where Scobie's weakness is shown in full play. Caught off guard with a contraband letter, the captain pleads with him for leniency. Scobie looks up and reads in the suppliant face the image of a victim: the captain "kept on wiping his eyes with the back of his hand like a child—an unattractive child, the fat boy of the school." Immediately the millstone begins to grind on Scobie's breast. The reduced aspect of the captain evokes pity; he feels in some way responsible. "Against the beautiful and the clever and the successful, one can wage a pitiless war, but not against the unattractive." The captain mutters something about the blow it would be to his daughter should he lose his job, and with that all Scobie's doubts are cleared away. He will not turn the letter in, although that amounts to a betrayal of his profession. But even as the flames lick up the last scrap of what had been the captain's letter, his guilt at betrayal has begun to haunt him. With that one act he has set himself on a new course. The carefully nurtured sense of integrity, now torn to shreds, lies crumbled with the ashes in the incinerator. Neither is he consoled to think that neither money nor any ordinary passion has lured him off the straight path, or that no one is privy to the act. It is not others but his own conscience that accuses him. "His own heartbeats told him he was guilty—that he had joined the ranks of the corrupt police officials." (p. 55)

The scene is revealing inasmuch as it shows up the true nature of Scobie's emotion and the modality of its functioning. The effect of pity on the protagonist is well defined and its potential for effecting his ruin is delineated powerfully and with great conviction. Later, in his office, Scobie rehearses the scene he must enact with his wife at home. Every gesture and word is scrutinized and weighed ahead as it may either enhance her misery or arrest it till later on. "So much of life was putting off unhappiness for another time," Scobie pleads. "He had a dim idea that perhaps if one delayed long enough, things were taken out of one's hands altogether by death."

But deferring a problem never solved it, as Scobie himself had learned on a previous occasion. Then, with his urge to salvage the night from the onslaughts of her growing misery, he had promised his wife a holiday, an expensive one in far off South Africa. He thus had committed himself to something beyond his means. Now he must go on pretending that somehow the money is being found. "People talk about the courage of condemned men walking to the place of execution: sometimes it needs as much courage to walk with any kind of bearing towards another person's habitual misery." (p. 56)   With the bank having refused him the loan, his options are considerably reduced. For the only person who could, and would, lend him the money is Yusuf; and Yusuf is a corrupt man, a Syrian and a merchant. He is of such reputation that no responsible officer would even be seen with him. "It would have been safer to accept the Portuguese captain's bribe." (p. 96)

Anxiety continues to grow in Scobie. It pursues him through the tour of Bamba where he is to investigate a case of suicide. More than the suicide itself it is the 200 pounds that occupies his thoughts. He simply must find the money, and fast, failing which he imagines what terrible calamities lie ahead. Pemberton has left a suicide note signed, "Your loving son, Dicky." Now Scobie's delirious mind reads it modified as "Your loving husband, Ticki." And Ticki is Louise's nickname for him. It is his subconscious sounding the alarm.

The tour completed, Scobie returns home. "Slowly and drearily he had reached the decision to tell her that the money simply could not be found," that she must stay on for another six months. But coming home he finds his wife strangely subdued. It is as if their roles were sudenly reversed, as if it was he who needed her pity and protection. "The sense of failure deepened around him." He feels "oddly unmanned." And in a frenzy of anxiety he tells Louise that she may book her passage. His decision made, he can now relax, cushioned on the knowledge of his awful sacrifice.

Louise's passage is bought with a loan from Yusuf, and with that loan the last vestiges of Scobie's integrity are demolished. Visiting the Syrian's quarters later he recognizes his own guilt: "perhaps because he had returned to the scene of a crime." His experience in the colony assured him that every association with Yusuf spelt corruption. "Useless to tell himself that he had committed no offence. Like a woman who has made a loveless marriage he recognized in the room . . . the memory of an adultery." (p. 149)

This is a fine artistic contrivance: associating, in Scobie's mind, the financial deal with his own marriage. His relationship with both Louise and Yusuf is essentially of the noblest kind; either might have grown into trust and devotion and love. Each has the fullest potential implied in a solemn pledge to friendship. But Scobie, with his long years' experience, knows how sterile a marriage may be and how empty every sort of pledge. Besides, where is any guarantee that the vows and the pledges will be honored? "There are certain places one never leaves behind; the curtains and cushions of this room joined an attic bed room, an ink stained desk, a lacy altar in Ealing—they would be there so long as consciousness lasted." (p. 151) The fourteen years of life with Louise had belied his marital expectations; he cannot now believe that his new relationship with Yusuf will be any more sound or satisfying.

With this much information for background, we are now ushered to the scenes of the central conflicts. In most of Book One, Greene's concern was to define his protagonist's character and his fatal flaw. Scobie's proneness to disaster is portrayed sensitively and in a convincing manner. Book Two is given wholly to an exposition of the tragic action. Here we are at the very heart of the book's drama. It opens on a scene of shipwreck; Scobie is among the officers providing relief.

Scobie is deeply affected by the torpedo-victims. To him they are not merely some war-casualties, but immensely more: they are rather the dramatized links in a personal and a cosmic equation. Among the victims, two particularly hold his attention: a dying girl of six and a widow, the latter very young, worn and exhausted. As he stands watching the six-year old in the makeshift hospital, he imagines seeing "a white communion veil over her head." For that is how he remembered his own daughter whose death had left him with a sense of guilt. "It was a trick of the light on the mosquito net and a trick of his own mind." But the knowledge yields him no consolation. "He had been in Africa when his own child died. He had always thanked God that he had missed that. It seemed after all that one never really missed a thing. To be a human being one had to drink the cup." Now charged with intense feeling he begs God to look after this child. God must give her peace at any cost, even denying it to him "for ever." It happens that his plea is heard. The child dies in peace. Scobie might now heave a sigh of relief and move on. Only he does not, as if his mission were yet unaccomplished. His pity, newly excited by a death-bed, is looking about for another victim on whom it might lavish its attentions. And that victim is Helen Rolt, the young woman widowed in the shipwreck. But two days before he had watched her being carried past on a stretcher. "Her arms as thin as a child's lay outside the blanket, and her fingers clasped a book firmly," a stamp-album. He had also noticed "the wedding-ring loose on her dried-up finger." Scobie would now always remember "how she was carried into his life on a stretcher grasping a stamp-album with her eyes fast shut." (p. 121)

Helen excites a complex of feelings within Scobie. Unlike the six-year old, she is not simply child and victim but also a woman denied her fulfillment for ever. The child's hand clasping a stamp-album and "the wedding-ring loose on [the] dried-up finger" are both heraldic of Helen's personality. Both together must account for the sort of demands she makes upon the hero's sensibility and for the complex responses she elicits from him. "It seemed to Scobie that she had never known her way around—at least not since she had left her netball team; was it a year ago? Sometimes he saw her lying back in the boat on that oily featureless sea day after day with the other child near death and the sailor going mad . . ., and sometimes he saw her carried past him on a stretcher grasping her stamp-album, and now he saw her in the borrowed unbecoming bathing-dress grinning at Bagster as he stroked her legs, listening to the laughter and the splashes, not knowing the adult etiquette. . . . Sadly like an evening tide he felt responsibility bearing him up the shore." (p. 157)

When Scobie meets her again, Helen is discharged from meddical care and is housed in a Nissen hut adjacent to his own quarters. They immediately become friends. His advanced years signalled safety, and he feels well at ease with her innocence, her childish airs and enthusiasm. "It seemed to him that he had not felt so much at ease with another human being for years—not since Louise was young. But this case was different, he told himself: they were safe with each other. He was more than thirty years the older; his body in this climate had lost the sense of lust; he watched her with sadness and affection and enormous pity because a time would come when he couldn't show her around in a world where she was at sea." (p. 159) Scobie takes it as self-evident that he alone could, and would, guide her through a wayward world.

Towards the end of his visit, Helen turns to him suddenly: "It's so good to talk to you," she says. "I can say anything I like. I'm not afraid of hurting you. You don't want anything out of me. I'm safe." The tone is one of wondering rapport, like a child's or of young love: fresh and trustful. "We're both safe," he says, to which she responds with a compelling affirmation of faith: "I have a feeling that you'd never let me down." And Scobie takes her words as "a command he would have to obey however difficult." Right at that instant there is a knock on the door: it is Freddie Bagster drunkenly calling out to her to open up for him. Helen stands alerted, pressing close to Scobie's side, tensely watching the door. And he has "the sense of an animal which had been chased to its hole." With the sound of Bagster's steps receding, they kiss and subsequently make love. "What they had both thought was safety proved to have been the camouflage of an enemy who works in terms of friendship, trust and pity." (p. 160)

The scene is done to perfection. The complex emotion binding the lovers is sketched sensitively and with great regard for truth. Waking up, Scobie is surprised to feel Helen's body by his side and momentarily ("before his tenderness and pleasure awoke"), she seems like "someone who had been shot in escaping," as though he was only "looking at a bundle of cannon fodder." Helen too wakes up disturbed, mumbling "Bagster can go to hell." She had dreamt that she was lost in a marsh and Bagster found her. But there is also excitement: Scobie has even left his umbrella behind. Setting out homeward in the dark, he is conscious of "an odd jubilation, as though he had rediscovered something he had lost, something which belonged to his youth." But neither the thrill nor the joy seem to him important enough to remember.

Back in his own room, Scobie repents the trap he has newly laid for himself.

In the future—that was where the sadness lay. Was it the butterfly that died in the act of love? But human beings were condemned to consequences. The responsibility as well as the guilt was his—he was not a Bagster: he knew what he was about. He had sworn to preserve Louise's happiness, and now he had accepted another and contradictory responsibility. He felt tired by all the lies he would some time have to tell; he felt the wounds of those victims who had not yet bled. Lying back on the pillow he stared sleeplessly out towards the grey early morning tide. Somewhere on the face of those obscure waters moved the sense of yet another wrong and another victim, not Louise, not Helen. (p. 161-162)

Is the unidentified victim perhaps not the same as the "hooded" figure of Eliot's *The Waste Land?* Like Eliot, Greene too has shown a marked preference for mythic symbols; and to water, we know, is generally assigned a redemptive significance. The movement "on the face of those obscure waters" also evokes Genesis 1:2. where "the spirit of God was moving," drawing out a universe only to be violated by the First Man. Apparently Scobie has premonitions of a future when even God would be a victim of his betrayal.

The affair, thus begun, moves by its own momentum which urges it further on. But secrecy has already begun to tell. Helen, quite predictably, is irked by Scobie's discretion. She also feels somewhat guilty and reacts to his caution by challenging his motives. She wonders aloud if he is not after all putting on an act; she starts badgering him, demanding proofs of his devotion. Her tone reminds him "oddly of Louise." In their dissatisfaction they have become indistinguishable. "He wondered sadly whether love always inevitably took the same road. It was not only the act of love itself that was the same." Helen is less experienced, that is all; and perhaps less capable of giving pain: but the fury of wounded vanity is unmistakable. She made a proper companion for Louise. "She was like a child with a pair of dividers who knows her power to injure. You could never trust a child not to use her advantage." This indeed is his moment of truth. He must by now know himself and the direction his pity would inevitable take. He is at the crossroads and we, the readers, are observing the most significant crisis of all. He may yet come to grips with his own compulsion or allow the wheel to run to full circle. We watch him attentively because Scobie's response to Helen, to her "bitterness and frustration," we know, is of the greatest consequence.

It needs to be observed that often Scobie's pity has implications of the most abject self-denial. Attempting to comfort Louise he does not shame to call himself by a nickname he detests. He had no compelling reason to give his wife a long expensive holiday at the cost of compromising himself and his profession. That the death of an unknown child should move him so, that he offers up for her his "peace for ever" is indeed passing strange. Yet, given Scobie's character, all this is quite natural: it is the diverse expression of the same inner urge—compulsive, powerful, and self-destructive. There is no damming of its wild rush now. That is Scobie's fatal decision and the significance of his frenzied efforts to reassure Helen. For suddenly flinging all caution to the winds, he takes "a sheet of . . . official paper stamped with the government watermark" and with grave gestures there writes his convenant: "'I love you more than myself, more than my wife, more than God, I think.'" No one could have promised more; and no oath could have been more solemn. But he is suddenly struck by "the banality of [his words]; they seemed to have no truth personal to herself: they had been used too often. If I were young, he thought, I would be able to find the right words, the new words, but all this has happened to me before." (p. 181) Nevertheless he repeats the password, "I love you," before signing the letter. "In human relations," Scobie has always held, "kindness and lies are worth a thousand truths."

The letter to Helen is the high water mark of the novel's action. In fact it denotes the very climax. The solemn act of signing the letter makes it as stern as an oath. It commits him just as inexorably to Helen as he is already to his wife by the marriage bond. The letter to Helen also implies a conscious decision to sustain the complicity and the evasions to the very end, come what may. What began as a vague sense of responsibility is now weighted with a nuance, even a sacramental dignity. Soon afterwards this is further reinforced with a triple oath. Scobie says to

Helen: "I'll always come if you want me. . . . I promise. . . . I'll always be here if you need me, as long as I'm alive." (p. 187) The rest of the action is but an elaboration of this one tragic decision.

Immediately on the heels of that oath, disaster strikes the lovers. Helen informs Scobie that she did not receive his letter. The note has simply vanished. Suddenly it is as if in the dusk were enemy eyes watching, bodies lying in wait. "Somebody is getting something on you," she says hopelessly. It is as if the oath were the password to some infernal world. But the word has been uttered, the evil unleashed, and its forces now rushing converge on the harried lovers. Scobie walks home and is greeted by a message announcing Louise is on her way home.

> He sat down. His head swam with nausea. He thought: if I had never written that other letter. . . how easily then life could have been arranged again. But he remembered his words in the last ten minutes, "I'll always be here if you need me as long as I'm alive"—that constituted an oath as ineffaceable as the vow by the Ealing altar. . . .
> Leaning back against the dressing-table, he tried to pray. The Lord's Prayer lay as dead on his tongue as a legal document. . . (p. 189)

The implications of the responsibilities he has newly accepted now strike him with a sudden and stunning finality. His dilemma appears insoluble, as he cannot imagine his ever going back on commitments already made. Despair enters the scene and, hovering about a bit, has perched itself definitely by Scobie's side. He resents it as he now resents all the exacting demands made on his compassion. "Why me, he thought, why do they need me, a dull middle-aged police officer who had failed for promotion? I've got nothing to give them that they can't get elsewhere. . . . It sometimes seemed to him that all he could share with them was his despair." (p. 189)

He only sought to give happiness to those in his care; for himself solitude is all he asked. What he has achieved thus far is to infect them all with his hopelessness, and the revelation is a blow. "'I don't want to plan anymore,'" he cries out suddenly. "'They wouldn't need me if I were dead. No one needs the dead. The dead can be forgotten. O God, give me death before I give them unhappiness.'" Shaking some tablets of aspirin onto his palm, he is seen toying with the idea of suicide. "The unforgivable sin," the priests said, but had not Christ "killed himself"? "He had hung himself on the cross as surely as Pemberton from the picture-rail." (p. 190)

The mystery of the missing letter, however, is shortly resolved with Yusuf coming along to claim his involvement. He is transferring some of his contraband gems to relations abroad, and he has come to Scobie to ask a favor: would he kindly hand over a packet to the Portuguese captain. With that done, Scobie could immediately have his letter back. But if he refused, the Syrian warns him, Scobie's letter will find its way to Louise on her arrival: a neat gift for her homecoming. Yusuf knows his victim. Scobie is trapped.

There is to be no respite for Scobie anymore. Day by day now, his tragedy is gaining momentum. Even the reader feels deeply drawn into the unfolding action. There is growing absorption about the drama. Scobie's disintegration is now so quick it is nearly visible to the eye. He meekly submits to the blackmail and is immediately aware of the strring of a general distrust. This was his indictment against himself. Having betrayed a trust he can never again trust another human being, not even Ali, the boy who has served him loyally for the past fifteen years. And what a lot indeed Ali knew! "He could ruin me, he thought: he could ruin them"—his protegees, Helen and Louise. In his new corruption, Yusuf is his sole companion. The Syrian, he is confident, would understand his dilemma. Yusuf does. He reassures him, taking upon himself all his cares. Scobie must never again worry about things, and Yusuf's way is to have the boy murdered. Now looking down upon Ali's slashed body he cannot suppress a sigh:

> . . . if only I could weep, if only I could feel pain. . . . O God
> he thought, I've killed you: you've served me all these years
> and I've killed you at the end of it. God lay there under the

petrol drums and Scobie felt the tears in his mouth, salt in the
cracks of his lips. You served me and I did this to you. You
were faithful to me, and I wouldn't trust you. (p. 247-248)

Ali represented the "servant God," the God who is ever faithful;
and in Scobie's mind his involvement with his boy's death has
larger and more frightening consequences.

In fact, the consequences have already been showing. From the
first day of her arrival, Louise has been urging him to go to Communion with her: "a sign that we've started again—in the right
way." This is a twist of the screw Scobie never anticipated and it
has him pinned in an impossible situation. For if he refuses to go to
Communion, it will naturally arouse Louise's suspicion; and he
cannot Communicate without a proper Confession. Merely
confessing one's sins was of no account; it did not qualify unless he
first repented of his sin; and his sin is adultery. For his Confession
to be effective, Scobie must resolve to break off with Helen. This
he is not prepared to do. "Save my soul and abandon her to
Bagster and despair"? he broods instead. Besides, his commitment
to Helen was just as final and binding as the one to Louise. In the
circumstances, no repentance would be possible, and no Confession valid; and without proper Confession, Communion would be
a sacrilege, the "worst sin." Scarcely could he have caught himself
in a worse tangle.

Scobie flinches from even the thought of a sacrilege, but not
from fear of retribution. Should he even have to "pay terribly" in
an afterlife, in order in protect his loved ones he will pay any price.
The source of his concern is really his intense feelings regarding the
gravity of the offense. For, to receive Communion in a state of un-
repented sin was worse than murder. It was a desecration of God
who out of love had made Himself into a Victim. As he says to
Helen, "It's striking God when He's down—in my power."
(p. 211) Murder was small matter compared to this.

Helen dismisses it all as sheer humbug: "I don't understand a
thing you are saying. It's all hooey to me." But by mistaking
Scobie's anxiety for a ploy she does him an injustice. It also shows
her incomprehension of his person and the nature of the emotion

that binds him to her. Her failure at grasping his moral dilemma is nearly complete; and she is a total stranger to the religious scruples that riddle him, forcing decisions where he sees no options, only responsibilities. As a result, neither can she appreciate the intensity of his anguish. For him there is never a question of either abandoning Helen or allowing Louise to discover his infidelity. They must be spared their suffering. At whatever cost to himself he is resolved to protect them. And now, with Louise insisting on his Communion, he would have yet another Victim to protect, even God. But he has a sudden inspiration on waking up. He fakes chest pains, calls for a dose of brandy and spoils the day for the Communion. He has just about won himself a brief reprieve. But the reprieve, he well knows, is only temporary: who would, day after day, go on faking imaginary aches?

Scobie's moral dilemma is rooted in such conflicts as he is unwilling to face. He ought to have had the courage to clear up the welter of his motivations and beliefs: but this he has not. Wanting an ordered moral conscience to guide and untangle his confused sentiments, his responses to life situations are frightfully unbalanced. His decisions, too, are unguided by reason and are themselves often but acts of despair. Thus his decision: "once and for all now at whatever eternal cost, [to] clear himself in [Louise's] eyes and give her the reassurance she needed." (p. 223)

Accordingly he accompanies her to church on the following day, but upon entering it he is overcome by a terrible reluctance. Tears strain at his eyes; "and looking up towards the cross on the altar he thought savagely: Take your sponge of gall. You made me what I am." (p. 224)   At last the dreaded moment has come.

Father Rank came down the steps from the altar bearing the Host. The saliva had dried in Scobie's mouth: it was as though his veins had dried. He couldn't look up; he saw only the priest's skirt like the skirt of the medieval warhorse bearing down upon him: the flapping of feet: the charge of God. If only the archers would let fly from ambush, and for a moment he dreamed that the priest's steps had indeed faltered: perhaps after all something may yet happen before he reaches me: some incredible interposition. . . . But with open mouth (the time had come) he made one last attempt at prayer, "O God, I offer up my damnation to you. Take it. Use it for them," and was aware of the pale papery taste of an eternal sentence on the tongue. (p. 225)

That act, he is convinced, was "a blow, a stab, a shot" on the prostrate body of the divine Victim. Scobie now sees himself in the accursed role of the Roman centurion. Yet he was not damning himself in order to save himself or an abstraction like the State; he was only defending two helpless women. Now he is doubtful if even his sacrifices would yield the desired effect, if the knowledge and the pain would be withheld for long. What indeed had he about him save his corruption to share, and by which he might redeem?

In a subsequent scene, Scobie confronts Helen: " 'Never pretend I haven't shown my love,' " he tells her. The touch of resentment in his voice infuriates her. " Love for your wife, " she retorts; " You were afraid she'd find out. "

Anger drained out of him. He said, "Love for both of you. If it were just for her there'd be an easy straight way." He put his hands over his eyes, feeling hysteria beginning to mount again. He said, "I can't bear to see suffering, and I cause it all the time. I want to get out, get out." (p. 233)

There are many faces to love. Scobie's love, corrupted to pity, has spawned a monster that would leave nothing and nobody unharmed on its trail.

The corruption of God in sacrilege is only the newest number in the list of his sins. But to him it is the most heinous of all. Week after week, he fears, he must go on with his torment of God; he can foresee no respite, no end to the mockery and the scourging. He has chosen the accursed role of the Roman soldier which he must replay endlessly on holy days and feastdays—striking his God, piercing Him with nails and sword and spear. It would have been better were he never born. If he could only vanish from life, could escape into the shoreless void where nothing was and no demand may be made on his compassion!

Introducing the novel in the collected edition, Greene has said that "suicide was [Scobie's] inevitable end; the particular motive of his suicide, to save even God from himself, was the final twist of the screw of his inordinate pride." (p. xv) The explanation, though valid to a degree, seems to me to overstate the case. The muddled reaction from the reading public and from reviewers naturally irritated the novelist, and in the end may well have provoked him to underplay some of the book's complexity. But is it really fair to lay the whole burden of Scobie's tragedy upon his own shoulders? Was he so entirely responsible, he and no one else? And did he deserve so unqualified an indictment from his author? Although Scobie is responsible for much of the muddle, his responses to his world are convincing because they are supported by the reality which we know of as objective.

Scobie's is an *ersatz* emotion, but only when contrasted with *our* idea of compassion and love. The novel's standard, however, is not the same as ours; nor does it seem to encourage a contrast. Indeed, it presents us with nothing more genuine or sympathetic than what is characterized in Scobie; and pride implies a contrast. Without a notable difference between the real and the illusory, and a clear perception of the difference, there can be no alleging pride. For pride, after all, is but a deliberate and willful decision in favor of an illusion. It must assume an alternative. But in the novel no such alternative course of action is indicated. Scobie's response to his situation is so favorably treated that one has the impression that another response would be neither right nor satisfactory. Given a relation of near conformity between the reality as shown and the response, it hardly becomes us to judge a character or to indict him against standards largely alien to his own world view.

What then is *The Heart of the Matter* finally about? What meaning is one to glean from it, or what message does it convey? Although critics have been greatly exercised over these questions during the past three decades, a consensus has yet to evolve. Arnold Kettle, for instance, says the work is a "moral fable."[20] But George Orwell thinks the emphasis is theological, and none the better for it.[21] To attempt "to clothe theological speculations in flesh and blood" is surely a debatable experiment, and Orwell doubts if it has ever yielded good art. Theology is more likely to tilt the scales; it must seek to guide and, in forcing the artist's hand, it must produce psychological absurdities. The stronger the theological intent, the greater the liability to abstraction, and the novel is an art form that is concerned with life in the concrete. Nothing but the real conflicts of life can animate it, no thoughts must interfere, and nothing must distract it from the flow of lived experience. This is the correct position and a rule to insist on. Father Martindale is not unaware of this, and yet he too, like Orwell, has chosen to underscore the theological interest. But he qualifies: theology in *The Heart of the Matter* is not notional nor an abstraction, but apparently a drive, and hence woven into the emotional pattern. That Scobie's "sins caused him such agonies" is then gravely significant; and nowise should it appear objectionable that the book seems to "suggest a profound conviction of the horror of sin and the miseries it brings about."[22] Father Martindale even thinks it has been a gain, enhancing the experience and hence the total effect of the work.

Most other views either play variations on these themes or are supplementaries to them. Thus the book has been taken as an illustration of the thesis, "that human action as such doesn't really matter much at all."[23] Allegedly neither "the ethics [nor the] aspirations of a sinful humanity" are of primary concern; in the book it is "the relation between man and God that is important." It has been further suggested that "the heart of the matter is the innate sinfulness of man and his need of divine mercy." In a parallel vein, the protagonist too has been variously described as a saint and a glorified sinner. He is thought to be fashioned after the very image of Jesus, "an all-suffering *alter Christus*."[24] Evelyn Waugh has opined that Scobie's behavior is indeed actuated by the love of God.[25]

The opinions are too various and confusing and, to an author, this is scarcely a circumstance to be proud of. Greene's own reaction to them is to that extent typical. He replies by disowning the book as a whole, as one he does not much care for at all. He admits a measure of authorial uncertainty in the craftsmanship. "In the six years [preceding] the start of *The Heart of the Matter* my writing had become rusty with disuse and misuse." (p. vii)   "In 1945 I felt myself at a loss. How had I in the past found the progressions from one scene to another? How confine the narrative to one point of view, or at most two? A dozen such technical questions tormented me as they had never done before the war when the solution had always come easily." (p. xii).   Insofar as there is a flaw in the book's artistry, this would seem to be centered about Greene's managing the point of view. It was very unwise of him to confine himself to a single perspective when that perspective was a defective one: Scobie, an imperfect and deluded hero. Viewing the whole, or even most, of the drama from Scobie's side gives him an undue importance in the reader's eyes; and the advantage so gained is no help in correctly defining his character. The scales are too heavily weighted in his favor and, as a result, instead of suspecting his motives, we feel persuaded to take them as accepted, if not as the most honorable. Consequently the book's larger world-view escapes us. A partial view is imposed on us, and the whole is confused and there is an unnecessary blurring of the philosophical scheme.

In trying to decode the final and weighted meaning of the novel we must look to the first chapter of book two, part I. It is here that the theme-passage occurs. The scene is the rescue of those torpedoed. Scobie, having just seen the survivors to their temporary shelter, is visibly disturbed; their pitiable aspect lies heavily on his mind; and the author feels advised to take us more fully into his confidence.

> [Scobie] went restlessly out on to the verandah, closing the netted door carefully behind him. . . . The lights were showing in the temporary hospital, and the weight of that misery lay on his shoulders. It was as if he had shed one responsibility only to take on another. This was a responsibility he shared with all human beings, but that was no comfort, for it sometimes seemed to him that he was the only one who recognized his responsibility. In the Cities of the Plain a single soul might have changed the mind of God.

. . .   .

Outside the rest-house he stopped again. The lights inside would have given an extraordinary impression of peace if one hadn't known, just as the stars on this clear night gave also an impression of remoteness, security, freedom. If one knew, he wondered, the facts, would one have to feel pity even for the planets? if one reached what they called the heart of the matter? (p. 122-24)

"The Cities of the Plain" is a reference to Genesis 18, where the degenerate towns of Sodom and Gomorrah are threatened with the direst of divine anger. To Abraham's importunate pleas God at last assents: He will spare the towns should there be even ten righteous men found amoung them. But the patriarch's anxious search is in vain. Not only are there not so many as ten righteous men in the two towns, Abraham fails to find even a single soul such as might "change the mind of God." This is Scobie's reading of his own situation. His world is no less decrepit than were Sodom or Gomorrah; it is just as decadent morally, and spiritually as barren. Under the semblance of virtue, of security, and of happiness, there lurks an "extreme egotism." Spite and malice fester; and everywhere one is met with signs of injustice, hatred, and violence. Scobie wonders that a God should have conceived of such a world; and once created, it could be so abandoned as to be so irredeemably lost. But lost indeed is his world, and this is a fact that must make one pity even the planets. With God having washed His hands clean of all responsibility, Scobie must bear the entire weight of the burden as best as he may.

This is a strange and startling cosmography. Here indeed is the world of Newman's description, a world without a God, a world from whose terrain the Creator has long since withdrawn and which is now denied both His power and His energizing presence. In a sense He is seen in the far distant horizons, like the faint streak of light that reminds one of stars that once were. The light that shines on Scobie's world is inert. God is a cold notion reminding one of some sacrifice of long ago and now demanding an equal response. The Cross is a scandal, a disgrace, and yet it holds him in its thrall.

In Greene's earlier fiction we have often had some sense of a God who courted death in order to give fuller life. Whether or not we accept this doctrine as historically objective, in the contexts of these books they do make sense, and we cannot escape the impression that the God thus presented is indeed a force to contend with. Thus, in *Brighton Rock*, Rose's God is a source of strength and her ultimate support; even Pinkie acknowledges Him as his supreme challenge and a tireless Pursuer. But to Scobie, God is a spent force, an imbecile. In *The Heart of the Matter*, as in the other works, it is around the Crucified that the religious motif is rallied: for Scobie the image symbolizes the God who failed. Failure he reads as the final meaning of Jesus's death. Despair was the reason for Calvary, not sacrifice; and this being so there is hardly anything further to hope for: not victory, nor regeneration. The last word was said when Christ "had hung himself on the cross." (p. 190)

The religious motif has a much greater bearing upon Scobie's destiny than is at first realized. Because the Cross means to him the ultimate in despair it cannot be a source of consolation and strength; but neither is there anything further for him to appeal to, nor higher Powers to invoke. His needs and aspirations, his schemes for his painstricken protégeés must in consequence depend entirely upon his own resources. His religious convictions are not any help to him coping with his personal dilemmas. Thus in an early scene in Book Two we observe him inside a church. For a long moment his eyes stay riveted on the image of the Crucified, until "the awful languor of routine fell on his spirits" (p. 153); and the routine reminds him that his proper place is among those "anonymous Romans" who kept order a long way off, and not by the Cross where His friends kept their sorrowful vigil. He is simply a "spectator—one of those many . . . over whom the gaze of Christ must have passed, seeking the face of a friend or an enemy." And so he proceeds to the Confessional, indifferently and without so much as a flicker of hope. If the Scriptures sometimes spoke of signs and miracles, they happened in the hoary past; and Scobie could not be expected to know them. The priests that he knows have neither power nor grace nor the gift of prophecy. They are dry

and stiff and their words do not carry conviction. And so, for
Scobie the words of absolution are only a meaningless routine.
They "brought no sense of relief because there was nothing to
relieve. They were a formula: the Latin words hustled together—a
hocus pocus." (p. 154)

Greene has since written defending his treatment of ecclesial
priesthood in *The Heart of the Matter*,[26] but he insists that the
picture is historically conditioned. In 1940 Vatican II had not yet
been called to take stock of the Church's role in the contemporary
world. Angelo Roncalli was not yet John XXIII and at the helm of
Peter's bark. The Church was fiercely jealous of its institutional
prerogatives. Doctrines set quickly into fixed patterns and the
Church would rather steer by doctrinaire theology. The stress was
on defining faith and on regulating worship and morals; the
individual was not deemed very important, and his personal
dilemmas could at best evoke only a programmed response.
Greene's reaction to such unhelpful ecclesiastic attitudes comes
through more compellingly in a play he published only four years
after *The Heart of the Matter*. Father James, the speaker in *The
Living Room*, is an invalid who has been confined to his
wheelchair for many years. For some time now his niece, Rose, has
been carrying on an affair with a married psychologist, but lately
she has been disturbed and only two days ago she came to him
begging for his advice:

> *Rose:* Uncle, what am I to do? (*She flings herself on the
> ground beside him.*) Tell me what to do. Father!
> *James:* When you say "Father", you seem to lick my mouth.
> There are only hard things to say. (II, i)

We see him "struggling for words" but he "can find none—except
formulae," and subsequently she commits suicide with an overdose
of sleeping pills. The next day the priest is unburdening his soul to
the psychologist (their roles now fittingly reversed):

> *James:* For more than twenty years I've been a useless priest.
> I had a real vocation for the priesthood—perhaps you'd
> explain it in terms of a father complex. Never mind . . . To

me it was a real vocation. And for twenty years it's been imprisoned in this chair—the desire to help. You have it too in your way, and it would still be there if you lost your sight and speech. Last night God gave me my chance. He flung this child, here, at my knees, asking for hope. That's what she said, "Can't you give me anything to hope for?" I said to God, "Put words into my mouth," but he's given me twenty years in this chair with nothing to do but prepare for such a moment, so why should He interfere? And all I said was, "You can pray." If I'd ever really known what prayer was, I would only have had to touch her to give her peace. (II, ii)

The words may well belong to Father Rank in *The Heart of the Matter*. But the novelist is here not to apportion blame. Indeed the two priestly characters are treated with the utmost regard and affection. There is no bitterness, no attempts at satire, although, in the total collapse of their vocation, they might have been made into objects of derision. Greene's intention, though, is not to mock but to portray a real situation which is the pitiable inadequacy of a priesthood to deal with "the human problems they were made to face." The blame is laid not on individuals but on the class that was called, by vocation, to a "deeper comprehension" of the human heart but was incapable of responding to the pains and dilemmas that faced an ordinary person. The portrayal of Father Rank is as much sympathetic as it is a complex one.[27]

But Greene's attitude to religion is one thing, his protagonist's quite another; and it will not do for us to confuse the two. Scobie holds his God responsible for what is objectionable in his world; he wonders that God could have created a world so evil, that He is unable to guard it from the gloom that is gathering all about it. And he is pained to see Him made so cheaply available; like "a popular demagogue," so accessible "to the least of His followers, at any hour." "Looking at the cross he thought, He even suffers in public." (p. 154) The spectacle overwhelms him not so much with wonder or gratitude but with the pangs of guilt of one who has in some way contributed to the suffering. God's vulnerability must seem improbable to the conceptualist, but in the context of Scobie's aroused sensibility it is amply convincing. The vision of a

God who has opted to go on suffering, unendingly, simply to share the human lot and with the vain dream of redeeming man's destiny—this indeed is far too moving for words. Creator and help-less onlooker: he is so much like that fabled "King of a West African tribe, the slave of his people, who may not even lie down in case the winds should fail." [28] His vision of God, however, does not infuse confidence in Scobie's heart.

Inasmuch as Scobie's driving passion is pity, even God is drawn into the magic circle of his victims. God too is in need of his pro-tection, he imagines; and he is not one to disown his responsibility.

> It seemed to him for a moment cruelly unfair of God to have exposed himself in this way, a man, a wafer of bread, first in the Palestinian villages and now here in the hot port, there, everywhere, allowing man to have his will of Him. Christ had told the rich young man to sell all and follow Him, but that was an easy rational step compared with this that God had taken, to put Himself at the mercy of men who hardly knew the meaning of the word. How desperately God must love, he thought with shame. (p. 213)

Pity and shame and resentment—these are the shifting hues on the spectrum of his pathetically aroused soul. God's being so reckless is like a handcuff on his sense of pity, and Scobie feels caught.

The peculiar notion of God we observe here is perhaps only the "projection" of Scobie's own pathological urge. Carl Gustav Jung has described in detail the working of this psychic process and he demonstrates how pervasive its incidence really is. [29] The effect on Scobie of his self-projection is to reproduce the pattern over and over again. We are well acquainted with the process: the keen eye for a victim, the urge to help, the unreasonable demands made on self, the failure of the redemptive role, its recognition and, finally, resentment at what had at first seemed an objective demand. The action is triggered more often than not by a girl or a young woman in distress, and ugliness is always a stimulant. This is Scobie's self, redeemer and victim; and his God, apparently, takes after him, as though He is none other than his own self projected outside and blown to cosmic dimensions. Clothed in the usual regalia of the Christian God, though, He nearly escapes identification. Scobie evidently "knew" his God, for he does not trust Him for an instant. Being but a creature of Scobie's imagination, His is a phantom existence; and a phantom cannot move, does not create or renew.

We have laid considerable stress on deciding the exact nature of Scobie's religion because without this it is not possible to see either the person of the protagonist or his tragedy in correct perspective. Consider for instance his reaction when urged by Louise to go to Communion. Being in "a state of sin" he is technically in no condition to do so until he has repented of his sins and confessed them; he must also undertake to terminate his illicit relations with Helen. Scobie reacts to his wife's suggestion by driving frantically and "unsteadily down the road, his eyes blurred with nausea." We hear him emitting heart-rending sighs: "O God, the decisions you force on people, suddenly with no time to consider." (p. 219) Even granting his is a real dilemma, the reaction is still rather extreme. He tells himself that Helen's claims on him are surely more pressing than God's, but he cannot dismiss the thought that God may suffer even more because He is infinitely more vulnerable; and it is quite beyond all possibility to protect all three—Helen, Louise, and God—at once. For to protect the women he must desecrate his God, and this means mocking and striking his God and piercing Him with nails and spear. This is the crux of Scobie's tragic dilemma, and it convinces only in so far as we accept his religious neurosis.

The two related elements we must distinguish as we set about resolving the problem of the book's meaning, then, are Scobie's private neurosis and the unhelpful attitudes of institutional religion. These twin factors combined bring on an awesome pressure upon Scobie's sensibility and we notice this in a later scene where he is going about preparing for his confession. Walking into the church he tumbles down on his knees, praying "for a miracle":

"O God convince me, help me, convince me. Make me feel that I am more important than that girl." It was not Helen's face he saw as he prayed but the dying child who called him father: a face in a photograph staring from the dressing-table: the face of a black girl of twelve a sailor had raped and killed glaring blindly up at him in a yellow paraffin light. "Make me put my own soul first. Give me trust in your mercy to the one I abandon." He could hear Father Rank close the door of his box and nausea twisted him again on his knees. "O God," he said, "if instead I should abandon you, punish me but let the others get some happiness." (p. 220)

This impassioned haggling with God over "others' happiness" is truly remarkable in one whose faith assures him that the sparrows of the air and grass in the meadow are both in God's safekeeping. Walking subsequently up to the Confessional, Scobie is quite understandably "unaware of the slightest tremor of hope." There follows the routine of the ritual and Father Rank's exhortations (but to Scobie a "hocus pocus"):

Father Rank said, "I don't need to tell you surely that there's nothing automatic in the confessional or in absolution. It depends on your state of mind whether you are forgiven. . . . And you must have a real purpose of amendment." (p. 221)

The wash of words presage no relief: the author does not mean them to. The hackneyed phrases anyway cannot have quickened the spirit or conveyed a sense of hope, because they are quite dead. They are altogether useless and it is this sense of hopelessness that comes through in the weary tone of the officiating priest. Scobie thinks how foolish he was "to imagine that somehow in this airless box I would find a conviction." He goes away without having received absolution.

Never again is it to be easy for Scobie to avoid offending God. He is already feeling like one condemned to the role of executioner. Through adultery and lies and, worst of all, through conscious acts of desecration, he will now day after day go on inflicting pain on God. There will be no let up to his tragedy, no end to the strange affliction, until the infection has altogether consumed him and he is dead. This is the price he pays in order to steady the sagging morale of a young woman and to keep an otherwise unattractive wife from a none-too-comfortable piece of information.

> Only a miracle can save me now. Scobie told himself, . . . but God would never work a miracle to save Himself, I am the cross, he thought, He will never speak the word to save Himself from the cross, but if only wood were made so that it didn't feel, if only the nails were senseless as people believed. (p. 225)

Resentful of the role to which he feels condemned, yet he has himself plugged off every route to escape and now he "savagely" cries out at God: "Take your sponge of gall. You made me what I am." His inner conflicts have been drawn out into the open, and the vision he has of himself in the guise of the Roman Soldiers, scourging and mocking and striking his God is dizzyingly frightening. It were better could he do the act and cease his own existence; if only he could "die and remove [himself] from their blood stream," they might be safe yet: all of them, Louise, Helen, and even God would be cured of him once and for all.

The novel's argument suffers, albeit not significantly, as the theological issues are insufficiently orchestrated among themselves and in relation to the hero's character. Notice for instance Scobie's outburst at the Communion rail: "O God, I offer up my damnation to you. Take it. Use it for them." The hysteria and the sacrilegious act and the vision "of the bleeding face, of eyes closed by the continuous shower of blows, the punch-drunk head of God reeling sideways": these various elements are not easily reconciled with the character of one who can plan out his own death so coolly and with such precision, oblivious apparently of how deeply this worst sin of his must hurt the divine Victim. "I've preferred to give You pain rather than give pain to Helen or my wife," he excuses himself before God, "because I can't observe Your suffering." Even granting the anguish and the moral confusion, his argument does not altogether convince us; as a result, we tend to discredit some of the importance the novel's rhetoric adduces to God in the working out of Scobie's tragedy.

The ambivalence between what is shown and what the rhetoric urges on the reader has occasioned not a little confusion among the critics. It has also exposed the author to some acrimonious debate regarding his good faith. A very extreme case is a reviewer who held him responsible for "a vulgarization of faith." He found him guilty of "grossly degrading" "theological dogma into melodrama," and "of hotting up . . . religious belief for fictional purposes."[30] To this charge the author's reply is perhaps his own best defense. He begins by denying that in *The Heart of the Matter* he is portraying the tenets of whatever faith. A novelist's task, he adds, is strictly confined to creating characters, and these must live and seem plausible; but their beliefs and motivations are entirely their own affairs and the author is not accountable for them. Concerning his own work Greene asserts he himself never shared any of Scobie's beliefs: "I was not so stupid as to believe that [salvation or damnation] could ever be an issue in a novel. Besides, I have small belief in the doctrine of eternal punishment (it was Scobie's belief not mine)." (cf. p. v Greene's introduction to The Collected Edition)

To some critics his epigraph proved an easy bait. They misread Peguy's words to mean that he, and Greene after him, preferred the sinner to the man of holy deeds; and this was indeed a perversity. But there really need not have been any misapprehension. For Peguy is not quoted as saying that the sinner is nearer to the heart of Christianity *than* the holy man, but only that (*"nul n'est aussi compétent que le pécheur en matiére de chrétienté. Nul, si ce n'est le saint"*) *excepting* the saint, there is perhaps none so well conversant as the sinner with the mysteries of Christian experience. And this should not cause too much concern. For, after all, is it not agreed that in the person of Christ the sinner and the saint are inextricably linked? They are the primary symbols, and typify for the believer his own essence on the one hand and his inspiration on the other; the only terms on which he may fulfil his vocation. They both embody his call to virtue and his natural reluctance. It is significant that Greene should want to emphasize this cardinal doctrine of the Bible: that although the Almighty may long suffer the sinner, and even loves him, He might not be so gracious towards the complacent.[31] In Greene's own catalogue there is hardly a sin more grievous.

The epigraph makes better sense if taken to mean an apology for Scobie's character and behavior. Although he is not exactly anybody's idea of a saint, in his fierce rejection of pose and pretension his claims to authentic humanity must be recognized as truly genuine. Admitting his helplessness and his sinful state, he also acknowledges his communality with a fallen race. He thus is able to appreciate the urgent need for the redemptive act. In his deeper perception he is linked naturally with the hell-bound Boy of *Brighton Rock*, just as he also compares with the priest-martyr of Tabasco. With both of them he shares this extra dimension of understanding; and this, the author insists, is all that is important about the three characters.[32] All of them resist to the end the temptation to mediocrity, each is rich in daring and undaunted even to the point of plumbing his "capacity for damnation." They dream too; but as they dream, their thoughts, like Jacob's in flight, are a ladder reaching up even to the high Heavens. And in the end all of them understand the ultimate meaning of humanity's destiny.

It is this greater sensitivity to the truth of human existence that vindicates Scobie and raises him high above the common run of men. His errors the author does not condone; on the contrary, their consequences for Scobie and his protégeés are fully recognized and presented in painstaking detail. If the muddle he has made of his life convinces us, not any the less does his candor. His sense of truth and the nobility of his compassion set him off as truly exceptional in an uncaring, decrepit world. Perhaps this is all Father Rank has in mind when, chiding Louise on her self-righteousness, he admonishes: "Don't imagine you—or I—know a thing about God's mercy. . . . The Church knows all the rules. But it doesn't know what goes on in a single human heart." And the priest says: "It may seem an odd thing to say—when a man's as wrong as he was—but I think, from what I saw of him, that he really loved God." (p. 272) To this we would readily respond: he was a sinner, and he was sinned against, but he was no worse than most of us; what evil he caused he did not himself will, but it was the fruit of his confusion; he was truly a better man than most.

Scobie's story only dramatizes the pathos that is intrinsic to human existence.

Typologically, Scobie ought to be counted among Eliot's "hollow men," although he is a most sensitive and articulate one: his proper milieu is contemporary wasteland. He is Tiresias in modern garb; experienced in much, and having foresuffered all, he does not belong to any one particular moment in history. Nor is he bound by the particularities of a race or culture. About him there is this sense of being undefined by time and space. He is all humans, every person unguided by the light of faith; and if his vision is thus gravely impaired, his weakened eyes yet have a power that is penetrating, and a gift to understand. "All is cheerless, dark, and deadly," intones Kent at the close of *King Lear*. *The Heart of the Matter* ends on no less a foreboding note. No sense of liberation is indicated, except perhaps the final relief that comes of death. No Thunder has yet spoken though the land is parched, no rain-laden clouds spot the skies. The oracle is mute. There is but the strained tones of a moral "complaint against the nature of life," against the blight and the curse nobody has understood or can atone for. With a God either withdrawn into the farthest horizons or just impotent, there is indeed nothing for the world to hope for. All is lost, in darkness, gloom and death.

The gloom and loss follow us to the next novel; but the situation in *The End of the Affair* is quite a different matter. The complaint is no longer that God is too little in evidence. It is that He is too interfering; He would not leave humanity alone.

THE END OF THE AFFAIR

You have created us for Yourself, and our heart is restless until it rests in You.

—St. Augustine, *The Confessions*

The End of the Affair (1951) is just what the title informs us it is, the story of an extraordinary love affair. It is told with a winsome simplicity. For several years Sarah Miles and Maurice Bendrix have been lovers when something mysterious happens, disturbing their security. Bendrix is the narrator and, for much of the book, our perspective. As the novel opens we find him in a mood of sober reflection. A great deal of the action is presented by means of flashback, and the rest through the contrivance of a diary—Sarah's. Thus the point of view is fairly divided between the two lovers. To sort out the affair after the mysterious event—this is the whole point of the novel. This is the task for Bendrix. Flashback is the artist's tool best suited for this purpose. The narrative starts on a "bleak wet January night on the Common, in 1946." But it keeps bouncing back and forth reaching down as far as 1939 when the affair had its actual beginning.

Sarah is the wife of a civil servant and it is at a party for government officials that Bendrix first met her. In wanting to be further acquainted with her, he had apparently no other motive than the "cold-blooded intention of picking her brain." (p. 7) He was working on a new book, and Henry Miles was to serve as his model

---

All quotes from *The End of the Affair* (Penguin Books, 1979)

for a farcical sketch. A sublime way to begin a relationship! But the artist shares qualities with the scientist and the mathematician, and his ways may be just as heartless and calculating. Sarah was to be Bendrix's source of information about her husband—that, and no more. She was not a part of his design. But soon she has become not just a part but the whole of it. She has captured the center of the stage and suddenly all Bendrix's interest is on her. With her entry, his aesthetic vocation is now in ruins. He is no longer capable of detaching himself from persons and events, and detachment is the first condition for art. Bendrix is consumed by passion. But he is not quite reconciled to it. Habits, nurtured through years, cannot be easily dismissed.

To Bendrix art is not simply a hobby, nor just a profession. It is a cult. There are no claims to equal those of art—not even love could compete, until recently. The subliminal energies were channeled, and rigorously contained.

> When young, one builds up habits of work one believes will last a lifetime and withstand any catastrophe. . . . I have always been very methodical. . . . When I was young not even a love affair would alter my schedule. A love affair had to begin after lunch, and however late I might be in getting to bed—as long as I slept in my own bed—I would read the morning's work over and sleep on it. Even the war hardly affected me. . . . (p. 38)

The life impulse was guided carefully to well rehearsed ends.

Bendrix's response to life compares somewhat with that of Sarah's husband. The middle-aged civil servant had traded for the routine of his office whatever was quickening and soulful in life. His work was all his life—so he tells us. Bendrix says Henry was a man who "liked his comfort." (p. 4) But comfort is a continuum without heights or depths, a flat and endless terrain. No place this for passion. Passion generates conflict, as often it does challenge well-tended habits. One cannot foresee every event, and one cannot plan and regulate. One cannot be reasonable always—passion disturbs all that. The mental equilibrium, the equanimity so necessary to the artist, is once and for all destroyed by passion. There are the peak moments, the ecstasy, and then too the moments of doubt; and both intrude on one's awareness.

This occasional unease comes through in the style of narration. The note of stridency is heard already in the first paragraph.

> A story has no beginning or end; arbitrarily one chooses that moment of experience from which to look back or from which to look ahead. I say "one chooses" with the inaccurate pride of a professional writer who—when he has been seriously noted at all—has been praised for his technical ability; but do I in fact of my own will *choose* that black wet January night on the Common, in 1946, the sight of Henry Miles slanting across the wide river of rain, or did these images choose me? It is convenient, it is correct according to the rules of my craft, to begin just there, but. . . (p. 3)

The anxious concern over outlining motives, the italicizing of 'choose', the lame defense of "the rules of my craft"—all this is indicative of a lack of confidence, an inadequacy. The stridency carries through to the end in varying degrees.

The character of the protagonist is complexly drawn. He is the narrator, the subject of the story and the critic, all in one. In his creative role as artist, he imposes meanings on his relationships. His critical task is to doubt, to question these very same meanings. The interplay of such divergent roles within the same person cannot but fascinate. The novel is simply the thrilling account of Bendrix's self-discoveries. Whatever within him had caused him to doubt his commitment to beauty now challenges his new devotion to love. In the book is outlined the effect these various events have on the protagonist.

Thomas Merton has distinguished three kinds of persons. These are the 'sensual,' the 'pious' and the 'spiritual' types. Neither of the first two is truly open to truth. Only the third is able to understand reality in its wholeness, "in absolute simplicity."[1] A possible exception is the artist who is committed: he may have an occasional glimpse into the inner sanctum. For "the highest experience of the artist," allows Merton, "penetrates not only beyond the sensible surface of things into their inmost reality, but even beyond that to God Himself."[2] The poet has the gift of intuition. He has the vision that probes below the surface of things, that searches into the very core of their individuality. His genius is for the unique apprehension; and if his endowments be truly exceptional, he may even find himself in the great Presence, the ground and source of all. And this is what happens to Bendrix. His pursuit of beauty has "set in motion the . . . psychological process" that drives him on to further exploration.

There is no stopping once the process begins. Sarah's function is to have initiated it. Through contact with her his "self-imposed discipline" is upset beyond recovery. (p. 38) No longer can he believe in the ultimate sufficiency of art. Sarah has proved how unsatisfying art may well be. She has aroused in him urges that are more elemental and that craved for other food. We recognize in his *angst* the despair of one who is thwarted in his elected mode of life.

The artist's vocation may be very demanding. His strength is in his "insights into human nature," and for these he must depend on well entrenched habits—habits of careful observation and analysis. He must note the multiform presence of human drives and motivations. He must chart their course, their direction and progress. He cannot do all this unless he has a deeply felt sympathy for the essential person. This is the person who craves freedom, the ultimate release, and finds himself inextricable bound to the prison of self. His need for sympathetic identification with his subjects is the artist's vulnerability. It has caught Bendrix in the cross currents of passion.

The affair is apparently a thing of great intensity. There is also magic in it, a certain quickening of spirit. With thought held in abeyance, there is even a sense of freedom. Time does not belong at all. Love has drawn them both into the mainstream of a boundless eternity. There is no conceivable beginning to it, no end; there is only peace and rest and satiety. And like the wheel of the stars or the night of Brahma, it is dark and primordial. Here is the faltering account by Bendrix of the effect love has on him.

I felt that afternoon such complete trust when she said to me suddenly, without being questioned, "I've never loved anybody or anything as I do you." It was as if, sitting there in the chair with a half-eaten sandwich in her hand, she was abandoning herself as completely as she had done, five minutes back, on the hardwood floor. We most of us hesitate to make so complete a statement; we remember and we foresee and we doubt. She had no doubts. The moment only mattered. Eternity is said not to be an extension of time but an absence of time, and sometimes it seemed to me that her abandonment touched that strange mathematical point of endlessness, a point with no width, occupying no space. What did time matter—all the past and the other men she must from time to time . . . have known, or all the future in which she might be making the same statements with the same sense of truth? (p. 59-60)

The narrator has little doubt that this which has happened to him is extraordinary, somewhat ineffable. He even compares it to the transports of which mystics speak. He believes that in these moments are the apogee of human bliss. Nothing could be finer, nothing more sublime or thrilling than this joy. Nothing could compete with the brilliance of these instants of unmediated presence to another being. Here time hung loose. And there is a sense of release in the oblivion of self, in the rapture of love. This is how it was whenever the lovers met; and in their meeting were moments "of absolute trust and absolute pleasure. . . . when it was impossible. . . . to think." (p. 84) These were of such quality that Bendrix began to wonder "whether eternity might not after all exist as the endless prolongation of the moment of death." (p. 83) Even those saints who were divinely privileged could not have been more enraptured.

Love is like fire; it burns out of the human frame all that is dross. The dross is the lethargy, gathered in the routine of boredom; it is the clogging inhibitions of the ego. Love regales the spirit and renders it free. It purges the self, and releases new energies. This must both thrill and frighten; and naturally Bendrix fears for his "self-imposed discipline." (p. 38) He feels threatened lest he should lose his identity.

Love too resolves all that makes for differences. It checks the ephemeral ego, with its functions—thought, images, and sensation. Thus it is, according to mystics, when the soul is enraptured by God. That deed would be even more profound, done at the darkest core of one's being. The soul is swept up into "union and identification in divine charity. One knows God by becoming one with Him."[3] This becoming one is not a union of entities, but of relationships. It is knowledge, but gained through assimilation, not through definition or analysis. Consciousness is phased out, self awareness wanes, and the soul enters what is best described as a void. This is a darkness so vast it has no dimension, no color, smell or taste. Everything melts away before the Beloved. It is as if He alone has existence; anything besides Him, including the self, is not. In consequence, the self "dwells in emptiness, darkness and obscurity,"—understanding "nothing in particular."[4] It is as though the soul itself has ceased to be, has vanished "out of itself by the perfect renunciation of all desires and all things." It is only aware of the loved One.[5] However, this does not result in any sense of helplessness, as ordinarily understood. On the contrary, there is the suffusion of a quiet plenitude. One who loves and yields is plentifully rewarded. But, for the neophyte the prospect of losing all his faculties may be very frightening. The fear actually is about crossing the frontier. Mystics opine that the growing inner darkness is an indication that God is near; He has always started off thus—by shutting out "the half-light of created images and concepts." We are not really to worry for our confidence will be strengthened, our certainty increased "with this obsurity."[6]

Bendrix claims to have experienced something comparable in his union with Sarah.

The words of human love have been used by the saints to describe their vision of God; and so, I suppose, we might use the terms of prayer, meditation, contemplation to explain the intensity of the love we feel for a woman. We too surrender memory, intellect, intelligence, and we too experience the deprivation, the *noche oscura*, and sometimes as a reward a kind of peace . . . there was this peace. (p. 55)

This may be read from a Kierkegaardian perspective. Then, the lover's exultation may be understood to flow out as the natural result of an act of aesthetic apprehension. But to Bendrix the encounter has meant a great deal more. By his own admission, it has somehow challenged him at the roots of his self. It has roused the elemental man within: new urges have surfaced. Aroused thus, he is able to penetrate deeper than the aesthetic ranges, beyond "the sensible surface of things, into their inmost reality."[7] In other words, the ardor of love has paved the way for some kind of a mystical awakening.

This is immediately sensed by Sarah. And she is the first to credit her dawning release to the affair and to the new awareness it began. Her decision is to pursue it to its completion. Bendrix himself balks, fearing the demands such a decision would make of him. He would not yield up yet. With demoniac obstinacy he clings on to the partial view. The result is sustained spiritual conflict. Jealousy and irritation play on his passion and vitiate it. He is "sweet all day," and then his mood changes with renewed insecurity, being "jealous of the past and the present and the future." (p. 111)   "His love is like a medieval chastity belt," comments Sarah in her diary, "only when he is there, with me, in me, does he feel safe. If only I could make him feel secure. . . ." (p. 111)

Some of his reluctance to yield to the multiform demands of love may be traced to his profession. As a novelist he is somewhat circumscribed in his response to reality, circumscribed too by concepts, images and contingent emotions—the artist's tools. He must perforce place a high premium on observation and on analysis. To doubt, to question the data of observation—all this is correct for an aesthete to do. Only it interferes with the enjoyment of love. Bendrix demurs at minor errors in Sarah's behaviour. He is afflicted with insecurity, and this in turn breeds bitterness. Like a detective he is obsessed with amassing "his trivial material before picking out the right clue." (p. 26)   His one thought is: "How can I disinter the human character from the heavy scene?" Anxious lest he should lose Sarah, he is overly preoccupied with every deviance from her set pattern of behavior. In consequence even in his most perfect moments he is not free. "Even in the moment of love, I was like a police officer gathering evidence of a crime that hadn't yet been committed." (p. 60)

There is a "grim" appropriateness, as Herbert Haber has noted,[8] in connecting Bendrix's profession with that of the detectives, of Mr. Savage and his "comically grotesque" deputy. But Bendrix is more acutely perceptive. He can boast of a certain detachment from surface things. Indeed, he prides himself on his skill to probe behind appearances, and to disinter truth. He does not yet realize that even his skill is a snare, an impediment. Insofar as it causes him to project, and to identify with, a fictitious ego, it must carry him away from his authentic self. He is possessed of a pressing need for self-expression. In his obsession he fails to notice that his artist's *daemon* is at the root of his inability to transcend, to yield and to be free.

With the affair maturing, however, there is a growth in awareness. Bendrix's love is still possessive, but the realization has dawned upon him that such love cannot last. Hence the note of bitterness, of regret in his reminiscences. "I would not believe that love could take any other form than mine; I measured love by the extent of my jealousy, and by that standard, of course, she could not love me at all." (p. 64)   The same bleary picture is sketched in Sarah's diary: "Sometimes I get so tired of trying to convince him that I love him and shall love him for ever. He pounces on my words like a barrister and twists them. I know he is afraid of that desert which would be round him if our love were to end, but he can't realize that I feel exactly the same. . . . What can one build in the desert?" (p. 111)

Insecurity is the blight of newborn love. The narrator is sorely conscious of the harm his insecurity was doing to their relationship. It "twists meanings and poisons trust. In a closely beleaguered city every sentry is a potential traitor." (p. 65)   Bendrix knows anxiety is the cruelest of love's enemies. Stretched on its crossbeams, love is doomed to a slow death. But the distrust had its beginning with the affair itself. He would check on her furtively, catching her in small lies and evasions which he would find out later "meant nothing except her fear" of him. He would magnify every little error into a betrayal—in his profession one read meanings into the plainest statement. "Because I couldn't bear the thought of her so much as touching another man, I feared it all the time, and I saw intimacy in the most casual movement of the hand." (p. 65)

The insecurity is shared by both the lovers; but there is a difference. Sarah does not show the gross egotism of one who must possess all. She can contemplate, with a measure of equanimity, his sleeping with another woman, should he need to. She is so much more concerned *for* him. It is his "being unhappy" that she cannot bear; she is not anxious over her loss. "I don't mind anything you do that makes you happy," she assures him. Her love has reached a depth which his would not attain without a soul rending struggle. His speech betrays a preoccupation with surfaces. "I'd rather be dead or see you dead. . .than with another man," he cries at her. That is to be a self-fulfilling prophesy. He is not being eccentric, he says. "That's ordinary human love. Ask anybody. They'd all say the same—if they loved at all. . . . Anyone who loves is jealous." (p. 66)

Does an affair ever "go on and on and never. . .get less"? Bendrix has wanted it to, for sure. But he cannot have doubted "that one day this must end." (p. 66)   Yet,

> when the sense of insecurity, the logical belief in the hopeless future, descended like melancholia, I would badger her and badger her, as though I wanted to bring the future in now at the door, an unwanted and premature guest. My love and fear acted like conscience. If we had believed in sin, our behaviour would hardly have differed. (p. 66)

Every artist has a heightened sense of time. He is keenly aware of the morrows and the days after, of moments that pass out and fade away. Such a keen sense of time must necessarily plague a love affair. The feeling of transience breeds "self-pity and hatred," and it incites quarrels. "When I began to realize how often we quarrelled, . . . I became aware that our love was doomed." Their love might have been secure and trusting. Instead, it "had turned into a love affair with a beginning and an end. . . . I was pushing, pushing the only thing I loved out of my life." So long as he could make believe that love lasted, he "was happy—I think I was even good to live with, and so love did last. But if love had to die, I wanted it to die quickly. It was as though our love were a small creature caught in a trap and bleeding to death; I had to shut my eyes and wring its neck." (p. 39)

Sarah has a good deal "more capacity for love"; and her love is immensely more trusting. It is Bendrix's misery that he is unable to trust, that he cannot "bring down that curtain round the moment." "I couldn't forget and I couldn't *not* fear." He is obsessed with time flowing out: "To me the present is never here, it is always last year or next week," (p. 60) And as a result, the most perfect of moments is for him riddled with anxiety.

Ecstasy and bitterness, doubts and joy crisscross their relationship. On the mystical plane, too, insecurity sometimes casts its shadow. But the mystic is ever attuned to the groundswell of God's presence. It may be faint, it may be distant; but one who believes never doubts its reality. This is not the case with our harried lovers. Their love is not all a pure glow. There are instants of "absolute trust and absolute pleasure," but those are nearly negated by an enveloping gloom. "What are we doing to each other?" says Sarah, perplexed. "Because I know that I am doing to him exactly what he is doing to me. We are sometimes so happy, and never in our lives have we known more unhappiness." (p. 112) Insecurity has become the most prominent object on the horizon now. Sarah fears being driven "into such complete isolation that I would be alone with nothing and nobody—like a hermit."

Love normally works to quicken life. In each other's arms there is indeed a promise of release, but their growing insecurity signalled a warning. Soon they would discover the desert was much nearer home than they ever suspected. The desert was where love ended. It was in every insignificant lie, was the reason for every evasion. It lurked even at the edge of love. Thus reads an entry in Sarah's diary:

> Sometimes after a day when we have made love many times, I wonder whether it isn't possible to come to an end of sex, and I know that he is wondering too and is afraid of that point where the desert begins. (p. 111)

Indeed, Bendrix did. "In a way—we'd got to the end of love. There was nothing else we could do together." (p. 66) He would thus sum up the matter later on. They had already in some way "lost each other." What remained of love, their anxiety did away. "What do we do in the desert . . .?" cries Sarah. "How does one go on living. . .?" (p. 111)

If they only could trust, love would be secure. "If only I could make him feel secure," muses Sarah, "then we could love peacefully, happily, not savagely, inordinately and the desert would recede out of sight. For a lifetime perhaps." Her thoughts wander off at a tangent, and she yields faintly to the suggestion: "If one could believe in God, would He fill the desert?" (p. 111) But that "if" is like a large question mark. She did not believe. Nor was she proposing to do so now. Besides, she has wanted to have "everything all the time, everywhere." It is just that the desert is too distracting, and she might try anything that might soften it, anything that may make it less frightening. Could faith do that? Would God give her the ultimate assurance that love has failed to give? Claims have indeed been made on His behalf. "God loves you," it has been said, "God is everything." Could He then satisfy one's longings as Bendrix could, but more lastingly? And would she be satiated in Him so that she would no longer be in need of admiration, would not even "need to sleep with a man?" (p. 112) These thoughts take a hold on her, growing on her pain raked sensibility, and suddenly she is aware of unseen hands. It is as though a master Magician were working on her and Bendrix, using their affair as an excuse, even as an occasion. She is now certain of His presence forcing her hands, guiding her destiny. But His purposes are yet dark and hidden. Sarah thinks of Him as a sculptor. "It's as if we were working together on the same statue, cutting it out of each other's misery. But I don't even know the design." (p. 112)

The Master's design unfolds progressively from the climactic scene. This scene is worked against the background of the London blitz and marks a turning point in the story. Sarah is spending an afternoon with Bendrix in his apartment, and they are making love, when a bomb lands causing severe damage. Bendrix, going down to the basement to search for the landlady, is caught by another explosion and buried in rubble. Sarah rushes down looking for Bendrix. But he is no where to be seen; only his arm stuck "out from under the door." (p. 115) And she is certain that he is dead. "Extinct. There wasn't such a thing as a soul. Even the half happiness I gave him was drained out of him like blood. He would never have the chance to be happy again—with anybody, I thought." (p. 116) And so she kneels down by his bed, just as she was, stark naked, her anguish working on the memory. And there, in the dark recesses of her memory, is kindled faintly a hope. And she cries out "to anything that might exist." She asks for a sign, a miracle—"They happen, don't they, to the poor, and I was poor." (p. 87) "Let him be alive," she says, "and I *will* believe. Give him a chance."

> But that wasn't enough. It doesn't hurt to believe. So I said, I love him and I'll do anything if You'll make him alive. I said very slowly, I'll give him up forever, only let him be alive with a chance. . . and then he came in at the door, and he was alive, and I thought now the agony of being without him starts. . . . (p. 116-17)

A vow has been made to, and accepted by, "anything" that existed. Sarah takes her vow seriously. She stops meeting with Bendrix. One knows another only through surrendering oneself to him; and this means trust, and it means faith and love. If Sarah ever stopped loving Maurice, she "would cease to believe in his love." Inasmuch as one loves another, one cannot doubt the other's

love. "If I loved God, then I would believe in His love for me. . . .
We have to love first." (p. 112) The various entries on her diary
are proof of an overwhelming trust. "I have no need to. . .talk to
You," she writes addressing God.

> You. . .know everything before it comes into my mind. Did I
> ever love Maurice as much before I loved You? Or was it
> really You I loved all the time? Did I touch You when I
> touched him? Could I have touched You if I hadn't touched
> him first, touched him as I never touched Henry, anybody?
> And he loved me and touched me as he never did with any
> other woman. But was it me he loved, or You? For he hated in
> me the things You hate. He was on Your side all the time
> without knowing it. You willed our separation, but he willed
> it too. He worked for it with his anger and his jealousy, and
> he worked for it with his love. For he gave me so much love
> and I gave him so much love that soon there wasn't anything
> left when we'd finished but You. For either of us. I might have
> taken a lifetime spending a little love at a time, doling it out
> here and there, on this man and that. But even the first time,
> in the hotel near Paddington, we spent all we had. You were
> there, teaching us to squander, like You taught the rich man,
> so that one day we might have nothing left except this love of
> You. But You are too good to me. When I ask You for pain,
> You give me peace. Give it him too. Give him my peace—he
> needs it more. (p. 150-51)

There is peace here, and also an inexplicable confidence. Sarah is
carried away by an upsurge of faith. This is like the foretaste of
what bliss may be hers forever.

That confidence, that ineffable joy may be Bendrix's too. Sarah
is now certain that the sexual phase of their love was only a stage to
something more profound and more sublime. It was but part of a
larger plan. And she knows too that Bendrix was being drawn to it,
and no less powerfully than she. They were being guided, their
every move was watched. Even their love was not private. They
were totally exposed to an all seeing eye. They had some brief

moments of ecstasy, but without any means to support these, they came crashing to the ground on their inadequacy. Their longings were like a chasm which they knew not how to bridge. They were not Berkin and Ursula Brangwen. Lawrence's lovers read into their love an unbounded promise. Either was aware of "a lovely state of free proud singleness." They were born aloft on the crust of self-confidence. When they loved and yielded, this was almost a concession to the race. What particularizes Greene's lovers is their anguish, their pained sense of inadequacy.

Sarah would not deny that there was daring in their surrender—and pleasure, even ecstasy, as reward. But there was no denying either the awful desolation in which these moments were nearly lost. Anxiety preceded them, doubts and insecurity followed upon them; and all this went to mar the enjoyment. The book's motto aptly describes their plight: The affair has burnt into their souls spaces that were not in existence, but have begun to exist by the suffering that was filling them. Their passion, and the intensity of it, has rendered them greatly vulnerable. It was no good any more pretending otherwise: they were out in the cold, homeless and weary, without anything to call their own. The great Void was on them; there was no running away from it.

Sarah is the first to get to grips with her Void. It is a painful process, but by it she is purged, and made ready for her eventual transformation. Now and again she is carried aloft on the wings of ecstasy, her soul soaring, and suffused with joy. Her decision also effects an echoing response within Bendrix. Though not quite resigned to it, he also is forced to a crisis, the second in the book—the London blitz being a crisis for Sarah. It is as if the sequence were being replayed for his benefit. The process is similar, beginning with a death, and a sense of irreparable loss. But he cannot cope with her lead. Indeed he lags behind by miles. At any rate her decision is the most crucial, and the progress from thereon is what the book is about.

Sarah's decision is to accept the Void simply, without preconditions. She might thus be condemning herself to perhaps a lifetime of loneliness, to days and nights, even years of sterility. It might even be a death trap for her soul. There might be nothing to hope for, no future to look forward to. The future is bleak, foggy. There is no promise in it at all. This is what mystics are wont to call a *kenosis*. That is the death of the ephemeral ego. But this death is only the first stage to a deeper discovery. It initiates a search for the Inner self, and this is a primary motif in most religious myths. It is laid down that trials must precede the discovery of the true self. It is only when the individual is purged of attachments, desires, and illusory ambitions, that this individual is deemed worthy to be admitted to the truth of his own self. Merton put it very succinctly. "The deepest spiritual instinct in man," he says, "is this urge of the inner truth which demands that he be faithful to himself: to his deepest and most original potentialities. Yet at the same time, in order to become one's true self, the false self must die. In order for the inner self to appear the outer self must disappear, or at least become secondary."⁹ In other words, the human spirit must divest itself of its passions before it can enter the inner sanctum of being. "Simple, pure, detached from all kinds of natural affection, actual and habitual," says St. John of the Cross, is the soul that shares "in the breadth of the spirit of the divine wisdom."¹⁰

These are the paradigms of mystical life. And now they are typified in Sarah's case. Her diary gives us some idea of the nature of her adventures, the stages thereof, and the pained soul searching that is part of that process. "Even a God can't love something that doesn't exist," reads an entry. "He can't love something he cannot see. When he looks at me, does he see something I can't see? It must be lovely if he is able to love it. That's asking me to believe too much, that there's anything lovely in me." (p. 123)   One did want of course, to be admired, she admits. But that was only because one needed an illusion to live by—"a soothing drug that allows me to forget that I'm a bitch and a fake. But what are you supposed to love, then, in the bitch and the fake? Where do you find that immortal soul they talk about? Where do you see this lovely thing in me—in me, of all people?" (p. 123)   Not the voice of doubt this, but of rapture. It is as if a shaft of light has suddenly burst into the gloom, and she is dazzled by its brilliance.

Of all the enigmas of the mystical way of life, perhaps none is more elusive to reason than what is known as "the paradox of the illuminative way." This may be stated thus: the inner self is awakened to the degree the ego is denied satisfaction. So long as the individual is active on the sensual or the ego level, his true self remains inert; it cannot emerge, cannot bloom. Let him die to the senses, and to his ego, and he is already at the threshhold. Saints speak of this point as the *Sunya*, the Tao, *le point vierge* and "the centre of nothingness." It is only reached by a leap in faith, and only the one who is possessed by God can take such a leap. The extraordinary decision of Celia Copleston in Eliot's *The Cocktail Party* is a case in point.

Sarah too is progressing towards the still-point, which is at the "center of nothingness." Her thoughts become more and more detached from self, her pain, her loss. It is now the other that engages her—Henry, her husband, Maurice, and even Smythe, a stranger who has just walked into her life. She exclaims she could well imagine a God loving Henry—"he's gentle and good and patient"—or "Maurice, who thinks he hates, and loves, all the time—even his enemies. But in this bitch and fake where do you find anything to love?" (p. 124)   This is the fire-test, the emptying of self; and Sarah has stood it well. She accepts her insignificance, her utter helplessness, and so can be trusted to honor the gift that will be bestowed on her. She is ready for the divine Spouse to possess her. She even does "not seek fulfilment." Nothing does she claim for herself. But God's entry into the soul is like a feast, and she is altogether contented. In the embrace of the divine Guest is true fulfilment. She writes of a "sense of peace and quiet and love," and is confident that "life was going to be happy" after all. (p. 151)

There is no longer evidence of any anxiety. On the contrary there is the stillness of quiescence. The spirit is at rest, "perfectly unified" in herself. She is not afflicted by the contrary pulls of sensation and feelings. All faculties and powers are aligned "into contact with reality by an immediacy that forgets the division between subject and object." There is no tension because everything is "recollected in the centre of [the soul's] humility."[11] This unification of the soul's energies is a proper effect of God's visitation.

The self-confidence in Sarah's exultation parallels that of the *Magnificat*. It is a recurring theme in the Scriptures that God's chosen ones are inevitably led through the desert, through the test of fire and water, before they see the Promised Land. Even Jesus was not spared; He was brought low, "made obedient unto death, even the death of a cross." Even He needed to be humiliated before He was raised up in glory. This apparently is the mystique of transcendent love, divinely sanctioned, and valid universally. Sarah too must accommodate herself to its rulings. She does so willingly, and to the very end. Bendrix would recall later:

> She had said to me—they were nearly the last words I heard from her before she came dripping into the hall from her assignation—"You needn't be so scared. Love doesn't end. Just because we don't see each other. . ." She said, "My dear, my dear. People go on loving God, don't they, all their lives, without seeing Him?" . . . I suppose I should have recognized that she was already under a stranger's influence; . . . As I shone the torch carefully to light her way across the devastated hall, she said again, "Everything must be all right. If we love enough." (p. 82)

Indeed, Sarah had need of this assurance. For the ecstasy, the "sense of peace and quiet and love," is transitory. It is a foretaste, and is meant to urge her on to a more thorough-going surrender. Her need, and her longing, for human love are yet unquenched; her loss of Bendrix keenly felt. "I'm not at peace any more," she confides in her journal.

> I just want (Maurice) like I used to in the old days. I want to be eating sandwiches with him. I want to be drinking with him in a bar. I'm tired and I don't want any more pain. I want Maurice. I want ordinary corrupt human love. Dear God, You know I want to want Your pain, but I don't want it now. Please take it away for a while and give it me another time. (p. 151-52)

A lifetime without the comfort of human love is quite frightening. Sarah thinks perhaps if she could dispel her belief things might yet be as before. If only she could persuade herself "that nothing happened," that her promise did not really count, she might then "write to Maurice and ask him if he wants to go on again. Perhaps I'll even leave Henry. . ." (p. 128)   She goes to consult a rationalist, Richard Smythe. Smythe has a strawberry mark on his cheek, a source of great embarassment to him. At one point in their discussions he blurts out: "'You believe in God, . . . That's easy. You are beautiful. You have no complaint, but why should I love a God who gives a child this?'" (p. 149)   Smythe was simply angry with God—a poor way of proving His nonexistence. Sarah had hoped to cure herself of belief; Smythe's impassioned rhetoric has it the more hopelessly "fixed" into her. She had gone to him "to rid me of a superstition, but everytime I went his fanaticism fixed the superstition deeper." (p. 140)

Rationalism did not work, not with her anyway. And so she looks around for other diversions. But nothing any longer satisfied, and she has altogether lost taste for casual affairs. In utter desperation, she makes a phone call to Bendrix. And again she is thwarted: the voice that comes through is not Bendrix's. He has moved, and has not left her his address.

> I said to God, so that's it. I begin to believe in you, and if I believe in you I shall hate you. I have free will to break my promise, haven't I? But I haven't the power to gain anything from breaking it. You let me telephone, but then you close the door in my face. You let me sin, but you take away the fruits of my sin. You let me try to escape with D., but you don't allow me to enjoy it. You make me drive love out, and then you say, "There's no lust for you either." What do you expect me to do now, God? Where do I go from here? (p. 122)

The tone is near despair. The future is uncertain.

Coming out of Smythe's one day, she sees Maurice on the road. She follows him almost up to his favorite bar. She was hoping he would turn and see her. If he did, she would go in too, and they might begin again as before. However, Maurice does not turn round, and she has to walk back home alone. At home she is about to ring up Bendrix to tell him she was going back to him, when

Henry, her husband, staggers in much too early than is his custom. Henry is looking ill and harassed. He pleads with her not to leave him, and seeing his misery she is compelled to promise. That was another vow to keep, as if the one at the London blitz were not burden enough. Dazed and in pain, she rushes out of the house. When she returns home it is with a crucifix—a cheap ugly one because I had to do it quickly." But the act signalled a further decision.

This is an act of momentous significance. It means that she is through with her vacillation, that she is ready for the plunge. In the dark of her faith she was surrendering. Down on her knees before the crucifix she makes a fervent plea: "I wish I knew a prayer that wasn't me, me. . . . Let me forget me. Dear God, I've tried to love and I've made such a hash of it." (p. 146-147) All claims are yielded up in these words, all that is her, and hers. The decision is solemnized in a Roman Catholic church, though that was not planned. She had just blundered into a church that happened to be on her walk and she had gone in because she needed the quiet. At first the plaster figures on the walls revolt her. She is even repulsed by the crucifix, and "all the emphasis on the human body."

The church scene marks an important event in Sarah's mystical growth. It is an epiphany, with undertones of tremendous consequence for herself. What had been only an idea, vague and distant, has now become part of a personal equation. Having closed her affair with Bendrix, she thought she could not stand any suggestion of the human body and its needs.

> I thought I could believe in some kind of a God that bore no relation to ourselves, something vague, amorphous, cosmic, to which I had promised something and which had given me something in return—a Thing which had stretched out of the vague into the concrete human life, like a powerful vapor moving among the chairs and walls. One day I too would become part of that vapor; I would escape myself forever. (p. 133)

The crucifix confronts her with the possibility that there may be no escape. It presents her with a human body, ripped naked, and stretched on the bed of a cross.

Thus, by degrees, Sarah is led to the heart of a mystery—the mystery of Incarnation. The plaster statues are the statement of a proposition, repulsive to her at this stage, that God, because of His love for men and women, has taken unto Himself a human nature—body and soul—and thus has admitted all to His grace. Half believing yet, Sarah is the focus of a debate between the Incarnational faith and the louder assertions of rationalism. This latter philosophy is supported by Smythe, by the scientists generally and, to a limited extent, by Bendrix. Sarah flirts with the idea, but is compelled to reject it. Disgusted as she is with the crudity of the images, she remains with them. But she cannot help noticing that to dismiss them altogether would be to deny whatever was uplifting in her relation with Bendrix.

> I thought of certain lines life had put on his face, as personal as lines of his writing. I thought of a new scar on his shoulder that wouldn't have been there if once he hadn't tried to protect another man's body from a falling wall. He didn't tell me why he was in hospital those three days; Henry told me. That scar was part of his character as much as his jealousy. And so I thought, do I want that body to be vapor—mine yes, but his? And I knew I wanted that scar to exist through all eternity. But could my vapor love that scar? Then I began to want my body that I hated, but only because it could love that scar. We can love with our minds, but can we love only with our minds? Love extends itself all the time, so that we can even love with our senseless nails: we love even with our clothes, so that a sleeve can feel a sleeve. (p. 134)

Looking up she sees the *corpus*, wounded and bleeding, erected at the centre of the altar. Surely that was no vapor! "Could the world have nailed a vapor there? A vapor of course felt no pain and no pleasure." Perhaps it was only her superstition that imagined it could hear her prayers. She ought not to have addressed it, Dear God; she should have said, Dear Vapor. "I had said I hate you, but can one hate a vapor? I could hate that figure on the Cross with its claim to my gratitude—'I've suffered this for you'—but a vapor. . . . ." (p. 136)

The argument is compelling. Incarnation forces trust and surrender by the very logic of its love. It admits of no ambiguity, and therefore no excuse for indecision. The laugh, thinks Sarah, is on the rationalists. In her words: "Richard believed in a vapor. He hated a fable, he fought a fable, he took a fable seriously." (p. 136) "Believed," "hated," "fought"—all verbs indicative of a most personal intercourse. None in his senses would be so engaged with something that did not exist. Not only was God real, even the Rationalist has taken Him seriously. Richard thought Him enough of a foe to want to fight Him. Sarah sees no option but to believe and, at this stage, belief means surender of her whole being—thoughts, desires, will—to the divine pleasure.

The incarnational mystery is not a little demanding on one who puts his faith on it. Here is Sarah: "I thought, sometimes I've hated Maurice, but would I have hated him if I hadn't loved him too? Oh God, if I could really hate you, what would that mean?" (p. 136) Suppposing this God did exist, she must already love Him. And "suppose he was a body like that. What's wrong in believing that his body existed as much as mine? I can't love a vapor that was Maurice. . ." (p. 136) All doubts vanish, and "in a flaming rage," she steps out of the church, to ratify her surrender by a ritual act. "And, in defiance of Henry and all the *reasonable* and the *detached*, I did what I had seen people do in Spanish churches: I dipped my finger in the so-called holy water and made a kind of cross on my forehead." (p. 137. Italics added).

The consequences of that action are far-reaching. There is no going back on the decision already made. This is how she expresses herself in her last letter to Bendrix:

I believe there's a God,—I believe the whole bag of tricks; there's nothing I don't believe, they could subdivide the Trinity into a dozen parts and I'd believe. They could dig up records that prove Christ had been invented by Pilate to get himself promoted, and I'd believe just the same. I've caught belief like a disease. I've fallen into belief like I fell in love. I've never loved before as I love you, and I've never believed in anything before as I believe now. I'm sure. I've never been sure before about anything. When you came in at the door with the blood on your face, I became sure, Once and for all. Even though I didn't know it at the time. I fought belief for longer than I fought love, but I haven't any fight left. (p. 182)

There is a new confidence about Sarah. Her faith has decidedly influenced her and changed her outlook on life. What appeared ugly before, what was revolting, is now accepted with gratitude. Sarah is suddenly very concerned about "the strawberry mark, ... Henry's face with tears falling." She dwells with compassion on all the misery round about her. These give her life a fresh orientation. It is no longer "me" that is at the center, but "they". "Dear God," she prays, "I've tried to love and I've made such a hash of it. If I could love You, I'd know how to love them. . . . Teach me to love. I don't mind my pain. It's their pain I can't stand. Let my pain go on and on, but stop theirs." (p. 147)

Such detachment is extraordinary in real life. But Sarah is of course possessed of a divine fire, and her actions are dictated by its glow. "If I could love You, I could love Henry," she addresses her new Lover.

God was made man. He was Henry with his astigmatism, Richard with his strawberry mark, not only Maurice. If I could love a leper's sores, couldn't I love the boringness of Henry? . . . I imagine I'm ready for the pain of Your nails, and I can't stand twenty-four hours of maps and Michelin guides. Dear God, I'm no use. I'm still the same bitch and fake. . . . (p. 147-48)

Love has sent her soaring. The desire of the beloved is to be with the Lover, to merge with him even physically were that possible: but she must seek to be closely identified with him. Sarah is in love, and her one desire is to be more like her Lover. She cries out with passion: "Dear God, if only You could come down from Your cross for a while, and let me get up there instead. If I could suffer like You, I could heal like You." (p. 147)   She would be with Him even in death, most of all in death.

It is an axiom in mystical life that the surest sign of God's indwelling is when the soul grows more and more forgetful of self and concerned for her fellows. The facility and willingness with which she reaches out to serve them are a measure of her union with God. God's love is a fire that consumes all that comes its way. No one may try to bottle it, to shut it away; it shoots out its tongues in every direction, until everything is upgathered, is suffused with its energy. But this is a fire that quickens life. To be "present to God" in faith, says Merton, is to be "present to ourselves in Him (and) present to everything else also in Him."[11] Elsewhere he says: "Our ability to sacrifice ourselves in a mature and generous spirit may well prove to be one of the tests of our interior prayer."[12] Mystics would generally agree. The inner awakening, we are told, "will unconsciously and spontaneously manifest itself in a habitual spirit of sacrifice and concern for others that is unfailingly generous though perhaps we may not be aware of the fact."[13] Indeed, God does not give Himself for the individual only, "but also for others."[14]

This is the context of Sarah's prayer to bring healing to those about her. Her response to Smythe's anguish is a clear sign of her progress. She has "an enormous wish to touch" his deformity, "to comfort it with words of love as permanent as the wound." She would "offer up some inordinate sacrifice if only he could be healed. . ." (p. 131)   Her previous attempts at love now seem to her too inadequate—a "precarious and a painful thing, full of labor and sorrow."[15] Now more closely united with God, the source of love and vitality, and "identified" with Him, her life is fuller and more satisfing. One with Him, she also feels "with all the others who are identified with Him."[16]

Her concern for the stricken Rationalist takes some unusual shapes. We read thus in her diary:

I shut my eyes and put my mouth against the mark. I felt sick for a moment because I fear deformity, and he sat quiet and let me kiss him, and I thought, I am kissing pain, and pain belongs to You as happiness never does. I love You in Your pain. I could almost taste metal and salt in the skin, and I thought, how good You are. You might have killed us with happiness, but You let us be with You in pain.

I felt him move abruptly away and I opened my eyes. . . . I couldn't tell him I envied him, carrying the mark of pain around with him like that, seeing You in the glass everyday instead of this dull human thing we call beauty. (p. 149-50)

An unusual fare for the reader? But it is vintage Greene.

God's indwelling is said to unify all the faculties and the energies of the human soul. It renders it 'simple', free "of all conflict, all confusion and hesitation."[17] It brings about a sea change within. This apparently is Sarah's experience, too. She now enjoys "a simplicity that simplifies [her] whole life and draws all the powers of [her] being together."[18] And hers is "a clarity that is profound and clean and embraces more than a universe."[19] By the time we close the book we have observed the various stages of her progress; her death is only the final one. The transformation does not preclude pain. But in her suffering we notice an unusual freedom, maybe because it is willed, and accepted with love. Sarah's final hours are spent about the Still-point. She has attained to a stage of identification when life "has become completely simple. It consists of one thought, one preoccupation, one love: God alone."[20] In that loving, suffering communion has she found her true self.

The diary entry for 10 January 1946 describes the events on which the novel opens. The tone is unmistakeably lovelorn.

I couldn't stand the house tonight, so I walked out into the rain. I remembered the time when I had stuck my nails into my palms, and I didn't know it, but You moved in the pain. I said, "Let him be alive," not believing in You, and my disbelief made no difference to You. You took it into Your love and accepted it like an offering, and tonight the rain soaked through my coat and my clothes and into my skin, and I shivered with the cold, and it was for the first time as though I nearly loved You. I walked under Your windows in the rain and I wanted to wait under them all night only to show that after all I might learn to love and I wasn't afraid of the desert any longer because You were there. I came back into the house, and there was Maurice with Henry. It was the second time You had given him back; the first time I had hated You for it, and You'd taken my hate, like You'd taken my disbelief, into Your love, keeping them to show me later, so that we could both laugh—as I have sometimes laughed at Maurice, saying, "Do you remember how stupid we were?. ." (p. 138)

This would seem to close a story. But it also begins one. The entry marks the last phase of Sarah's awakening. Within some few hours she would be dead, gathered forever in the divine embrace. To Bendrix, however, it is simply the opening of a new chapter.

The novelist-narrator is no less infected with Sarah's faith, but he does not yet know it. Nor does he know that Sarah has been long pursued by her divine Lover. He had her marked for His own years ago. From her infancy she had carried within her the seeds of His grace. (She had been baptized as a child; her mother now gives out her secret). "It's an extraordinary coincidence isn't it?" Henry says when he learns of it. "Baptized at two years old, and then beginning to go back to what you can't even remember. . . It's like an infection." That grace is like a contagion, even Sarah would agree. That is exactly what she wrote on her deathbed: "I've caught belief like a disease." (p. 182)

To Bendrix all this is very disturbing. For now he has begun to see Sarah as a frightening precedent. And if she were susceptible to grace, so might he be. Alive, Sarah was a temptation, strong enough to ruin his career; dead, she has destroyed all his interest in life. He dares not even acknowledge that God has taken her away: that would be to admit defeat. It would also be to allow reality to the irrational, and the artist must proceed on rational lines. And according to the rules of reason he must certify "that it was his own driving will and not that of God which took Sarah from him."[21]

Nothing would please him better, and half the book is about his fretful efforts at giving credence to his story. Still, he is often afflicted by a "doubt that. . .comes when I begin to write, the feeling that after all perhaps she was right and I was wrong." (p. 65)

To doubt is already halfway to belief. Bendrix is confronted with two sets of evidence—neither to be lightly brushed aside. The first has to do with Sarah's diary which reported in minute detail both the events that have lately afflicted his mind and their motives. Other evidence had to do with some extraordinary happenings following on Sarah's death. Their cumulative effect is such as almost to engulf him. That he feels threatened is obvious from his own words: "If Sarah is right, how unimportant all the importance of art is." It would take a struggle before he can settle that question.

Bendrix had once dismissed Smythe's agnosticism as "hysterical." If Smythe's disbelief is that, how about his own? Why the impassioned, though vain, efforts at defending himself against belief? Surely, his lies and his childish refusal to take cognizance of vital evidence do not constitute sanity. The element of hysteria is enough proof that his own defenses are crashing. Bendrix is only too aware of this. He himself admits: "I would only have to shut the eyes of my mind for a long enough time, and I could believe that you came to Parkis's boy in the night with your touch that brings peace. Last month in the crematorium I asked you to save that girl from me and you pushed your mother between us—or so they might say. But if I start believing that, then I have to believe in your God. I'd have to love your God. I'd rather love the men you slept with." (p. 227) The choppiness of the narrative here corresponds to his present state of mind.

His bluster does not really carry conviction. He claims that were there "to be a conflict between an image [meaning God] and a man, I know who will win. I could put my hand on her thigh. . .he-. . .couldn't move to plead his cause." Yet, he is quite helpless before a simple fever that has taken hold of her. With her coughing by his side, doubled up and in great pain, he only utters an impotent wish: "If only one had a touch that could heal." (p. 158)

The End of the Affair is not simple hagiography. Although the author does dwell at some length on Sarah's conversion and the extraordinary events that follow upon it, his focus really is elsewhere. It is Bendrix who commands the center of the stage, and the burden of the story is the effect Sarah's life and doings have on him. The point of view is weighted in favor of Bendrix, too. "The end of the affair" applies to him in more than one sense. It is not only his sexual affair that is brought to a close, but also his impassioned concern for beauty—even his very aesthetic outlook. Towards the end he is forced to a recognition that art of itself is not capable of giving to life its ultimate significance, its justification.

"All the world's a stage/, And all the men and women merely players. . ./ And one man in his time plays many parts," quips Jaques, the melencholy philosopher.[22] Bendrix can now see the truth of that saying. He thinks of himself as a character in fiction, flung about, observed, and guided by an unseen, unreachable will. There are some characters who, he says, "in a sense create themselves. They come alive. They are capable of the surprising act or word. They stand outside the plot, unconditioned by it." Such, in his reckoning, is Sarah. But not everyone rises to this freedom. There are also those who "stick," who refuse to "come alive," although there is nothing psychologically false about them. It is just that they "have the obstinacy of nonexistence," and consequently they need "to be pushed around." (p. 232) "We are inextricably bound to the plot, and wearily God forces us, here and there, according to his intention, characters without poetry, without free will, whose only importance is that somewhere, at some time, we help to furnish the scene in which a living character moves and speaks. . . ." (p. 232)

This is a new perspective for Bendrix; and the implications of it involve him in a loss of identity. He cannot even take comfort in the thought that he alone had Sarah for all these years, that it was he, Bendrix, and no God of hers, who 'took' her. For he has to admit that he was unable to keep her. God "won in the end." (p. 206)   His feeling of impotence before a superior Wisdom and Might is brought home strikingly in a dream. He is at a fair "shooting at bottles that looked as though they were made of glass but my bullets bounded off them as though they were coated with steel." (p. 207)   There is no winning against that greater Power. Still, he would go on struggling with It to the end. For if he gave in, he fears, he might lose himself. "If I begin to love God, I can't just die. . . . If ever I loved like that, it would be the end of everything. Loving you I had no appetite for food, I felt no lust for any other woman, but loving Him there'd be no pleasure in anything at all with Him away. I'd even lose my work, I'd cease to be Bendrix. Sarah, I'm afraid." (p. 229)

Bendrix's anxiety parallels Sarah's before her surrender. 'O God, if I could really hate you, what would that mean?" (p. 228)   So she wrote in her diary. "Sometimes I've hated Maurice, but would I have hated him if I hadn't loved him too?" Bendrix's thought now is a faithful echo of her words: "And I thought, hating Sarah is only loving Sarah and hating myself is only loving myself. I'm not worth hating. . . Nothing—not even Sarah—is worth our hatred if You exist, except You." (p. 228)

Hate or love—God's call commands some kind of response. From Bendrix too it wrings a cry of desperation.

> I have no peace and I have no love. . . . . For if this God exists,. . . and if even you—with your lusts and your adulteries and the timid lies you used to tell—can change like this, we could all be saints by leaping as you leapt, by shutting the eyes and leaping once and for all; if *you* are a saint, it's not so difficult to be a saint. It's something He can demand of any of us—leap. But I won't leap.
>
> I sat on my bed and said to God, You've taken her but You haven't got me yet. . . . I don't want Your peace and I don't want Your love. I wanted something very simple and very easy: I wanted Sarah for a lifetime and You took her away. With Your great schemes You ruin our happiness as a harvester ruins a mouse's nest, I hate You, God, I hate You as though You existed. (p. 238-39)

The strained note, disguised as hatred, and intolerably painful, is a prelude to surrender. Though he would be reluctant to the last, his resistance is being worn down, stage by stage, until he cannot possibly hold himself back. "I said to Sarah, all right, have it your way. I believe you live and that He exists, but it will take more than your prayers to turn this hatred of Him into love. . . ." He well knows, hatred is the beginning. Smythe and Sarah hated too, and were overwhelmed. So would he be.

The skeptic may demur at this conclusion. So Bendrix is at pains to explain. "Nobody knows the beginning of anything," he claims. Sarah had believed the end began when she saw Bendrix's body in the rubble. "She would never have admitted that the end had started long before: the fewer telephone calls for this or that inadequate reason, the quarrels I began with her because I had realized the danger of love's ending. We had begun to look beyond love, . . . When we get to the end of human beings we have to delude ourselves into a belief in God, like a gourmet who demands more complex sauces with his food." (p. 180)

Bendrix is no less a gourmet. His whole career bears witness to this—whether he is nosing for "the right clue", or preoccupied with disintering "the human character from the heavy scene." (p. 26) Indeed, he is no less susceptible than Sarah to the allure of a divine feast. In *La Pharisienne* Francois Mauriac makes this observation: although people do not quite change with years, he says, certain impulses which they have striven tirelessly to suppress do at times assert themselves; and many people end up by succumbing to them. And he adds: "God is very often the good temptation to which many human beings in the long run yield." They would rather not have Him. They flee from Him; and silently but unfailingly He pursues; and they are overcome. They are changed through their surrender. They cease to be what they have hitherto been. This is a matter of some confusion. We noticed the anxiety in both Sarah and Bendrix. But the anxiety subsides as they are claimed by "the deep sea swell"; their doubts and worries are hushed "in whispers."

In the 'whirlpool' of divine love neither youth counts nor age. "Time's a strange thing," says Father Crompton towards the close of the novel. "St Augustine asked where time came from. He said it came out of the future which didn't exist yet, into the present that had no duration, and went into the past which had ceased to exist.

I don't know that we can understand time any better than a child."
(p. 225) One may spend an entire life riding with time, and still
may never reach its sources. For the lovers it was with an awareness of time that things began. Soon, however, they discover that
the Source is within, prompting and urging them. United with the
Timeless, they have their first taste of freedom.

One does not associate such a sense of freedom with Querry, the
hero of the next novel we will consider. No aura of holiness, nor of
joy surrounds him; but unlike Greene's earlier characters neither is
he quite so haunted. Querry is simply withdrawn from life, he
would have nothing to do with its variegated demands. In him the
faculties of feeling have long atrophied. He is, in terms of the
book's symbology, just "a burnt-out case"

A BURNT-OUT CASE

What happens if one's will-to-meaning remains unfulfilled?
What if the person finds himself frustrated in this most human
demand for a meaning to his existence? . . . What we can
observe in the majority of people is not so much the feeling of
being less valuable than others, but the feeling that life no
longer has any meaning.

—Viktor E. Frankl

A Burnt-Out Case is not one of Greene's elaborately planned religious novels; it is more in the nature of an afterword. With *The End of the Affair* the religious impulse was nearly spent and the author's interest shifted elsewhere. He still wore the helmet and the breastplate. The battlefield, however, was no longer the individual soul, but the soul of politics caught in transnational greed and manipulation. He was now gripped by the moral-political enigma of a Vietnam, a Haiti, and a socialist Argentina.. In *A Burnt-Out Case* Greene is, as it were, turning back to scribble a hurried post-script to his earlier preoccupation. We are, therefore, not surprised by undertones of an apologia; between the lines one reads the implied warning, Let Me Explain.

It should indeed seem ironical when an author's very success proves to be his undoing; Greene's situation was such as he set about writing *A Burnt-Out Case.* His recent work, particularly *The Heart of the Matter,* had set off waves of unprecedented enthusiasm; some reactions were high pitched and wild enough to seem zany. One young woman, reports Greene, sent him "a rather

All quotes from G. Greene, *A Burnt-Out Case* (Penguin Books, 1977)

167

drunken letter of invitation from a Dutch fishing boat enclosing a photograph."[1] Another wrote to him from Switzerland suggesting that he join her "where the snow can be our coverlet."[2] It was clear that these poor neurotics had equated him with Scobie, and Greene felt it urgent to let them know that he was no knight-in-arms ready to jump to the aid of every distressed damsel. He must correct his public image, and fast, if only to save his personal integrity.

The Heart of the Matter "appealed too often to weak elements in its readers," reports Greene.[3] The book brought in an enormous crop of correspondence from total strangers. One young man wrote from West Berlin urging him "to lead a crusade of young people into the Eastern Zone where we were to shed our blood for the Church."[4] The Green Knight had evidently entered the arena; long live the Knight, and his lady, and Mother Church. He craved peace, he prayed those who would urge him on to leave him alone; and they replied that he did not belong to himself anymore, they had taken him up. He had become as much a public property as the stationery stamped with government watermark. Even more intolerable to him was that priests and religious should join in the "hunt." There was a brand of the ecclesiastic with mystical illusions who would not be kept away; they were certain they had a kindred spirit in "Brother" Greene. *A Burnt-Out Case* is Greene's reply to them all: the romantic, the neurotic, and the self-styled but deluded mystic.

Marie Rycker is not a far too distant cousin to the young woman who beckoned the author to the icy embrace of Switzerland. Narcissistic to the core, she is an instance of arrested sexual growth; and not merely sexual but even emotional under development. Her immaturity seeps through in her speech with its phrase-book idiom; and her feeling of personal inadequacy is very much underscored. She fears the dark, dreads the moth and the rat in the wainscot. Married to a factory owner, a man old enough to be her father and a psychotic, Marie has written off her present estate as grossly unreal in contrast to the earlier, less painful phase of her adolescence. Her thoughts tend to hover about the convent school and Sister Therese with her broken ankle, and the *plage* in August with her parents. (p. 66)   All this was a willed diversion from the unpleasant demands and complications her husband represented. Rycker has not only failed to awaken her passion, he has the more firmly sealed her virginity; and it is no accident that it is the "smell of stale margarine which she would always associate with marriage." (p. 137)   Her unfortunate marriage has resulted in warping her sexuality, and Marie is already showing the split between her ardent eroticism and her capacity to enjoy sex. There are traits she shares with Helen Rolt, too, who at nineteen was cast adrift at sea and picked up a widow. Marie is a widow in the emotional, but nonetheless very real, sense; and her unfulfilled erotic impulses are hunting for a worthy object when Querry blunders onto the scene. But the retired architect is also retired from women; and she must do with mere daydreaming about him—and what havoc such daydreaming might do!

If the novelist would have nothing to do with Marie and her ilk, he felt the more hurt and mortified by demands made on him by his priestly suppliants. Greene recalls how a French priest kept harassing him "first with letters of a kind which should only have been addressed to his confessor, and then in person: he even popped up unannounced and inopportunely, one evening. . . . Other priests would spend hours in my only armchair, while they described their difficulties, their perplexities, their desperation."[5] All this, understandably, was very unnerving. Greene tells us how he felt:

> . . . in the years between *The Heart of the Matter* and *The End of the Affair* I felt myself used and exhausted by the victims of religion. The vision of faith as an untroubled sea was lost for ever; it was more like a tempest in which the lucky were engulfed and lost, and the unfortunate survived to be flung battered and bleeding on the shore. A better man could have found a life's work on the margin of that cruel sea, but my own course of life gave me no confidence in any aid I might proffer. I had no apostolic mission, and the cries for spiritual assistance maddened me because of my impotence. What was the Church for but to aid these sufferers? What was the priesthood for? I was like a man without medical know-

ledge in a village struck with plague. It was in those years, I think, that Querry was born, and Father Thomas too. He had often sat in that chair of mine, and he had worn many faces.[6]

In the character of Father Thomas we have a sense of Greene's impatience with that soulless religiosity which, in the suburban wasteland, passes, at times, for piety: "the piety of the educated, the established, who seem to own their Roman Catholic image of God, who have ceased to look for Him because they consider they have found Him."[7] But their religion is quite barren: it cannot save or quicken their lives. How very different was the simple faith of the Mexican Indian about whom Greene wrote with such touching admiration.[8] Both in Mexico and in the African bush, belief was something primal and hence likely to release in the believer's veins an elixir of the purest trust and joy. Neither is there joy nor freedom evidenced in Father Thomas. On the contrary, he scares off even the most ordinary comfort; he makes his companions feel guilty that they should enjoy an occasional drink. Joy is the farthest from where Father Thomas is. He is indeed an unusually blighted figure: frigid in company, and so scared of the dark that he is forced to keep many a sleepless night. (p. 89)   He is so grossly intolerant of human weakness[9] and so unlike the Incarnate God who in embracing the flesh also took on its weakness that we wonder at the audacity of his priesthood. One who understood so little of the Master could ill function as his vicar!

Father Thomas belongs to that priestly tribe who are overly self-confident of their spiritual insights but, strangely enough, are also so confused and so lost in their theological labyrinths that they must borrow a taper from any passerby to light their way out. He has very little in common with Greene's earlier priest characters, except perhaps with the perpetually agitated Father Clay. Both Father Rank of *The Heart of the Matter* and Father James of *The Potting Shed* are mature characters; and even if they are not much use to their flock, still their helplessness is balanced by their very genuine compassion. Father Thomas in his pride and spiritual immaturity is a proper match only for Marie.

The priest's character is brought out in clear relief in the scene just preceding the climax. Doctor Colin and the priests are discussing Querry who has just gone out of the room. A scientist with no pretensions to religious belief, Colin describes him simply as a "burnt-out case." In the milieu of the leprosarium this diagnosis is amply expressive. Simple truths, however, are not for the complicated mind; and Father Thomas retorts with "The better the man the worse the aridity," hinting that if Querry were not a saint already, he is well on the way. "A man with little faith doesn't feel the temporary loss of it." (True, even Colin suspects a virulent condition, as he tells Querry: "You're too troubled by your lack of faith. . . . You keep on fingering it like a sore." But we are not concerned with Querry's faith or lack of it.) What bowls us over is the priest's impudence in appropriating to himself such extraordinary ability for spiritual guidance. He is quite satisfied that Querry is only passing through a difficult phase of his mystical ascent; his loss of faith is no more than apparent: he is actually slogging through the Dark Night ("Perhaps even now you are walking in the footsteps of St. John of the Cross, the *noche oscura*."), at the end of which awaited the divine Spouse with outstretched arms, and the crown of bliss for an eternal reward. When the doctor warns him against reading too much into Querry's "loss" of faith, the other retorts:

> "You talk, doctor, like all atheists, as though there were no such thing as grace. Belief without grace is unthinkable, and God will never rob a man of grace. Only a man himself can do that—by his own actions. We have seen Querry's actions here, and they speak for themselves." (p. 178)

"I hope you won't be disappointed," says the doctor, and the other's reply is quite patronizing: "You are a very good doctor, but all the same I think we are better judges of a man's spiritual condition. . . . You can detect a patch on the skin where we see nothing at all. You must allow us to have a nose for—well. . ." Father Thomas hesitates and then says ". . . heroic virtue."

His behavior envinces not the shadow of a doubt in his own skill in diagnosing another's spiritual condition. Querry, he has decided, is one especially favored of God. He is quite determined that neither sickness nor boredom has driven the architect into their midst; it was nothing but heroism of an unusual order. Soon, however, it becomes clear what sort of nose the priest has for heroic virtue. Even as he is speaking, the Mother Superior rings up to pass on the "terrible news" that Querry has got Marie Rycker with child (p. 179), and the priest is thrown into the worst tam-trums of despair: "He could not have given a more extreme signal of distress."

> Father Thomas said, "I envy you your skin test, doctor. You were right to warn me against disappointment. The Superior too. He said much the same thing as you. I have trusted too much to appearances." (p. 179)

If this priest repels our finer instincts, it is not merely due to his bigotry and proud self-assurance which, however, he cannot long sustain. Nor are his pretensions to be an all knowing doctor of souls vindicated by his life or deeds. Few men would ever dare make such sweeping claims as Father Thomas. Even the moder-ately sensitive Greene character is conscious of his inadequacy, painfully aware how little he knows himself, how much less another human being.

Father Thomas typifies Unamuno's believers: "Those who believe that they believe in God, but without passion in their heart, without anguish of mind, without uncertainty, without doubt, without an element of despair even in their consolation, believe only in the God Idea, not in God Himself."[10] Their God, being but a concept cannot save or heal the soul of its guilt; it is after all a mental construct and, at best, only a pale reflection of the living God.

Father Thomas is, of course, the villain of the piece. But even before he takes Querry up in earnest as exemplifying his own mystical tenets, others had surveyed the field and erected a little, vulgar shrine for this latter-day saint. Rycker is the secular coun-terpart of Father Thomas, and the author spares no love for him at all. Rycker is the owner of a margarine factory and during the long lonely years in the bush, he has built himself a tragic profile. He is to himself a man much to be pitied, not for his personal immaturity and lack of understanding (which might have passed for true self-knowledge) but for his "spiritual problems." "When a man has nothing else to be proud of," the Superior says perceptively, "he is proud of his spiritual problems. After two whiskies he began to talk to me about Grace." (p. 21)

Ryker is a character straight out of a common farce, and part of the comic effect is that he doesn't know it. His marriage to the adolescent Marie was a calculated affair. "In a post like this it's necessary to have a companion. . . . But I look ahead. If you believe in marriage you have to. . . I've still got twenty years of— let's call it active life ahead of me, and what would a woman of thirty be like in twenty years?" (p. 36)   Rycker is obsessed with sex and St Paul—in that order:

> "There are enough problems without sex I can assure you. Saint Paul wrote, didn't he, that it was better to marry than burn. Marie will stay young long enough to save me from the furnace." He added quickly, "Of course I'm only joking. We have to joke, don't we, about serious things. At the bottom of my heart I believe very profoundly in love." (p. 36)

Later he makes the proud claim: "I'm a good Catholic, I hope, but that doesn't prevent me from having spiritual problems." (p. 39)

Here, indeed, is a soul mate for Father Thomas. "A lot of people take their religion lightly." he says, "but I had six years when I was a young man with the Jesuits. If a novice master had been less unfair you wouldn't have found me here." (p. 39)   And so he has been spending his long years in the bush meditating on palm nuts and love: "the love of God. Agape, not Eros," he qualifies.

> "In the seminary I formed the habit of thinking more than most men," Rycker said. "A faith like ours, when profoundly understood, sets us many problems. For instance—no, it's not a mere instance, I'm jumping to the heart of what really troubles me, I don't believe my wife understands the true nature of Christian marriage." (p. 39-40)

A strangely twisted character, Rycker has sex, love, and religion all mixed up in his mind. He claims a right to have sex with his wife whenever and anyway he desired, never mind her own wishes in the matter. His lust is divorced from any hint of affection, and altogether unattended by romantic sentiments. "Sometimes she even refuses her duties," he blurts out to Querry on their first meeting. "Her duties to me. Her married duties." Did one really think of those as duties? "You know very well the Church does. No one has any right to abstain except by mutual consent." (p. 41) He is tortured in turn by a sterile, brute lust and the dread that she might any day leave him. Instead of making himself more appealing, his strategem is to preach to her on St. Paul and the love of God. "Because if she loved Him, she wouldn't want to offend Him, would she? And that would be some security." (p. 40) God is but a handy means to hold up his tottering marriage. One suspects that for Rycker Querry also is a means: he is not only an acquiescent dummy on whom Rycker may exercise his need for "intellectual conversation", he is also the famed architect whom it is Rycker's privilege to "rediscover"— itself a short-cut to world fame. In every way it has been profitable to latch on to Querry. Unlike Father Thomas, Rycker does not so much exemplify a "vulgar lust for holiness"[11] (which might have done him some credit), as a pathetic need to boost up his sagging morale by whatever means—through a reference to religion if that helped, or to a famed name.

Rycker's portrait is cynical. But even less sympathetic is the author to the seedy British journalist, Parkinson. He is vulgarized beyond any hope of recovery. The representative of a cheap Sunday newspaper, he makes loud claims of his articles being '"syndicated in the United States, France, Germany, Japan, and South America. No other living journalist. . .'" (p. 108) He has quite forgotten that there might be some small distinction between falsehood and truth.

If Father Thomas rouses us to anger and Rycker to scorn with their self-importance, Parkinson elicits no emotions at all—only laughter. This is perhaps because he is not really built up as a character; he is only the clown whose role is to keep us amused between scenes; and this he does well and without any apparent effort. He appears to be incensed that Querry has not come forward to meet him: "It's stupid of him to pretend to hide away. No one really wants to hide from Montagu Parkinson. Aren't I the end of every man's desire? Quote. Swinburne" (p. 105) "Parkinson," he shouts out to Colin who has asked his name, "Montagu Parkinson." He added with disappointment: "Doesn't the name mean anything at all to you?" (p. 106) Shortly afterwards he ejaculates again.

> "Have neither of you," Parkinson said sorrowfully, "heard my name Montagu Parkinson? Surely it's memorable enough." It was impossible to tell whether he was laughing at himself.
> Father Thomas began to answer him. "To be quite truthful until you came. . ."
> "My name is writ in water. Quote. Shelly." Parkinson said. (p. 107)

". . . [W]hat are you? What are your motives? I know a lot about you already. I've briefed myself," cries he as soon as he has Querry alone and in his power. "You aren't exactly a man who loves his fellows, are you? Leaving out women, of course." (p. 109) "There is a strong allurement to corruption," notes the author,

> . . . and there was no doubt of Parkinson's? he carried it on the surface of his skin like phosphorus, impossible to mistake. Virtue had died long ago within that mountain of flesh for lack of air. A priest might not be shocked by human failings, but he could be hurt or disappointed; Parkinson would welcome any kind of failing. Nothing would hurt Parkinson or disappoint him but the size of a cheque. (p. 109)

Parkinson is but a small time reviewer; but the author uses him to larger purposes. In him is seen the type descriptive of critics and connoisseurs of literary art, the kind about whom Querry speaks in his parable of the Jeweller:

They began to write books about his art; especially those who claimed to know and love the King wrote about him. The books all said much the same thing, and when our hero had read one he had read them all. (p. 157)

And quite unashamedly Parkinson announces to Querry his intention of "building him up" as a hero and a saint. Greene perhaps had similar experiences as Querry; at any rate he could not but have been exasperated by all the critical attention. It was not only the cynic who loved to finger "faults [he] was tired of facing"; he was even more irritated by claims made of discovering in his work "buried significance . . . of which [he] was unaware."[12]

It is quite important to recognize the bond that connects Father Thomas with each of the other two. All three of them are intent on using Querry or at least his name to personal advantage. While Rycker would have him boost his self image and thinks him in some vague way a surety against his marriage breaking up, Parkinson cynically employs his name for the purpose of earning a livelihood. For Father Thomas, the most interesting of the three, he is a sainted hero, an angel sent to stand guard over his troubled faith. And all three get along beautifully. Rycker sets Parkinson upon Querry; and the priest aids them both in their pursuit. No sooner has Parkinson landed on the leprosarium than the priest and he become intimate friends, to the great surprise of Dr. Colin. Parkinson arrived a total stranger of whose existence nobody knew before his arrival. Not all of Father Thomas's motives are spiritual either. "There is another side to all of this," the priest tells Colin who has rebuked his encouraging Parkinson. The "other side" is that the reportage might bring fame to the leprosarium—money too: "and the British, one has heard, are a generous people." (p. 108) The imputing of a materialistic motivation is the author's only revenge on this ecclesiastical type who pursued him for months with complicated spiritual problems.

He did not, of course, want the clerical hounds; he was punished enough with a handy religious tag. Had he never rebelled, the label might have stuck and tied him down to a lifetime of humbug. Greene however did rebel; and his counter thrust is in all earnestness. The blow is dealt with force and accuracy. If irony is his only tool, it is no mean weapon. But Greene does not strike to kill; his only aim is self-defense. He owed it to himself to guard the little germ of sincerity: "All I have left me is a certain regard for truth," Querry tells Rycker at one stage. "It was the best side of the small talent I had." (p. 145) *His* "small talent, no less than Greene's, was widely noticed: "Everyone said he was a master technician, but he was highly praised too for the seriousness of his subject matter." (p. 155)

The Jeweller of the story which Querry tells Mme Rycker in Luc to put her to sleep is his own mask. Querry speaks for Greene; and the story is a masterpiece in comic invention. The jeweller was shot into world fame on account of his intricate designs in enamel and gold—"a little gold figure sitting at a table and a little gold-and-enamel egg on the table, and when you opened that there was a little figure sitting at a table and a little gold-and-enamel egg, and when you opened that . . ." and so on, and on top of each egg "a gold cross set with chips of precious stones in honour of the King." (p. 155)   No one ever doubted that he was a very clever jeweller, but it was the gold cross that caught the imagination of a certain type. For this religiously fervid type, the artist had stamped himself with an indelible seal; no use his wanting ever to scrape off the marks. The only trouble was that the jeweller had meanwhile become tired of it all: he had worn "himself out with the ingenuity of his design." But this the world would not recognize; it would not see that with neither ambition nor a faith to guide him he was as much out in the cold as the next person, that he did not even have the excuse of love to give purpose to life. And so he had simply given up. "He never wanted to turn his hand any more to mounting any jewel at all. He was finished with his profession—he had come to an end of it. Nothing could ever be so ingenious as what he had done already, or more useless, and he could never hear any praise higher than what he had received." (p. 156)

But still the rabble clamored; they would have more eggs and with crosses on them too. He was some rare bird, and they were not about to let him just fly off. He must produce more of the kind, they said; "it was his duty to the King and the King's followers.

Seeing no scope for flight, he flings them some more pieces, not gold-and-enamel eggs now, but nevertheless something to divert them. What he gave them was a series of satires on society and morals—"stones [cut] frivolously . . . exquisite little toads for women to wear in their navels." And avidly they lapped it up until "navel-jewels" became the rage of the season. The jeweller was beginning to enjoy his joke. Now he bettered his own previous mark by making "little soft golden coats of mail, with one hollow stone like a knowing eye at the top, with which men might clothe their special parts—they came to be known for some reason as Letters of Marque and for a while they too were quite fashionable as gifts. (You know how difficult it is for a woman to find anything to give a man at Christmas.) So our hero received yet more money and praise, but what vexed him most was that even these trifles were now regarded as seriously as his eggs and crosses had been. He was the King's jeweller and nothing could alter that. People declare that he was a moralist and that these were serious satires on the age." (p. 157)   The moral of the story is clear enough, the tone unmistakeable. Greene is having his belly laugh at the expense of his persecutors—the religiose and the peddlers of 'significance'.

But of course as is characteristic with Greene, the laughter is directed against himself insofar as the target is the milieu of which he is no less a part. With a ringing humor he probes the suburban religious standards and finds them hollow and meaningless. "When a man and a woman married," so they had told the jeweller, the King "was pleased by their marriage because when they came to litter it would increase the number of his subjects." (p. 152)   The use of the word "litter" and the King's sublime motive are all too amply expressive to need comment. The jeweller had been briefly taken in by the god talk; but when he woke up he found "he had deceived himself. . . . He had believed quite sincerely that when he loved his work he was loving the King and that when he made love to a woman he was at least imitating in a faulty way the King's love for his people." (p. 158)   This is the casuist's trap into which he fell, and it took some doing on his part to ease out the door. As Querry tells Mme Rycker, "it isn't easy leaving a profession" or a habit. "People talk a lot to you about duty." (p. 156)   Religion, the suburban habit, has a stranglehold on Querry/Greene, and his breaking out of it is, therefore, a significant event in his career as artist. The consequence of that rebellion is the new freedom with which he can meet Father Thomas's religious zeal: "The King after all had so loved the world that he had sent a bull and a shower of gold and a son. . ." (p. 158) Not blasphemy, this; but only the play of a mind newly freed from stifling thought patterns.

And if there is a serious intent in this new mocking manner of Greene, it is somewhat in the style of Jesus as he goes about cleansing the temple.[13] Jesus makes a whip and drives out those who bought and sold in the sacred precincts, and lets free the pigeons to their home in the skies. It is remarkable that objections should come primarily from the chief priests and theologians who take alarm at the straightforward simplicity of the new teaching.[14] Greene's mockery, too, is directed to the complacent: those who clutch their dogmas as though that guaranteed their salvation but without an active faith to animate them; those who mouth doctrines of faith as they might cheap political slogans. They tell the jeweller "that, even though the King was far away, he was watching everything that went on everywhere. When a pig littered, the King knew of it, or when a moth died against the lamp. When a man and a woman married, he knew that too." (p. 152) What irked Greene was the smug insensitivity of the half-believing.

The notions of divine reward and retribution are a cliché with the preacher. Whether or not he is wholly convinced of its truth, he has few qualms at flinging them on Sundays and holy days at a bored congregation. Those who pleased the king, it was claimed on His behalf, never missed the reward, although the reward was not always evident to the eye: "but, after all, you cannot see the air—and yet it exists according to those who know. . ." (p. 152) Similarly, when an act went clean against the divine law, such as "when a servant slept with another servant in a haystack, the King punished them. You couldn't always see the punishment—the man found a better job and the girl was more beautiful with her virginity gone and afterwards married the foreman." But all that made no difference, for the punishment was sure to come, and if it failed in the present time, it was only being "postponed until the end of life, but that made no difference because the King was the King of the dead, too, and you couldn't tell what terrible things he might do to them in the grave." (pp. 152-53)

Querry's life in a general way follows the pattern of irony detailed above. So long as he lived a blameless life, "he made no progress in his profession"; his only child, moreover, had died. Come the gradual lapse into 'immorality', and he begins to thrive, to be a "famous jeweller, for one of the women whom he had satisfied gave him money for his training, and he made many beautiful things in honor of his mistress and of course the King." Money too flows in, and prizes; and everyone is agreed that all this was his reward from the King. The perversity of the ecclesiastical logic is that he should come clean of it and become a hero; even the churchmen cannot help joining in the general chorus. "He left his wife and his mistress, he left a lot of women, but he always had a great deal of fun with them first. They called it love and so did he; he broke all the rules he could think of, and he must surely have been punished for breaking them, but you couldn't see the punishment, nor could he." (p. 153) The only punishment he knew was that he grew ever richer and the women were kinder and more generous to him. "He had, everyone agreed, a wonderful time." (p. 153)

No one can long withstand such indulgence; nor could the jeweller. The heat of success and adulation all but withered up his soul. His heart, swollen with pride, could no longer beat to the subtle rhythm of the Spirit. The shock of suffering might have revived his faculties; but "nobody ever made him suffer—it was always the other people who suffered." The result is a wilting boredom, but the worst is yet to come. His moment of truth occurs when he realizes suddenly that he has lost his capacity for feeling. He has left only the faint nostalgia of the burnt-out: the wish for even "the pain of punishment that the King must all the time have been inflicting on him." (p. 153) For if he could feel the pain, other emotions might be reactivated too-when he is jolted by a further discovery.

This is the sudden foreboding lest the King would, after all, prove to be a philosophical hoax. And if there were no King, then "anything that he had ever done must have been done for love of himself. How could there be any point any longer in making jewels or making love for his own solitary pleasure?" (p. 158) Over stimulation has killed the appetite; and the jeweller's sensibilities are quite jaded. Only, in moments "he wondered if his unbelief were not after all a final and conclusive proof of the King's existence. This total vacancy might be his punishment for the rules he had wilfully broken. It was even possible that this was what people meant by pain. The problem was complicated to the point of absurdity. . ." (p. 158)

Belief however has little to do with the logic of reason; it operates in a region that far exceeds understanding. Scientific methods are here of no avail; if God's existence could be proved "by historical, logical, philosophical, and etymological methods" (p. 154), similar methods may be employed to prove the reverse, as the jeweller learns too late, much to his dismay. To overstress reason may well be to deal the death blow to an incipient faith; and Querry, says the author, was "a victim of theology."[15] So was Greene's earlier character, Morin. What Morin says to his non-Catholic interviewer has a close relevance to Querry's condition:

A man can accept anything to do with God until scholars begin to go into details and the implications. A man can accept the Trinity, but the arguments that follow. . . I would never try to determine some point in differential calculus with a two-times-two table. You end by disbelieving the calculus. . . I used to believe in Revelation, but I never believed in the capacity of the human mind.

One could hardly be more emphatic.

Here one must sound a warning against too closely identifying the author and his characters. Querry/Jeweller may speak with Greene's voice; he may even be lent some of the author's passion. There the parallel must end. Querry's progress is from a complacent variety of belief to a tortured unbelief; Greene's seems to have followed the reverse course. At twenty-one he had believed "in nothing supernatural."[16] He reports in *A Sort of Life* that he never really intended to be received into the Church. "For such a thing to happen I would need to be convinced of its truth and that was not even a remote possibility."[17] His was not a theological problem: it had nothing to do with doubts and perplexities regarding God's goodness or love, or any other divine attribute. Greene's "primary difficulty," he tells us, "was to believe in a God at all. The date of the Gospels, the historical evidence for the existence of the man Jesus Christ: these were interesting subjects which came nowhere near the core of my disbelief. I didn't disbelieve in Christ; I disbelieved in God."[18] But as with Querry's disbelief, Greene's too was apparently of that painful kind that cannot deny faith a chance should it press its claims.

> If I were ever to be convinced in even the remote possibility of a supremee omnipotent and omniscient power I realized that nothing afterwards could seem impossible. It was on the ground of a dogmatic atheism that I fought and fought hard. It was like a fight for personal survival.[19]

This is the young Greene, the quester. When he met Vivien Dayrell-Browning, his future wife, he thought he might as well find out "the nature and limits of the beliefs she held."[20] That he was thus led to the Catholic Church is something of an accident; his reception into it, he recalls, was not even a joyful event.[21] The arguments that brought about the change could scarcely have been important. He couldn't even remember them. All he remembers is "that in January 1926 I became convinced of the probable existence of something we call God."[22] In the more than four decades since, his faith has become purer and more distilled, attuned to the groundswell of the Silent Music,[23] purified even of concepts. In 1970 he wrote: "Now I dislike the word [God] with all its anthropomorphic associations and prefer Chardin's Noosphere."[24] His belief, he tells us, "never came by way of those unconvincing philosophical arguments which I derided in a short story called "A Visit to Morin"; neither would he be bothered with them now. His final stage is one of unqualified surrender: "I accept. With the approach of death I care less and less about religious truth. One hasn't long to wait for revelation or darkness."[25] It should help us to remember that the man who created Querry is himself one of profound and well-tempered faith.

Thought has no power to heal, neither any to save, nor any to free us. Insofar as Querry's faith is based on rational arguments, it must remain tortured, riddled with anguish and uncentainty. Querry is in Unamuno's words—Greene quotes them—one of those "in whom reason is stronger than will, they feel themselves caught in the grip of reason and hailed along in their own despite, and they fall into despair, and because of their despair they deny, and God reveals Himself in them, affirming Himself by their very denial of Him."[26] The words recall to us Georges Bernanos's young women, particularly Mlle Chantal of *Jounal d'un Curé de la Campagne* who would do evil to get her own back, "out of spite"; and the priest's reply is memorable: "And when you do, you'll discover God."[27] The Querry we meet at the outset is no less in despair, although he does not quite know it. "I don't wish to believe," he cries at Father Thomas who plagues him with his zeal. "I am cured. . . . I don't want any of the things I've known and lost. If faith were a tree growing at the end of the avenue, I promise you I'd never go that way. I don't wish to say anything to hurt you, father. . . . " (p. 92) One cannot help the suspicion that Querry, with his impassioned denial is still nearer to God than the priest with his insecure faith.

Querry certainly is not offered to us as a hero. Had he challenged God like Faustus, or even like Job, or gone and damned himself with the boy hero of *Brighton Rock*, we might speak of some strain of heroism. But Querry belongs to none of these types. He is an anti-hero like most Greene characters. True, he is tenaciously honest in his dealings and in his refusal to pay lip-service to a faith he does not share. But his motivation is not a heightened moral sense, as dread of involvement; he prefers to stay on the outer fringes. He is done with life, the success, money, and women. None of this interests him now. All he asks is to be left alone. "If there were a place called Pendélé, he thought, I would never bother to find my way back." (p. 172) In Querry, we might say, the seed of faith has taken deep roots but it must struggle hard against "worldly cares and the false glamor of wealth and all kinds of evil desire," if it is to yield fruit.[28]

In his dedicatory note Greene said that the book was "an attempt to give dramatic expression to various types of belief, half-belief, and non-belief, in the kind of setting removed from world-politics and household-preoccupations, where such differences are felt acutely and find expression." The Fathers and the nursing nuns of the leprosarium offer variations on belief and half-belief which, as we have seen, Father Thomas gives the most obnoxious expression. But the institution does not escape censure, either. Evidently Greene has not set out to canonize the Fathers nor their way of life. One sees no reason why he should: he has not held any brief for them. The Fathers are what they might be in any real situation—men rooted up from their home and country, living a hard life in unfriendly circumstances. Their eccentricities are what naturally attend on such difficult conditions. "The too easy laughter, the exaggerated excitement," Querry notes, "over some simple game of cards with matches for stakes had the innocence and immaturity of isolation—the innocence of explorers marooned on an ice-cap or of men imprisoned by a war which has long passed out of hearing." (p. 14) For him, howerer, to be irritated by these, as he is at the beginning, shows a lack of understanding. With acquaintance comes appreciation, though the first impressions linger. "Those who marry God," thinks Querry as he surveys the scene before him, "can become domesticated, too."

> . . . —it's just as hum-drum a marriage as all the others. The word "Love" means a formal touch of the lips as in the ceremony of the Mass, and "*Ave Maria*" like "dearest" is a phrase to open a letter. This marriage like the world's marriages was held together by habits and tastes shared in common between God and themselves—it was God's taste to be worshipped and their taste to worship, but only at stated hours like a suburban embrace on a Saturday night. (p. 14)

The nuns' community is a counterpart to the priests', and Greene has not thought it necessary to linger here. Among the nuns, too, one might note shades of sensitivity and motivation. Some, maybe, were forced into religion by circumstances; others, the true leprophiles, attracted by the disease. Doctor Colin recalls how one such un had once complained to him bitterly because the D.D.S. tablets had begun to reduce the number of her patients: "It's terrible, doctor," she had wailed. "Soon we'll have no lepers at all." (p. 23) Others had perhaps been entranced by a grand vision which, with years, had grown dim and vague and blunted. As the Superior suggests, for such the leprosarium was both an asylum and a battlefield. "An old maid," says the priest, "without imagination, anxious to do good, to be of use. There aren't so many places in the world for people like that." (p. 23) But the priest warns against probing too deeply into motives lest one should "find some terrible things." Yet if we dug further, "who knows? The terrible too might be only a few skins deep. Anyway it's safer to make superficial judgments. They can always be shrugged off. Even by the victims." (p. 23) The nuns' behavior on the mere report of Querry's having fathered Rycker's child is odious enough to list them with Father Thomas and his kind. The other priests of the leprosarium are treated with a gentle reverence, even with affection; and the most affable of these is the Superior.

The Superior's manner is in total contrast to Father Thomas's. On the one side exists a joyless asceticism, a ceaseless searching for motives both in oneself and in others and a strained seeking after perfection. There seem to be some Calvinistic traits in the making of Father Thomas. The Superior's faith, on the other hand, is confident, warm, trusting, and joyful; and his relationship with fellowmen and women touched with the saving grace of a tolerant magnanimity. Their differing attitudes to life are focussed in a discussion on Marie Akimbu, the promiscuous woman catechist. The Superior tells the other priest that the nuns were surely fortunate in having such an efficient woman for a catechist: "She works very hard, I'm told by Mother Agnes." "Certainly," the other replies sarcastically:

"if you call having a baby every year by a different man hard work. I can't see that it's right allowing her to teach with her cradle in the class. She's pregnant again. What kind of an example is that?"

"Oh, well, you know, *autres pays autres mœurs*. We are here to help, father, not condemn, and I don't think we can teach the sisters their business. They know the young woman better than we do. Here, you must remember there are few people who know their own fathers. The children belong to the mother. Perhaps that's why they prefer us, and the Mother of God, to the Protestants." The Superior searched for words. (pp. 85-6)

In his abashed fury over sexual functions and processes, and in his puritanical refusal to acknowledge that moral standards differ according to regions and peoples, he is very much a kindred spirit to the pious Catholic spinster of *The Power and the Glory*. This Catholic woman was the first to recognize the martyr in the whiskey priest; she does so in the prison cell and after he had told them how much a sinner he was—a drunkard and father of a bastard child. But she had made allowances for all those past lapses, and the priest thinks admiringly, "What a worthy woman she was"[29] when from the far corner of the cell there comes the breathless shuffle and then the cry of pleasure. This she cannot bear: "Why won't they stop it? The brutes, the animals!"[30] She grasps his knees, digging in, begging the priest to intervene and stop them: "it's a scandal."[31] He wouldn't: there is such beauty in love, he says, even in "unhappy love," and besides, "we're all fellow prisoners." She takes offence at him. "I can see you're a bad priest," she says. "I wouldn't believe it before. I do now. You sympathize with these animals."[32] Similarly, Father Thomas is early in recognizing Querry's heroism; yet with the mere suggestion of a sexual sin he is scandalized.

Here are two virgins who have blundered into celibacy because they cannot quite accept their bodily nature, its functions and drives. The Superior however is well reconciled to the human condition: its urges, ecstasies, as well as weaknesses. His God is a compassionate Father, not the Policeman who kept count of every human foible. The supreme test to the Superior's magnanimity is his reaction when he is told about Rycker after the latter has shot Querry dead: "We don't know enough about Rycker to condemn him," he tells Doctor Colin, inviting the retort: "How persistent you are, father. You never let anyone go, do you?" (p. 199) He could not have been better complimented. A truly noble soul, the Superior accepts the human material given to him, no questions asked, and no motives sought for.

Querry and Doctor Colin embody differing shades of unbelief. Yet, just as the Superior's faith is at opposite poles from Father Thomas's, so is Doctor Colin's disbelief of a different order from Querry's lack of faith. Colin is a far too intricate character to be dismissed with a simple difinition. Evidently he does not share the priests' faith, yet he is no less persevering than they in his difficult vocation. If Colin does not believe, his non-belief needs qualification. Discussing the suffering one necessarily meets within a leprosarium, Colin tells his friend that some people would prefer death to the shame of illness.

> "Wouldn't you rather suffer than feel discomfort? Discomfort irritates our ego like a mosquito-bite. We become aware of ourselves, the more uncomfortable we are, but suffering is quite a different matter. Sometimes I think that the search for suffering and the remembrance of suffering are the only means we have to put ourselves in touch with the whole human condition. With suffering we become part of the Christian myth." (p. 122)

It is essentially the mystique of the cross that the doctor enunciates here—a doctrine not always well understood. By exalting the Cross the Christian tends at times to forget that the glory of the Cross is Christ's triumph over it.[33] The doctor, by his manner of life, imitates that victory. He takes pain for an evil, and yet suffers it himself in order to eliminate it for others.

Without employing the worn categories of Christian theology, Colin does celebrate the awful import of Christ's coming. His hard vocation is sustained in hope, and at the heart of that hope is found Christ. Christ is the *elan vitale*; historically but a link in the vast unfolding of the life-force, as the agnostic doctor thinks of Him, He is nevertheless the most important link, Colin admits. He is the "fertile element, looking for a crack in the wall to plant its seed." (p. 124)   The metaphors play variations on the New Testament imagery of the Sower and again of the Vine that sustains and quickens life: dwelling in Him (the Vine), everyone "bears much fruit."[34]

"I want to be on the side of change," is how the doctor explains his sense of vocation.

> If I had been born an amoeba who could think, I would have dreamed of the day of the primates. I would have wanted anything I did to contribute to that day. Evolution, as far as we can tell, has lodged itself finally in the brains of man. The ant, the fish, even the ape has gone as far as it can go, but in our brain evolution is moving—my God—at what a speed! I forget how many hundreds of millions of years passed between the dinosaurs and the primates, but in our own lifetime we have seen the change from diesel to jet, the splitting of the atom, the cure of leprosy. (p. 124)

A grand vision this; but Colin agrees that humankind has not always made the most of its vast potential. Nor has it used to advantage the enormous energies released by the evolutionary process. Humanity has all too often failed in its vocation, but that is no reason to deny the grandeur that is shaping up all about us. The doctor himself has no doubts that "we are riding a great ninth evolutionary wave." (p. 124)

"Even the Christian myth is part of the wave," says the doctor, "and perhaps, who knows, it may be the most valuable part. Suppose love were to evolve as rapidly in our brains as technical skill has done. In isolated cases it may have done, in the saints. . . in Christ, if the man really existed." (p. 124)   That "if" is quite necessary as it is part of his atheist's mask. Rather than search for God in the frozen fringes of the universe where many a pious Christian soul has lost Him, Colin has found Him right in the midst of this petty human world with its stale joys and sorrows, but enlivening it all, charging it with a new significance. The one most vital link in the process of evolution, Christ might guide it still, channel its energies, see to its flowering and fruition.

Colin however is no doctrinaire prophet of evolution. He faces up to the fact that there have been, and must be, "blind starts and wrong turnings. . . Evolution today can produce Hitlers as well as St. John of the Cross." (p. 124)   And it could not be otherwise, for evil is lodged firmly in the human psyche. "We have become cynical about progress," continues the doctor,

> "because of the terrible things we have seen men do during the last forty years. All the same, through trial and error the amoeba did become the ape. . . . I have a small hope . . . that someone they call Christ was the fertile element, looking for a crack in the wall to plant its seed. I think of Christ as an amoeba who took the right turning. I want to be on the side of the progress which survives." (p. 124)

There is little doubt, from what we know of Colin, that he *is* on the side of the "seed" that survives.

Einstein is reported to have said that "everyone who is seriously involved in the pursuit of science becomes convinced that a spirit is manifest in the laws of the Universe—a spirit vastly superior to that of man, and one in the face of which we with our modest powers must feel humble."[35] A serious thinker must need fathom the depths of the mind and would sooner or later come to realize how small indeed one's powers are. And when the individual has touched the botton one would find too the Ground of all, surrounding all, and containing all; but to be so contained is our glory, for in Him every creative impulse has its source.

To Querry's poser, "Are you a happy man?" Colin replies simply: "I suppose I am. It's not a question that I've ever asked myself. Does a happy man ever ask it? I go on from day to day." (p. 125)   "Swimming on your wave," the other says with a twitch of envy. The Greene hero is never at a loss to express pain. It may be, as one of them puts it, that "in misery we seem aware of our own existence," whereas in pleasure we don't. "This pain of mine is individual, this nerve that winces belongs to me and no other. But happiness annihilates us: we lose our identity."[36] His capacity to forget himself so completely surely bespeaks the doctor's dedication. And it may well be a pointer to the inner peace and harmony which flows over in service of his fellow men and women. Through service he fulfils himself.

Greene wrote in a recent introduction: "The doctor, whom I like best as a realized character, represents a settled and easy atheism; the Father Superior a settled and easy belief (I use easy as a term of praise and not as a term of reproach), Father Thomas an unsettled form of belief and Querry an unsettled form of disbelief."[37] And through these diverse characters he has purposed to "give expression to various states or moods of belief and unbelief." This however is only part of his intentions; at least the realized life in the novel evinces more than just a picture gallery. There is action and movement; and the dramatic action centers on Querry's slow progress towards recovery.

At the beginning of the novel, the protagonist is no more than half alive. "I feel discomfort, therefore I am," he scribbled in his diary a parody of Descartes, then sat pen in hand with no more to record. The malignancy we note here is underscored by the author's choice of epigraphs. *Io non more, 'e non rimasi vivo* reads the line from Dante ("I did not die, yet nothing of life remained."). The quotation, playing on our modern sensibility, evokes within us images of the wasteland. The setting is carefully planned to enforce the impression: Querry is in the limbo, his spirit is quite dead. The second epigraph clinches the suggestion in the title that the protagonist be taken as an advanced 'case' of leprosy. The disease is far too advanced for him to feel the pain anymore.

In one of his rambling conversations Querry tells the doctor how he came to lose interest in life. He had begun well as an artist. Soon, however, his career had become all important. It had him so fully engrossed that there was no time for anything besides, not even for love.

"Before I went to sleep, even if I was with a woman, the last thing I had always to think about was work. Problems which seemed insoluble would often solve themselves in sleep. I had my bedroom next to my office, so that I could spend two minutes in front of the drawing-board the last thing of all. The bed, the bidet, the drawing-board, and then sleep." (p. 45)

"It sounds a little hard on the woman," comments the doctor.

But the artist, insofar as he is a professional, cannot be bothered with feelings, either his own or other peoples'. Emotions have a way of interposing themselves between the artist and his work. They not only hamper the work at hand by ruining habits and the concentration necessary for sustained effort, they destroy the very condition for art. Hence every artist in a way is wary of feelings. Passion whittled down and destroyed the artist in Maurice Bendrix.[38] Gilbert Osmond, Henry James's model of the aesthete, who has set out to fashion his life into a fine art, ends up an emotional fossil.[39] Querry's fate has been comparable to Osmond's.

Querry, like Osmond, has had to pay a price. His instincts, spurned and long neglected, have atrophied. The wellsprings are dried up and, drained of passion, he can find no motive for carrying on. Art taken in proper measure may have seasoned life: used as staple diet it becomes poison. Too late Querry discovers that he has substituted an illusion for life, and art indeed is a dangerous illusion. "Self-expression is a hard and selfish thing. It eats everything, even the self. At the end you find you haven't even got a self to express." It ate the parent in him, too. He has lost his children: since they went out into the world he had not kept in touch. And the result is a loss of interest "in anything." "I don't want to sleep with a woman nor design a building." (p. 46)

Art had become a career, had enslaved his spirit. He became an addict to work, such that there was no room for anything, even God although he had begun as a believer. "Even in the days when I believed. . . It would have got in the way of work." On another occasion Colin remarks: "You must have had a lot of faith once to miss it the way you do." And Querry's reply is couched in irony:

"I swallowed their myth whole, if you call that belief. This is my body and this is my blood. Now when I read that passage

it seems so obviously symbolic, but how can you expect a lot
of poor fishermen to recognize symbols? Only in moments of
superstition I remember that I gave up the sacrament before I
gave up the belief and the priests would say there was a
connection. . ." (p. 192)

This is a characteristic note with Querry whose unbelief is mixed
with nostalgia and a tortured sense of loss. "Oh, well, I supose
belief is a kind of vocation and most men haven't room in their
brains or hearts for two vocations. If we really believe in something
we have no choice, have we, but to go further. Otherwise life slowly
whittles the belief away. My architecture stood still. One can't be a
half-believer or a half-architect." (pp. 192-93)

The demands faith makes on the believer are well expressed in
the brusque "either/or": it forces a choice and a definitive
commitment. No wonder Bendrix was frightened: "it would be the
end of everything . . . loving Him there'd be no pleasure in
anything at all with Him away. I'd even lose my work. I'd cease to
be Bendrix."[40] Nor can one evade the choice, and not bear the
consequences.

A major consequence for Querry is his drifting into a vague pro-
fessionalism. He is no longer the inquiring artist he once gave
promise of: he has become just a "builder". Another is that he has
nearly lost the trick of feeling. Emotionally he is burnt-out. So
much so it has become an urgent necessity for him to be left alone.
He dreads company; he would not know how to react to another
human being any more. On his very first meeting with the Superior
he blurts out: "I suffer from nothing. I no longer know what suffering is. I have come to an end of all that too." "Too?" said the
Superior. "Like all the rest," Querry replies: "To the end of everything." (p. 16) When the doctor suggests a little later that perhaps
Querry meant to "just come and die here," he replies: "Yes. That
was in my mind. But chiefly I wanted to be in an empty place,
where no new building or woman would remind me that there was
a time when I was alive, with a vocation and a capacity to love—if
it was love. The palsied suffer, the nerves feel, but I am one of the
mutilated, doctor." (p. 46)

Querry recovers gradually. The healing begins by a return to that earlier time when "he was alive, with a vocation and a capacity to love" and to suffer. The process is signalled by his new responsiveness to pain. His African servant, Deo Gratias (the name perhaps is symbolic) had gone out into the jungle and apparently is lost. By midnight there is still no trace of him, and so Querry sets off into the sodden dark scanning the vaguely twisted forms for a human shape. At long last he comes upon his man on the edge of a marsh, knee-deep in the slush and crippled with fear. Querry pulls him out and, because the man would not be moved, despite the damp and the mosquitoes, keeps the nightlong vigil with him.

There, in that instant, Querry discovers a new tenderness within himself. He speaks of the vigil as "a night when things begin." And he is right. For after all it takes a good measure of compassion to forget one's comfort and answer another's need. Querry explains: "I had an odd feeling that he needed me." Yes, but why "odd"? "Odd to me," says Querry. "I've needed people often enough in my life. You might accuse me of having used people more than I have ever loved them. But to be needed is a different sensation, a tranquilizer, not an excitement. . ." (p. 57-8)   Thus with one daring deed the prison gates are flung wide, and he is free; and the proof of that freedom is that he laughs now for the first time. (p. 59)

Doctor Colin sums up Querry's life thus: the architect had told him once that "all his life he had only made use of women":

". . . but I think he saw himself always in the hardest possible light. I even wondered sometimes whether he suffered from a kind of frigidity. Like a woman who changes partners constantly in the hope that one day she will experience the true orgasm. He said that he always went through the motions of love efficiently, even towards God in the days when he believed, but then he found that the love wasn't really there for anything except his work, so in the end he gave up the motions. And afterwards, when he couldn't even pretend that what he felt was love, the motives for work failed him. That was like the crisis of a sickness—when the patient has no more interest in life at all. It is then that people sometimes kill themselves, but he was tough, very tough."

"You spoke just now as though he had been cured," [says the Superior].

"I really think he was. He'd learned to serve other people, you see, and to laugh. An odd laugh, but it was a laugh all the same. I'm frightened of people who don't laugh." (p. 198)

Colin's report both contains the diagnosis and testifies to the cure.

The ending is a masterful stroke of comic irony. When he sees the first instalment of Parkinson's story on him in a prurient news magazine, Querry decides he must go and urge Rycker to put a stop to anymore such pious canards about him. Rycker receives him with a beaming smile; however their discussions get nowhere, and Querry only succeeds in involving himself innocently with Rycker's young wife. Marie comes to him with tears in her eyes and her face dark with despair. She fears being with child, she says—a child nobody wanted. Rycker would berate her for not having taken precautions ("But he wouldn't allow me to be safe," either). She wants to check with a doctor before Rycker got to know: would Querry give her a lift to Luc? Querry suggests that she first tell her husband where she was going, but he does not insist. In Luc, when the medical test delays their departure, Querry spends the night telling Marie the parable of the Jeweller. And, "Spent night with Q." Marie jots down in her diary. (p. 169) The seemingly innocent remark however is not without a purpose. She had said the same thing to him as he was ending the fairy tale: "I could almost say to him, couldn't I, that we'd spent the night together. Do you think that he'd divorce me?"—the thought uppermost in her mind. (p. 159) She badly needed a divorce, and if the diary was not enough evidence, she has left tell-tale signs of her presence all over his room: smudges of powder on his towel, hair on his comb ("Women are disgusting, aren't they?"). (p. 163-164) She has even trapped him into lunch. Marie hated and despised her husband and a young Rycker was the last thing she would want but, as she suspects, the child is perhaps on the way and so she has her strategem all worked out. By noon, Rycker too is in Luc, has been shown into Querry's room and, courtesy of

Parkinson who has been scouting around, noted the powder smudges and the comb, read the latest entry on Marie's diary, and is raving mad.

Ryker's metamorphosis is truly fascinating. It is an instant transformation and too fantastic for words. When Querry had stopped at his place the day before asking him to leave him in peace ("or must I go again the way I came?") Rycker had protested from his bed under the crucifix: "It's a penalty of genius to belong to the world." Querry apparently has been a source of great inspiration to him ("You have set an example to all of us . . . [of] Unselfishness and humility.") (p. 145); and nothing Querry might say or do now would change his view of things. He is quite determined to make Querry a saintly example and is in raptures over his own power: "Saints used to -be made by popular acclaim. . . We have taken you up, Querry." (p. 145)   Come a night and a day and when the two meet again in Luc, Rycker is an altogether changed man. He waves his wife's diary at Querry and threatens him, "I can imagine what the courts would say to this." (p. 170)   Since Querry would not play the role he has assigned him, he would change his own role. If not a saint maker, at least a cuckold: there was a kind of dignity about being cuckolded by a famous man. And the world, knowing Querry's reputation, was sure to sympathize. As Parkinson comments with a perception unusual in him: Rycker has wanted such a chance: "he *wants* to believe the worst. It makes him Querry's equal, don't you see, when they fight over the same girl." He added with a somewhat surprising insight, "He can't bear not being important." (p. 189)   Ryker pursues Querry to the mission. "I am a man in agony," he raves.

> "I'm suffering from a terrible shock, father. I opened my soul to that man, I told him my inmost thoughts, and this is my reward." (p. 190)

"He laughed at me and despised me," he growls. "What right had he to despise me? We are all equal in the sight of God. Even a poor plantation manager and *the* Querry. Breaking up a Christian marriage." Muttering "There isn't a jury that would convict me," he walks out into night. (p. 190)

The comic contortions of Father Thomas are still more remarkable. The pious priest has been no less responsible than Rycker for ruining Querry's quiet retreat. He had aided and encouraged Parkinson by spreading tales about him, and a second instalment has been promised in a Paris rag sheet ("Next Sunday. A Saint's Past. Redemption by Suffering. The Leper Lost in the Jungle.") The threat of publicity urges the action on to its crisis. For, "I must silence him," Querry tells Father Thomas. "This mustn't go on. I'm fighting for my life. . . . My life here. It's all I have."

> He sat wearily down on the bed. He said, "I've come a long way. There's nowhere else for me to go if I leave here." (p. 135)

And Father Thomas's reply is, "For a good man fame is always a problem." The priest, like Rycker, is determined to hold Querry to the role he has quite gratuitously assigned him. No use Querry's protesting he was "not a good man"; that the role did not fit him; that he wouldn't play ("I had no good motive in coming here. I am looking after myself as I have always done.") For every such objection, the priest has an answer ready: "You have a truly wonderful quality of humility," he declares smugly. In the three days following Querry has been to the Ryckers, then proceeded to Luc, and is back for the feast, the raising of the roof tree for the new hospital. There is champagne after meals, and a lot of harmless raillery at which all except Father Thomas takes part. When Querry has left the room, Father Thomas complains that they forgot to toast "the man to whom we owe most," and that they "ought to express the gratitude of the community, formally, when he comes back. . . It was a happy day for all of us when he arrived here," he expostulates. "Who could have forseen it? The great Querry." (p. 177)

Meanwhile Marie has arrived at the mission with the tale that she is carrying Querry's child. As soon as he hears of it, Father Thomas goes pale; he is stunned. Bent over the telephone like a question mark, "suddenly he was again the nervy and despairing priest who couldn't sleep and was afraid of the dark." He weeps.

"We gave you a warm welcome here, didn't we? We asked you no questions. We didn't pry into your past. And in return you present us with this—scandal. Weren't there enough women for you in Europe?" (p. 180)

And soon he is busy devising plans to send Querry away. In vain the fathers protest that he was jumping to conclusions, that it was after all only the girl's word against his; besides Querry has been an asset to the mission. "We've reason to be grateful—" Father Paul says echoing Father Thomas' phrase of a while ago. "Grateful?" cries he now.

"Can you really think that, father, after he's made us a laughing stock? The Hermit of the Congo. The Saint with a Past . . . I believed in him . . . I hadn't realized then what his true motives were." (p. 187)

But there was no doubt that Querry was a good builder, and Father Joseph insists that they could not afford to lose him now when so much work remained to be done. And Father Thomas raps out at him: "What do you propose then, that he should stay here in the mission, living in sin with Mme Rycker? . . . Do you suppose the General will be pleased when he reads at his breakfast table the scandal at our leproserie?" If the General does not hear of it, surely the bishop will. With an awful sense of self-importance he adds, "In the absence of the Superior I am responsible . . ." (p. 188) Querry has been more than proved right: he has always been suspicious of praise, and especially "the praise of priests and pious people—the Ryckers of the world." (p. 193)
Suddenly Querry has become an indecent word: the nuns peer at him from shuttered eyes, "as though he were the devil himself—with fear, distaste and curiosity." (p. 181) Marie sticks to her lie, that being her exit line from Rycker and Africa. To Querry's persuassions ("You know what you are saying is all nonsense. I'm certain you don't want to do me any harm.") pat comes her reply:

"Oh no," she said, "never. *Je t'aime, chéri. Je suis toute à toi.*" (p. 132)

She never wanted Rycker, she explains when they are alone. "The only way I could manage was to shut my eyes and think it was you . . . It was then that the baby must have started. . . If I hadn't thought all the time of you, I'd have been all dried up and babies don't come so easily then, do they? So in a way it is your child." (p. 183)

> He looked at her with a kind of respect. It would have needed a theologian to appreciate properly the tortuous logic of her argument, to separate good from bad faith, and only recently he had thought of her as someone too simple and young to be a danger. (p. 183-84)

Perhaps she would at least tell Father Thomas the truth? "Well, I've rather burned my boats, haven't I?" the girl replies, with a callousness one did not associate with her age. What if she also burnt the only home he had? "I just had to escape," she explains apologetically.

> "What do you expect me to do?" Querry said. "Love you in return?"
> "It would be nice if you could, but if you can't, they'll have to send me home, won't they?" (p. 185)

Querry had once been as much a selfish lover himself. But the egoism of this young woman was so absolute it surpassed all instances of selfishness he ever knew. Ryker meanwhile has been prowling about in the dark and, just as Querry comes out, he shoots him. And Querry dies amused at the ironies of fate, ironies he had always noted: that so long as you are selfish and greedy you are successful. The moment Querry renounced success and women, he dies their victim.

A NOVELIST'S CREED

What is the meaning of human life, or for that matter of the life of any creature? To find a satisfying answer to this question means to be religious.

—Albert Einstein

Rarely has an author enjoyed in his lifetime more resounding applause than Graham Greene. His career began in the early 1930's, and in the five decades that followed he has held his own in the world of letters. It is remarkable that he could retain his vast readership through the turbulence of our time. Through the shifting moods and emotions, ideas and attitudes, his books have addressed a steady audience. Nor is his readership confined to the British Isles; it extends far and wide, taking in the English speaking peoples of Asia and the Americas. In the Continent he is also widely read in translations. All this bespeaks a rare ability. Of his technical virtuosity much has already been said. His nearly magical effects, the skill that weaves meanings into a thriller, the precision of his portrayals, the deft handling of scenes, the strength of his dialogue, the economy and confidence in the narration—all this is truly remarkable. For the student of literary art Greene is an invariable treasure house. But here we are not to delve too deeply into questions of art. We shall have to be content with a more general discussion of his art, world, and vision.

Greene, we notice, displays a keen interest in the topical event. Perhaps this is part of his appeal. He certainly has a nose for where there is trouble—be it Mexico, Havana, Haiti, or Vietnam. But the topical sense is not the whole appeal in Greene; it is used as a bait, like a coating of sugar on a pill of uncertain taste. He has an uncanny knack for observing things from the inside. This is a rare ability: only the greatest literary writers have possessed it. Shakespeare had this capacity to an unusual degree. So did Tolstoy, Dostoevsky, and Dickens. It is the gift of total objectivity, and Greene shares it with them. It has enabled him to plunge straight into the action with but the minimum of stage setting. Whatever information is required is worked into the scene and the dialogue. And like every great dramatist he is deeply involved with his characters. A committed observer of people and events, he still evokes no partisan emotions. It is the affairs of the human spirit that matter to him, but they engage him profoundly. Perhaps this is why his books have not become dated. Each of his great works— *Brighton Rock*, *The Power and the Glory*, *The Heart of the Matter*, *The Quiet American*, *The Comedians*—deals with situations which have passed imperceptibly into history. But these books are no less insightful and enjoyed today.

Part of his appeal, too, is the quality of his obsessions. Obsessions are not unusual for an artist. They furnish the energy required for work. In this sense, in every artist there is something of a maniac. "Every creative writer worth our consideration," Greene himself admits, ". . .is a victim: a man given over to an obsession."[1] Greene cultivated his. Scorning caution, he would expose himself to situations of danger. He liked to taste anxiety which would have sent many another into flight.

But his obsessions work themselves into a kind of private world. The humanity he envisions is one that has reverted to its nature— not the "civilized" world as we know it. Indeed Greene would have nothing to do with the hamburger and the Coca-Cola. Like Lawrence and James, he too is haunted with what is primeval. He envies primitive Africa its energy. But he knows there is no remaking his own world. One has to make do with the remains of the culture as it obtains. Greene has no illusions on this score. His own characters are old and tired—prematurely old. And none of them is nostalgic for the comforts of civilization. Greene suspects the cultured person of playing truant with the human vocation.

Thought has not liberated us, on the contrary, our spirits are broken with new tyrannies. Our instincts have been most cruelly used. Greene is obsessed with whatever effort would make us free.

He gives us the sense of the Elizabethan or the Jacobean stage. Greene takes no less delight in heightened colors and in the goriest violence than did, for instance, Webster.[2] Edwin Muir was right to complain that in Greene "everything is shown up in a harsh light and casts fantastic colors."[3] This is very true of the early work. The later books are different—more discriminating, and done in tones of greater subtlety. Greene uses melodrama; but it is never an end, not the goal itself. He says it was simply "one of [his] working tools."[4]

What then are the goals melodrama is meant to serve? Greene points to Conrad and to James (a claim, perhaps, to the lineage?); the effects they have obtained, he says, are the same he strives for. He is full of praise for James for "the final justice of his pity, the completeness of an analysis which enabled him to pity the most shabby, the most corrupt, of his human actors. . . ."[5] Similarly in Conrad he has noticed an instinct for "the mental degradation to which a man's intelligence is exposed on its way through life"; an instinct too for "the passions of men short sighted in good and evil." In scattered phrases, Greene remarks, "you get the memories of a creed working like poetry through the agnostic prose."[6]

How relevant is all this to achieving the sort of effects he was after? First it says, Greene's effects are subtle, and hence hard to vocalize. They cannot be caught in neat formulae. It says, further, that pity is often the keynote. Indeed, one cannot read Greene without becoming aware of his profound concern for human beings. His characters—Pinkie, the whiskey-priest, Scobie, Fowler, Brown and Querry—each of them is of the most derelict and corrupt of the species. For his effects melodrama was indeed the right medium; they "would be unobtainable otherwise."[7]

His books deal generally with lawlessness, with social injustice, and moral anarchy. But underlying it all is a sense of lost spiritual dimensions. In the thirties he wrote about the crises and confusion of those years. He has captured in his novels a sense of that "moral desperation" that since has become part of our sensibility. It is fed daily with news of terrorism, police atrocities, violence on a global scale—all stuff for the thriller. "Maybe this is why we like reading thrillers," as Auden remarked; "because each of us is a creature at war with himself. Further he is a self-deceptive creature who thinks he is feeling one thing or acting from one motive when his real feeling and motive are quite different."[8]

The deception is everywhere, worked into the very texture of our civilized modern way of life. The thriller exposes it by accentuating the design. It thus forces us to recognize realities, which otherwise we would rather not face at all. Thriller has this merit: by projecting into "outer melodramatic action" our outlooks and motivations, it compels our attention. It has no need to prevaricate. It may speak the truth in all its stark details—the truth about "the struggles which go on unendingly in every mind and heart."[9] Greene's objective in choosing the thriller as his narrative scheme is made evident from the epigraph he chose for his first novel. The line is from Sir Thomas Browne's autobiography: "There is another man within me that's angry with me."[10] This is an adaptation of St. Paul's "law of the members" By blazing it above his book, Greene appears to suggest that the forces that conflict within are beyond reconciliation. Every individual is like a city in perpetual siege. The struggle would go on and on, until only death relieves the tension.

Greene is almost obsessed with the concept of moral dualism. In *The Lawless Roads* he compares human existence to a battlefield.

It is engaged everywhere in the same subterranean struggle, lying like a tiny neutral state, with whom no one ever observes his treaties, between two eternities of pain and—God knows the opposite of pain, not we. It is a Belgium fought over by friend and enemy alike.[11]

No one can deny the truths of one's perceptions. Juvenile fiction often attempted just this: it did not allow for "an unhappy ending. And none of them was disturbed by a sense of pity for the beaten side."[12] Greene's books scarcely ever end happily. And in each of them he is unabashedly on "the beaten side." He not only insists that it is most natural for the individual to fail, he even endows failure with an aura of the good.

Like Greene, Conrad thought of life in terms of a sustained moral struggle. To be a human being one had no choice but to take part in it. No one could evade the issue: so Conrad taught. Greene acknowledges the violence and the horror that may be whenever the two forces are ranged against each other, but he knows there is more to it than struggle. He allows that evil "is an intrinsic part of human life in every place."[13] But he cannot deny there are other and more complementary impulses in the human soul. He is not only aware of the immediate action; he sees further than ordinary mortals. It is his belief "where the eagles are gathered together, it is not unnatural to expect to find the Son of Man as well."[14] Greene's confidence sets him apart. Neither Conrad nor James had this assurance; and lacking faith they could not achieve his strength. Their work tended weakly toward a vague emotionalism.

Greene does not see good and evil as always on the warpath. Sometimes they are; at other times not so. He even links them strangely in a kind of wedlock. Pinkie of *Brighton Rock* notes Rose's goodness as something that completes him. He admits his evil, yet he is helplessly drawn to her. Even enemy troops may fraternize at Christmastime. Pinkie and Rose do understand and sympathize with each other. Similarly, the lieutenant, sworn enemy to the whiskey priest, ends up recognizing the other as a good man, even a hero.

Rarely indeed do we have a situation in Greene where good and evil are locked in conflict. Often they are not only unopposed, but are together against a common enemy. They appear to understand each other; they speak the same language, share the same anguish. The enemy often is complacency. Greene's heroes are never complacent. They are sensitive to various moral dilemmas, are imaginative even when they are evil. Between them and the indifferent, however, there is no love lost. To be cultivated, to be "law-abiding"—these are not values a Greenean hero would understand. "So many years have passed in England," says the author, "since the war began between faith and anarchy: we live in an ugly indifference."[15] A sorry state of affairs this for a nation, but fatal to individual human spirit. In the past faith supported painful explorations into the mysteries of life. It gave to life a certain substance and significance. Now naturalized, life was without the balm of faith; and it began to totter under the heavy burdens thrust on it.

Orwell has created for our benefit a vision of the naturalized man: his "tastes lie towards safety, soft beds" and curvacious women.[16] Such mundane pleasures do not ever tempt Greene's hero. He is always and preternaturally driven. Perhaps it is some voice from eternity that keeps urging him, guiding, ordering his destiny. All Greene's protagonists are haunted, afflicted by a "conscience, implicated in the full mystery and terror of their natures."[17] Pursued by some spiritual force, they either give in wearily, or turn on it with rage. Whatever the mode of the encounter and the outcome, the meeting is the thing; and life is never the same again. Not to be adequate to the situation—here is a sense of tragedy.

Tragedy, of course, has been defined variously in different ages. Both the ancient Greek and the Elizabethan worked their tragedies against a stated scheme of values. Implied therein were philosophical absolutes which might not be contested. To the Grecian mind the supreme deity was the pivot to the world. The most reliable of forces working upon the world, God was like the North Star, a point of reference. It was He who controlled the vagrancy of fate; He absorbed the shocks and the trepidations of temporal existence, and graced human destiny with a measure of meaning. The weakness and insignificance, the pathos of human existence on earth were not denied. But the dignity of the Godhead, His Power and unalterable Will somewhat restored the balance, and rekindled in the human heart a hope. For, if God were won over, since He could be won over, there was no cause for despair. With Him on one's side nothing could be amiss. There was danger only in questioning His Will. Aroused, He was a foe to contend with; and rebellion did rouse Him. Greek tragedy has its roots in this sense of divine retribution.

Like the Greeks, Shakespeare based his plots on offenses against harmony. But the disruption had not the same sense of finality. For Shakespeare no action is irretrievable, nothing so lost it could not be redeemed. The impulse that began the tragic cycle is allowed to run its course. There is pain, and much affliction, but these are surgical and passing. The playwright, as it were, is gazing over the murk and the violence to a future of peace, order and sanity. Shakespearean tragedy takes after nature and follows its rhythm. The day with its long scorching afternoon succumbs wearily to the night, but is miraculously restored in the cool of dawn. So with the seasons. Winter's assault on the aging summer does not quite stem nature's vitality, which would soon break into the juvenescence of spring. This regenerative intent is nearly always present in Shakespeare. True, he jolts us with his terror, but at the end of every story there is a sense of completion which, delayed though it may well be, is never wholly denied. "Ripeness is all," exclaims Gloucester in *King Lear*. Although the protagonists would suffer a reversal towards the end, still we know Gloucester is right—and not only in reference to Lear and Cordelia, but also with respect to us, the spectators.

Greene's tragic sense, were it permissible to describe it thus, is quite akin to Shakespeare's. His better works, discussed above, are all preoccupied with some spiritual malaise. Yet in each book one also notices a vein of redemptive grace. And particularly remarkable is his way of yoking together grace and failure. Greene does not admire success; but he seems intrigued by the possibilities of failure. Always the die is loaded heavily against his protagonists. But because they even attempt the big leap, because they dare the wrath of the world, they are ever alert to the Silent Step. And down and up the labyrinth It follows them, until wearied they must give in.

Thus it is with most of the works we have considered. *The Heart of the Matter* is perhaps the one exception. This book is unique in Greene's *oeuvre*, with a cosmography which stands it apart. There are comparisons to be made with Hardy's novels, and Hardy never believed in anything supreme. Weariness and frustration are the ultimate in Tess's experience. So with *Jude the Obsure*. So with Henry Scobie. There is no trace of a guiding benevolence. Only in death is there relief. Scobie is quite like a Brahma caught unwittingly in Maya's dizzying whirl.

Sin, grace, redemption—all properly religious motifs—are, perhaps, handy for the preacher and the polemist to peg their wares on; but they are not, some would protest, proper material for fiction. At any rate, they are not themes most novelists are wont to build on. How is it that Greene uses them so amply, and with no apologies? As artist he is beyond reproach because he takes religion as just another aspect of human experience and works it skillfully into his stories adding a certain weight and intensity to them. But this has not always been noticed. In fact he has been made a victim of all sorts of critical innuendo. One critic labelled him "a gourmet of sin."[18] Another descried an "edifying purpose" in his novels, of which *Brighton Rock*, he said, came "closest to Catholic apologetic."[19] Yet another scholar found in Greene's fiction a forum for sectarian polemics. All these are serious charges, and need to be looked into. For if they are proved right, so much the worse for the artist. If he uses his art to ends other than aesthetic, surely his claims as artist must seem weak.

First, the charge of apologetics. This has to do with "the argumentative defense of some doctrinal tenet, of a way of life or course of action."[20] More specifically it refers to a phenomenon that surfaced in the Church after the Reformation. The dictionary defines apologetics as a "systematic discourse in defense especially of the divine origin and authority of Christianity."[21] In every case it is a "systematic," argumentative "defense" of some view or other; the object thereof being ordinarily religion or dogma. John Henry Cardinal Newman is properly an apologist. His works, "Discourses to Mixed Congregations" and "Plain and Parochial Sermons," are some of the best extant specimens of this kind of writing.

But Greene's attitude to the Church is somewhat at variance with Newman's. He appears wary of the institution. In *The Heart of the Matter*, towards the end, Father Rank says: "The Church knows all the rules. But it doesn't know what goes on in a human heart!" Which is not simply a character's private judgment. For that matter, Father Rank is not conceived without sympathy. He is only voicing what everyone in the novel feels. Nor is this the only book to censure the Church leadership for its spiritual atrophy. In

The Power and the Glory the lieutenant's charges are not met even by the whiskey priest; he adroitly evades them. The priests and nuns in several books have seedy looks and awfully repugnant habits. And the best of them are fashioned after Greene's heart—as failures. One of the novels has a defrocked priest in the role of the protagonist.[22] Father Rivas is convincing as an honest rebel and his case against the Church bureaucracy is not easily rebutted.

Not all this has been lost on the critics. For instance, one of them claimed he noticed "clear signs that Catholicism's leading English author was suffering from doubts concerning the Church to which he had been converted" some years previously.[23] Another reported thus:

> The criticisms of Catholic doctrine implied by some of his most sympathetic characters, perhaps especially by Scobie in *The Heart of the Matter* (1948), were so devastating that many Roman Catholics concluded that the supposed apologist was really subversive. Not only has Greene always shown a more tender concern for his sinners than for his saints, but the intellectual doubts and moral anguish of the lost are never satisfactorily answered or assuaged by those who represent the religious point of view. When Greene does allow the arguments of the saved to prevail, as in *The Living Room* (1953) they are so sophistical as to be embarassing.[24]

The argument turns, finally, on the merits of literature when used for purposes other than literary. The condition for art is freedom from dogma; tied down to fixed patterns of thought it is never free. There would be no life in it, no scope for spontaneity, no growth. If, indeed, Greene ever allowed his faith to dictate to art, "the artist in him" would have been a casualty. But has he been so chained? An adult convert to Catholicism, he never displayed undue zeal in defending his choice. Besides, faith, admittedly, is everyone's private affair. Only when it threatens the integrity of art is it even in order to question it. Even if we grant that the "aesthetic attitude" is not ordinarily "compatible with religious commitment"[25] the question to ask then is, how deeply committed is he to faith.

The artist who is also a believer is faced with a real dilemma. Noxon puts this in perspective:

> The detachment and impartiality which are essential to making credible fiction are qualities alien to the religious propagandist. As a Roman Catholic, Greene must accept the interpretation of events and the evaluations of persons which are endorsed by his elected authorities. As a novelist, he must remain faithful to his own experience of the world and men. His "attempt to give dramatic expression to various types of belief, half-belief, and non-belief" requires neutrality as a condition for doing justice to the experience of those whose beliefs and values differ from his own. This is not simply a matter of tolerance or fair play. It is a matter of being driven, as artist, from the religious stage of existence to the aesthetic, where he must repudiate his authorities in order to look freely for whatever truth the world reveals. Only if the writer's own disinterested observation tended to confirm a Catholic interpretation of existence would Greene the novelist and Greene the convert be in harmony.[26]

In "an exchange of views" between Elizabeth Bowen, V.S. Pritchett, and himself, Greene admitted this was a difficult situation for the believer. Being a member of the Catholic Church, he owns, "would present me with grave problems as a writer if I were not saved by my disloyalty. If my conscience were as acute as François Mauriac's showed itself to be in his essay *God and Mammon*, I could not write a line. There are leaders of the Church who regard literature as a means to one end, edification. That end may be one of the highest value, of far higher value than literature, but it belongs to a different world."[27]

But the dilemma is not all that peculiar to Greene. Every Catholic novelist of note has had at some time to face the question of his loyalty. Thus François Mauriac spoke as if his Christianity had "enriched" him, only to add in the same breath: "It has also hampered me, in that my books are not what they might have been had I let myself go"[28] "One would have to be a saint, " he said on another occasion. "But then one could not write novels."[29] Leon Bloy's tone is more nostalgic: "I could have become a saint," he said, "a worker of wonders. I have become a man of letters."[30]

Georges Bernanos is scarcely remorseful about his choice. He apparently has no regrets that he courted the joys of art. But he, too, implies that the call of the one may be opposed to the demands of the other. "Saints have a genius for love," he observed, "but not that sort of genius which is the artist's. . . which is the privilege of a very small number."[31] Whatever the merits of a saintly way of life, it may not interfere with matters of art. Bernanos has no doubts that the two must be kept apart.

> May God preserve us from poets who are apologists! If there is one thing to be ashamed of, it is to see methods of propaganda, taken from politics, divide truths into those which can and those which cannot be said, into the convenient and the inconvenient, the regrettable and the consoling, the dangerous and the harmless—as if there were truths without risk. That is why I refused the name of Catholic novelist and why I said that I was a Catholic who wrote novels, no more, no less. . . .[32]

He cautions the aspiring novelist: "If you cannot harmonize without strain and contortions your faith and your art, then keep silent."[33] The warning merits careful attention.

Greene, too, disclaimed the title of Catholic novelist, protesting he was simply "an author who is a Catholic." Like Bernanos he gives primacy to art. He would not trade the pleasures of creative endeavor for the aged maxims of religion. He, too, is opposed to use of literature for propaganda. Art is nobody's handmaid is Greene's motto. "Literature has nothing to do with edification. I am not arguing that literature is amoral, but that it presents a personal moral, and the personal morality of the indiviual is seldom identical with the morality of the group to which he belongs."[34]

This is vintage Greene—he loves his privacy. But there is more than that. Greene is enunciating the principle by which he has tried to solve the dilemma of the believing artist. "A personal moral" is not only part of the artist's sensibility, it is at the source of it. Indeed, it is the springhead of his creativity. Destroy that, and you stifle his obsessions; you starve the artist in him. But to use art to upholster a dogma or a religious institution is quite another matter. That Greene ever succumbed to this error is an exasperatingly wild suggestion which causes him to retort denying that he is "a religious man, though it interests me." "Religion is important," he said, "as atomic science is."[35]

What then is his personal morality like? What is its shape, its dimensions? Greene appears haunted with images of evil—indeed, this is his obsession. It is in every work, a looming dreadful presence in varied forms. It may come dressed in worn seedy clothes; it may be pompous and hard. Or it may brazenly display its character in acts of cruelty. Sometimes evil comes disguised as light, seductive, and charming. The artist has a wide range from which to choose. Goodness on the contrary, has a limited scope. Perhaps this is why in Greene evil has an edge over its opposite. The scales are weighted to give it an advantage which has complicated the matter further. The Jansenists and the Manicheans emphasize the role of evil, too. And how does Greene stand *vis-a-vis* their doctrines?

George Orwell claimed he noticed in Greene a certain "conflict not only between this world and the next world but between sanctity and goodness."[36] That Greene has pitched "sanctity *versus* goodness" is a recurring complaint.[37] In his fiction "everything supernatural stands in implacable hostility over against everything natural and human," says R.W.B. Lewis.[38] His portrayals have been labelled "cruel" and "irrational" and on par with Hemingway's "Nemesistic Nada."[39] Greene's work has suggested to some minds the "frustrating spiritual determinism of Jansen."[40] The position is argued out at some length by Haber:

Granted that there is a God and a metaphysical existence beyond the one that is admitted to our limited faculties, is there no rational relationship between the two worlds; is not earthly goods rewarded by Heavenly sanctity and worldly wickedness by damnation? Is there no meaning, no dignity in man's actions and moral choices?[41]

The question smacks heavily of Brighton pubs where Ida Arnold is everywhere at home. Haber is deliberately on her side, and viewed from Ida's side Greene is a heretic or worse. He has utterly no sympathy for the life she represents. This is a matter of some chagrin to a number of his admirers. R.W.B. Lewis articulates their disappointment in these terms:

Despite its singularly uninviting character, the narrow and oppressive world of Pinkie Brown is clearly to be honored—in the terms of the novel—over the spiritual bourgeoisie of Ida Arnold. Her world, for all its robust good humor, is increasingly represented as sterile, and she as a hollow heartless menace. Ida, with her big breasts and warm enveloping body, remains childless; it is the angular, nearly sexless Rose who conceives at once, after a single sexual venture.[42]

Ida, for sure, is childless; but how is this Greene's responsibility? I do not like to think Ida is barren by a special design of his—any more than Rose is pregnant by his bounty. If Greene had worked these into symbols he could not deny some responsibility. But this he has not done. In the circumstances I would suppose Ida is welcome to do as she pleased. She was well in her rights to decide that children were a bother. Indeed, that would only be in character; since having children would spoil for her some "fun." What might become of the story were she otherwise than she actually is, or how she might behave in another situation: all this is difficult to say; nor is it within the scope of criticism to answer it. Criticism is just as helpless to decide the correlation between a woman's angularity and her chances of conceiving. It is hoped that some other discipline will elucidate the matter.

The charge of Jansenism is simply unfortunate, because it has no basis whatever. Cornelius Jansen, after whom the doctrine is named, held views quite different from what Greene's characters may be said to exemplify in his books. Jansen viewed human nature with apprehension, even with distaste; it is *a nature*, or in its very essence, perverse, he said. Human nature is ever turned to evil; hence nothing good may come of it: such is Jansenist doctrine.

Greene could never accept that! In fact many of his protagonists—such as Elizabeth in *The Man Within*, Rose in *Brighton Rock*, the whiskey priest in *The Power and the Glory* and Sarah Miles in *The End of the Affair*—represent in their various ways the human "temptation to goodness." Part of the charm of Pinkie's character is his hankering for peace, for goodness, and also the near possibility of his conversion. Scobie's troubles begin with his goodness, an untamed force in him, and his story is the wild raging of an otherwise good impulse.

"People who think they are getting at Jansenism in my novels," says Greene,

> usually do not know what Jansenism really means. They probably mean Manichaeism. This is because in the Catholic novels I seem to believe in a supernatural evil. One gets so tired of people saying that my novels are about Good and Evil. They are not about good and evil, but about human beings. After Hitler and Vietnam, one would have thought good and evil in people was more understandable. Still, I do not wish to judge any of my characters. I would hope it was common to most of us to have sympathy for the unfortunate part of the ordinary human character.[43]

Evil is an aspect of life, an essential part. It does not take a Jansenist to recognize that.

But Greene is no more a theologian than a moralist. He does not hold briefs either for the Church or society. If orthodoxy does not quite suit him, no heterodox doctrine can claim him either. Indeed, he is nobody's champion: as novelist he is answerable only to himself and, in a different sense, to the world he is to portray. "This world" is sketched at various levels, like the circles of Dante's *Purgatario*. Those enclosed places have each its unique manner of purging the human soul. Greene's characters are like the spirits in purgatory. Their punishments are of various types; but the worst is the charge of an impulse, dark, and unknown, which nevertheless is ripped from their soul. There is never any suggestion in Greene of superseding nature, no "implacable hostility against everything natural and human." Conflict is never worked in those terms. On the contrary, nature is blessed, honored, and enriched so long as it holds itself open. The more receptive the human soul, the more fulfilled it is. The stories of the whiskey priest and Sarah Miles, are cases in point.

Although Greene has denied he is a "religious man", he is quick to assert the importance of religion for humanity. And because it is important to humanity, there is no excluding it either from the "slice of life" that a novel purports to be. Integrally worked into the situation, scene, or sequence, it should cause no one offense. Indeed, it may even be a major artistic asset, as Greene has well shown us. It can add potency to energize an otherwise barren world; for religion is an impulse of great vitality. It is also "a system of thought, a source of situations, and a reservoir of symbols."[44] And Greene utilizes it to "order and dramatize certain intuitions about the nature of human experience."[45] If it catalyzes the aesthetic urge, certainly it is not "a crippling burden."[46] It cannot both enhance and hamper "his artistic freedom".

But his religion is not what marks him out among contemporary novelists. Religious motifs have been used in fiction before; and they will continue to be used after him. His writing craft does not quite distinguish him any more than the religious motifs. True, Greene is one of the better skilled in his profession, but surely there must be others no less talented. What sets Greene apart is the correlation he strikes between truth and suffering. Perhaps even this is not a discovery. It may be the inherited wisdom that sufferings make the person. The grain must fall to the ground, decay and die before it gives new life. You must die, said the Man from Galilee; unless you die, you shall not have life. A simple paradox to shame all complexities of thought. Greene has given it an easy novelistic expression.

"After the death of James a disaster overtook the English novel," said Greene. "For with the death of James the religious sense was lost to the English novel, and with the religious sense went the sense of the importance of the human act. It was as if the world of fiction had lost a dimension: the characters of such distinguished writers as Mrs. Virginia Woolf and Mr. E.M. Forster wandered like cardboard symbols through a world that was paper thin."[47] Many of those writing today are men and women of proved ability, but their works do not have a lasting effect upon us. The characters slide over our minds and hearts, without any real contact, leaving no great impression. Greene's characters stay with us, hauntingly. The thriller is there to shock us just to the degree needed for the larger effect to take place. "If you excite your audience first," he has said, "you can put over what you will of horror, suffering, truth."[48]

Quite early in his career, Green decided his art should be "to create something legendary out of the contemporary thriller." His view, accordingly, is fixed on the struggles of the human spirit that go on unendingly in every age. Nothing ever abates them. Neither culture, nor sophistication, nor all the comforts modernity has lavished on anyone is able to buy peace that lasts. This is Greene's rejoinder to the Naturalists; and on this premise has he built his vision. Because pain is a condition of human existence it cannot be removed once and for all. Still, Greene is no pessimist, nor is his vision in any sense negative. For he is able to look beyond the present of pain: or rather he finds, right in the heart of it, a limitless freedom.

Greene's effects verge on the magical. Magical, too, is his style which blends story, character, and meaning into an exquisite drama and evokes a compelling response. Such vision and style, such sublimity and spiritual insight, such dramatic power—it is rarely that a single author combines all these various attributes. In an age of great literary efforts Greene's work will shine among the best. It will continue to exercise its charm, which will endure for ages to come.

NOTES

A SORT OF BACKGROUND

1. Alfred Lord Tennyson, *In Memoriam.*
2. R.A. Scott-James, *Fifty Years of English Literature: 1900-1950.* 2nd ed. (London: Longmans, Green and Co., 1960), p.47.
3. W.B. Yeats, "The Second Coming," Norman Jeffares, ed. *W.B. Yeats: Selected Poetry* (London: Macmillan and Co., 1962), p.99.
4. Stephen Spender, cited in R.A. Scott-James, *op. cit.,* pp.212–13.
5. T.S. Eliot, "The Waste Land," *Selected Poems* (London: Faber and Faber Ltd., 1961), p.51.
6. T.S. Eliot *Ibid.*
7. Cf. Martin Shuttleworth and Simon Raven, "The Art of Fiction: Graham Greene," *Graham Greene: A Collection of Critical Essays,* etc. Samuel Hynes (New Jersey: Prentice-Hall, 1973), p.154.
8. Graham Greene, *Journey Without Maps* (London: Heinemann, 1950), p.31.
9. Graham Greene, *The Lawless Roads* (Penguin, 1971), p.15.
10. Eric Berne, *What Do You Say After You Say "Hello"?* (Bantam Books, 1973), p.53.
11. *Ibid.,* pp.172–73.
12. Graham Greene, *The Lawless Roads,* pp.13–14.
13. Graham Greene, *Journey Without Maps,* passim.
14. Graham Greene, *The Lawless Roads,* pp.13–14.
15. *Ibid.*
16. Graham Greene, *Journey Without Maps,* p.193.
17. *Ibid.*
18. Graham Greene, *The Lawless Roads,* p.14.
19. *Ibid.*
20. *Ibid.*

THE MAKING OF AN ARTIST

1. Graham Greene, *A Sort of Life* (Bodley Head, 1971), p.115.
2. Martin Shuttleworth and Simon Raven, *op. cit.*, p.160.
3. Cf. S. Karpman, "Fairy Tales and Script Drama Analysis," *Transactional Analysis Bulletin* 7 (April 1968), pp.39–43.
4. Graham Greene, *Journey Without Maps*, pp.7–8.
5. *Ibid.*, p.312.
6. Morton D. Zabel, "The Best and the Worst," *Graham Greene: A Collection of Critical Essays*, ed. Samuel Hynes (New Jersey: Prentice-Hall, 1973), pp.39–40.
7. Graham Greene, *The Ministry of Fear* (London: Heinemann, 1956), pp.71–72.
8. W.H. Auden, "The Heresy of Our Time," *Renascence* 1 (Spring, 1949), pp.23–24.
9. John Atkins, *Graham Greene* (London: Calder and Bogars, 1957), p.45.
10. Austin Warren, *Perspectives on Fiction*, ed. James L. Calderwood and H.E. Toliver (New York: Oxford University Press, 1968), p.82.
11. *Ibid.*
12. Graham Greene, *A Sort of Life*, p.198.
13. Graham Greene, *A Burnt-Out Case* (Penguin Books, 1977), p.185

BRIGHTON ROCK

1. Cf. footnote 12
2. Graham Greene, *Orient Express* (Pocket Books, 1975), p.132.
3. Graham Greene, "Bernanos, the Beginner," *Collected Essays* (London: Bodley Head, 1969).
4. T.S. Eliot, *The Waste Land*.

5. R.W.B. Lewis, "The 'Trilogy' of Graham Greene," *Modern Fiction Studies. 3: Graham Greene Special Number* (Autumn 1957), p.202.

6. Francis Kunkel, *The Labyrinthine Ways* (New York: Sheed and Ward, 1959), pp.110–111.

7. *Ibid.*

8. Gilbert Thomas, *How to Enjoy Detective Fiction* (London: Salisbury Square, 1947), p.26

9. Herbert R. Haber, "Two Worlds of Graham Greene," *Modern Fiction Studies, 3: Graham Greene Special Number* (Autumn 1957), pp.260–61.

10. R.W.B. Lewis, "The 'Trilogy' of Graham Greene," *Modern Fiction Series op. cit.*, pp.201–203.

11. Herbert R. Haber, "Two Worlds of Graham Greene, *Modern Fiction Studies op. cit.*, pp.261–63.

12. T.S. Eliot, "Baudelaire," *Selected Essays*. Third Enlarged Edition. (London: Faber and Faber, 1951).

13. Robert O. Evans, "The Satanist Fallacy of *Brighton Rock,*" ed. R.O. Evans, *Graham Greene: Some Critical Considerations* (Lexington: University of Kentucky Press, 1963).

14. *Ibid.*

15. *Ibid.*, pp.164–65.

16. A.A. DeVitis, "Allegory in *Brighton Rock*," *Modern Fiction Studies, 3: Graham Greene Special Number* (Autumn 1957), p.219.

17. Georges Bernanos, *The Diary of a Country Priest* (London: Boriswood, 1937), pp.270–71.

18. Robert O. Evans, "The Satanist Fallacy of *Brighton Rock*," *op. cit.*, pp.156-57.

19. Graham Greene, *The Lost Childhood & Other Essays* (New York: Viking Press, 1952), p.93.

THE POWER AND THE GLORY

1. "Lapsed" is a description that suits many a Greene-hero. Most of them did once cherish a great vision which only the harshest of experience could have dissolved. Dr. Czinner, Pinkie, the whiskey priest, Scobie were all once idealists.

2. Graham Greene, *The Lawless Roads*, pp.41–42.

3. *Ibid.*, p.42.

4. Graham Greene, *Journey Without Maps*, p.87.

5. Georges Bernanos, *Journal d'un Curé de la campagne*, pp. 270–71.

6. Graham Greene, *Brighton Rock*, pp.201–202.

7. See below in the chapter on *The Heart of the Matter*.

8. See below in the Chapter on *The End of the Affair*.

9. Graham Greene, *The Lawless Roads*, p.15.

10. Edwin Muir, *The Structure of the Novel* (London: The Hogarth Press, 1928), p.64.

11. Karl Patten, "The Structure of *The Power and the Glory*," *Modern Fiction Studies, 3: Graham Greene Special Number* (Autumn 1957), pp.225–30.

12. Edmund Wilson, "Theodore Dreiser's Quaker and Graham Greene's Priest," *The New Yorker* 22 (March 23, 1946), pp.88–94.

13. Dietrich Bonhoeffer, *Ethik*, ed. Eberhard Bethge and trans. Neville Horton Smith (London: Fontana Library, 1970), pp.240–41.

14. *Ibid.*

15. *Ibid.*, pp.241–42.

16. *Ibid.*

17. R.W.B. Lewis, "The 'Trilogy' of Graham Greene," *Graham Greene: A Collection of Critical Essays, op. cit.*, p.205.

18. *Ibid.*

19. R.W.B. Lewis finds special significance in the name Calver which "echoes two syllables of the Mount on which Christ was crucified." *Ibid.*, p.210.

20. Jn. 18:8.
21. T.S. Eliot, *The Waste Land.*
22. Mk. 15:39.
23. R.W.B. Lewis, "The Fiction of Graham Greene: Between the Horror and the Glory, *Kenyon Review*, 19, 1957, pp.56–75.
24. Kenneth Tynan, *The Observer* (London: April 8, 1956), p.11.
25. Goerges Bernanos, *Star of Satan* trans. by Pamela Morris (London: Bodley Head, 1927), p.209.

THE HEART OF THE MATTER

1. Graham Greene, *Brighton Rock* (Penguin, 1973), p.222.
2. Graham Greene, *The Power and the Glory* (Penguin, 1970), p.125.
3. Graham Greene, *Journey Without Maps*, p.11.
4. Graham Greene, quoted in John Atkins, *Graham Greene, op. cit.*, p.216.
5. Graham Greene, *England Made Me* Penguin, 1970), pp.34–35.
6. *Ibid.*, p.51.
7. Graham Greene, *Orient Express* (Pocket Books, 1975), p.193.
8. Graham Martin, A Pelican Guide to English Literature, 7, ed. Boris Ford (Penguin Books, 1961), p.407.
9. *Ibid.*
10. T.S. Eliot, "The Hollow Men," *Selected Poems* (Faber and Faber, 1961).
11. Graham Greene, *Brighton Rock,* pp.228–29.
12. Graham Greene, *The Power and the Glory*, p.25.
13. *Ibid.*, pp.24–25.
14. John Atkins, *Graham Greene, op. cit.*, pp.44–45.

15. Ecclesiastes, Ch. 1.
16. Ecclesiastes, Ch. 2.
17. W. H. Auden, "The Heresy of Our Time," *Renascence 1* (Spring 1949), pp.23–24.
18. Graham Greene, *The Ministry of Fear* (London: Heinemann, 1943).
19. "Introduction" to *The Heart of the Matter*. The Collected Edition (London: Bodley Head & Heinemann, 1971).
20. Arnold Kettle, *An Introduction to the English Novel* (Harper and Row, 1968), pp.337–41.
21. George Orwell, "The Sanctified Sinner," *The New Yorker* 24 (July 17, 1948), pp.66–71.
22. Barbara Wall, "London Letter," *America* 79 (August 28, 1948), p.471.
23. Arnold Kettle, *op. cit.*, pp.337–41.
24. Henry M. Robinson, *The Saturday Review* (July 10, 1948) p.9.
25. Evelyn Waugh, "Felix Culpa?" *The Tablet* 91 (June 5, 1948).
26. Graham Greene, *A Sort of Life*, p.189.
27. *Ibid.*
28. Graham Greene, *The Power and the Glory*, p.19.
29. Carl Gustav Jung, "Aion: Phenomenology of the Self," *Portable Jung*, ed. Joseph Campbell (New York: Viking, 1972), pp.139–62.
30. Philip Toynbee, *The Observer* (London, December 4, 1955).
31. Cf. Revelation, 3:14–16.
32. Cf. Gene D. Phillips' interview of Greene: "Graham Greene: On the Screen," *The Catholic World*, 209 (August 1969), pp.218–21.

THE END OF THE AFFAIR

1. Thomas Merton, "Spiritual Virginity," *Collected Essays*, 16 (1950-52), pp.67–71.

2. Thomas Merton, "Poetry and Contemplation: a Reappraisal," *Commonweal* 69 (Oct. 24, 1958), p.90.

3. Thomas Merton, passim.

4. St. John of the Cross, *Dark Night of the Soul*, trans. E. Allison Peers (New York: Image Books, 1959), p.119.

5. Thomas Merton, *New Seeds of Contemplation* (New York: New Directions, 1961), p.285.

6. *Ibid.*, pp.134–35.

7. Thomas Merton, "Poetry and Contemplation," *op. cit.*, p.90.

8. Herbert R. Haber, "The End of the Catholic Cycle," *Graham Greene: Some Critical Considerations, op. cit.*, p.133.

9. Thomas Merton, "Preface to the Japanese Edition" *The New Man* (October 1967), p.2.

10. St. John of the Cross, *op. cit.*, p.119.

11. Thomas Merton, *No Man is an Island* (New York: Harcourt, Brace and World, 1955), p.219.

12. Thomas Merton, *The Climate of Monastic Prayer. Cistercian Studies*, no. 1 (Spencer, Massachusetts: 1969), p.102.

13. *Ibid.*

14. Thomas Merton, *New Seeds of Contemplation*, pp.268–69.

15. *Ibid.*, pp.70–71.

16. *Ibid.*, p.65.

17. Thomas Merton, "The Gift of Understanding," *The Tyger's Eye*, 16 (December 1948), p.43.

18. *Ibid.*

19. *Ibid.*

20. Thomas Merton, passim.

21. Herbert R. Haber, "The End of the Catholic Cycle," *Graham Greene: Some Critical Considerations, op. cit.*, p.134.

21a. William Shakespear, *As You Like It*, II,vii.

A BURNT-OUT CASE

Lead quotation: Victor E. Frankl, *From Death-Camp to Existentialism* (Boston: Beacon Press, 1959).

1. Graham Greene's Introduction to *A Burnt-Out Case* in the Collected Edition of his works.
2. *Ibid.*
3. *Ibid.*
4. *Ibid.*
5. *Ibid.*
6. *Ibid.*
7. *Ibid.*
8. Cf. Graham Greene, *The Lawless Roads* (Penguin Books, 1971), pp.48–49.
9. His aversion to Marie Akimbu, noticed later in the chapter, is but one instance. Another is his reaction to Querry on the mere allegation of a sexual lapse.
10. Cited in Greene's Introduction to *A Burnt-Out Case* in the Collected Edition.
11. As claimed by Frank Kermode. Cf. Kermode, "Mr. Greene's Eggs and Crosses," in Samuel Hynes (ed), *Graham Greene: A Collection of Critical Essays*. Twentieth Century Views. (New Jersey: A Spectrum Book, 1973), p.129.
12. Cited by Frank Kermode, "Mr. Greene's Eggs and Crosses," *op. cit.*, p.126.
13. Mk. 11:15. The version used is The New English Bible.
14. Mk. 11:18.
15. Graham Greene's Introduction to *A Burnt-Out Case* in the Collection Edition.
16. Graham Greene, *A Sort of Life* (London: Bodley Head, 1971), p.161.
17. *Ibid.*, p.162.
18. *Ibid.*, p.164.
19. *Ibid.*

20. *Ibid.*, p.161.

21. *Ibid.*, p.166.

22. *Ibid.*, p.165.

23. St. John of the Cross, "My Beloved is the mountains, the solitary wooded valleys, strange islands . . . silent music." Also, the title of Williams Johnston's work on the Science and stages of mystical communion.

24. Graham Greene, *A Sort of Life*, p.165.

25. *Ibid.*

26. Quoted by Graham Greene in his Introduction to *A Burnt-Out Case* in the Collected Edition.

27. Georges Bernanos, *Journal d'un Curé de la campagne* (Plon, 1936), Trans. as *The Diary of a Country Priest* (London: Boriswood, 1937). pp.270–71.

28. Mk. 4:19, in The New English Bible.

29. Graham Greene, *The Power and the Glory* (Penguin Books, 1970), p.127.

30. *Ibid.*, p.130.

31. *Ibid.*, p.131.

32. *Ibid.*

33. Father Francis MacNutt, in his book, *The Power to Heal* says: "We have learned to accept evil as good, as God's will, and have learned a hopeless rather than a hopeful response to sickness. In this we act more like Buddhists talking about karma than Christians talking about redemption." He regrets that we have thus "been robbed of our heritage."

34. Jn. 15:5-6. The version used is The New English Bible.

35. Banest Hoffman and Helen Dukas (ed.), *Albert Einstein: The Human Side* (Princeton University Press). Excerpt taken from *Time* (February 19, 1979).

36. Graham Greene, *The End of the Affair* (Penguin, 1962), p.46.

37. Graham Greene's Introduction to *A Burnt-Out Case* in the Collected Edition.

38. Refer above, chapter 6.

39. Cf. Henry James, *The Portrait of a Lady*. The latter half of the book is of special interest.
40. Graham Greene, *The End of the Affair* (Penguin, 1962), p.179.

A NOVELIST'S CREED

1. Martin Shuttleworth and Simon Raven, "The Art of Fiction: Graham Greene," *Graham Greene: A Collection of Critical Essays, op. cit.*, p.154.
2. *Ibid.*
3. *Ibid.*
4. *Ibid.*
5. Morton D. Zabel, "The Best and the Worst," *Graham Greene: A Collection of Critical Essays, op. cit.*, pp.39–40.
6. *Ibid.*
7. Martin Shuttleworth and Simon Raven, "The Art of Fiction: Graham Greene," *Graham Greene: A Collection of Critical Essays, op. cit.*, p.154.
8. W.H. Auden, "The Heresy of Our Time," *Graham Greene: A Collection of Critical Essays, op. cit.*, pp.23–24.
9. *Ibid.*
10. Graham Greene, *The Man Within* (New York: Bantam Books, 1964), The epigraph is quoted from Browne's *Religio Medici*.
11. Graham Greene, *The Lawless Roads*, p.33.
12. W.H. Auden, "The Heresy of Our Time," *op. cit.*, pp.23–24.
13. Graham Greene, *The Lawless Roads*, pp.33–34.
14. *Ibid.*
15. Thus Greene's reading of the present state of literature. Faith and the conflicts, it engenders in the human heart — the *angst* caused by an Either/Or — may have quickened life, and made art a soulful thing.

16. George Orwell, "The Art of Donald McGill," *Critical Essays* (London 1946), pp.96–97.

17. They experience in full the anguish of one who has to choose between two enternities. Indeed there could be no hard options between absolute good and absolute evil. It is harder to choose between a present of pain and a future glory, but these are not Greene's terms. To prefer enduring pain to anaesthetized sensibilities is more heroic still.

18. Jack Kroll "Sin and Sentimentality," *Newsweek* (November 3, 1975), p.87–88.

19. Robert O. Evans, "The Satanist Fallacy of *Brighton Rock*," *Graham Greene: Some Critical Considerations, op. cit.*, pp.163–66.

20. Cf. *Oxford Universal English Dictionary on Historical Principles*, ed., C.T. Onions (Oxford University Press, 1937): "The defensive method of argument; often *spec.* The argumentative defence of Christianity."

21. *Webster's Seventh New Collegiate Dictionary.*

22. Graham Greene, *The Honorary Consul* (New York: Pocket Books, 1974).

23. James Noxon, "Kierkegaard's Stages and *A Burnt-Out Case, Review of English Literature, op. cit.*, p.90.

24. *Ibid.*

25. *Ibid.*, pp.100–101.

26. *Ibid.*

27. Graham Greene, *Why Do I Write? An Exchange of Views Between Elizabeth Gowen, Graham Greene and V.S. Pritchett* (London: Marshall, 1948), pp.46–52.

28. François Mauriac, in an interview with Jean le Merchand for *The Paris Review*. Reproduced in *Writers at Work*, ed. Malcolm Cowley (New York: Viking, 1958), p.49.

29. Quoted by Herbert R. Haber, "The End of the Catholic Cycle: The Writer versus the Saint," *Graham Greene: Some Critical Considerations, op. cit.*, p.127.

30. *Ibid.*

31. *Ibid.*

32. Georges Bernanos, *Bulletin de la Société des Amis de Georges Bernanos*, nos. 15-16, pp.13–14.

33, *Ibid.*

34. Graham Greene, *Why Do I Write? op. cit.*, p.48.

35. Gene D. Phillips, "Graham Greene: On the Screen," *Graham Greene: A Collection of Critical Essays, op. cit.*, p.157.

36. George Orwell, "The Sanctified Sinner," *The New Yorker*, 24 (July 17, 1948), p.66.

37. Herbert R. Haber, "Two Worlds of Graham Greene," *Modern Fiction Studies, op. cit.*, p.256–57.

38. R.W.B. Lewis, "The 'Trilogy' of Graham Greene," *Modern Fiction Studies, op. cit.*, p.200.

39. Herbert R. Haber, "Two Worlds of Graham Greene," *Modern Fiction Studies, op. cit.*, pp.256–57.

40. *Ibid.*

41. *Ibid.*

42. R.W.B. Lewis, "The 'Trilogy' of Graham Greene," *Modern Fiction Studies, op. cit.*, p.202.

43. Gene D. Phillips, "Graham Greene: On the Screen," *Graham Greene: A Collection of Critical Essays, op. cit.*, p.175.

44. David Lodge, *The Novelist at the Crossroads* (London: Routledge and Kegan Paul, 1971), p.89.

45. *Ibid.*

46. *Ibid.*

47. Graham Greene, "François Mauriac," *Collected Essays*, (London: Bodley Head, 1969), p.115.

48. Gene D. Phillips, "Graham Greene: On the Screen," *Graham Greene: A Collection of Critical Essays, op. cit.*, p.172.

BIBLIOGRAPHY

1. Primary sources

A. Novels

Greene, Graham. *The Man Within.* London: Heinemann, 1929. New York: Bantam Books, 1964.

———. *The Name of Action.* London: Heinemann, 1931.

———. *Rumour at Nightfall.* London: Heinemann, 1932.

———. *Stamboul Train.* London: Heinemann, 1932.

———. *It's a Battlefield.* London: Heinemann, 1934.

———. *England Made me.* London: Heinemann, 1935.

———. *A Gun for Sale.* London: Heinemann, 1936.

———. *Brighton Rock.* London: Heinemann, 1938.

———. *The Confidential Agent.* London: Heinemann, 1939.

———. *The Power and the Glory.* London: Heinemann, 1940.

———. *The Ministry of Fear.* London: Heinemann, 1943.

———. *The Heart of the Matter.* London: Heinemann, 1948.

———. *The Third Man and the Fallen Idol.* London: Heinemann, 1950.

———. *The End of the Affair.* London: Heinemann, 1951.

———. *Loser Takes All.* London: Heinemann, 1955.

———. *The Quiet American.* London: Heinemann, 1955.

———. *Our Man in Havana.* London: Heinemann, 1958.

———. *A Burnt-Out Case.* London: Heinemann, 1961.

———. *The Comedians.* London: Bodley Head, 1966.

———. *Travels with My Aunt.* London: Bodley Head, 1969.

———. *The Honorary Consul.* London: Bodley Head, 1973.

———. *The Human Factor.* London: Bodley Head, 1978.

B.   Other Works

Greene, Graham. *The Basement Room and Other Stories*. London: Cresset Press, 1935.

——. "Bernanos, the Beginner," *Collected Essays*. London: Bodley Head, 1969.

——. *The Complacent Lover*. London: Heinemann, 1969.

——. "Edgar Wallace," *Collected Essays*. London: Bodley Road, 1969.

——. "Ford Madox Ford," *Collected Essays*. London: Bodley Head, 1969.

——. "François Mauriac," *Collected Essays*. London: Bodley Head, 1969.

——. "Frederick Rolfe: Edwardian Inferno," *Collected Essays*. London: Bodley Head, 1969.

——. "Frederick Rolfe: From the Devil's Side," *Collected Essays*. London: Bodley Head, 1969.

——. "Frederick Rolfe: A Spoiled Priest," *Collected Essays*. London: Bodley Head, 1969.

——. "Henry James: The Private Universe," *Collected Essays*. London: Bodley Head, 1969.

——. "Henry James: the Religious Aspect," *Collected Essays*. London: Bodley Head, 1969.

——. *In Search of a Character*. London: Bodley Head, 1961.

——. "Journey Into Success," *Collected Essays*. London: Bodey Head, 1969.

——. *Journey Without Maps*. London: Heinemann, 1936.

——. "The Last Buchan," *Collected Essays*. London: Bodley Head, 1969.

————. *The Lawless Roads*. London: Longmans, 1939.

————. *The Living Room*. London: Heinemann, 1953.

————. "The Lost Childhood," *Collected Essays*. London: Bodley Head, 1969.

————. *Lost Childhood and Other Essays*. London: Eyre & Spottiswood, 1951.

————. *May We borrow Your Husband? And Other Comedies of the Sexual Life*. London: Bodley Head, 1967.

————. "The Portrait of a Lady," *Collected Essays*. London: Bodley Head, 1969.

————. *The Potting Shed*. London: Heinemann, 1958.

————. "Rider Haggard's Secret," *Collected Essays*. London: Bodley Head, 1969.

————. *A Sort of Reality: Four Short Stories*. London: Bodley Head, 1963.

————. "Simone Weil," *Collected Essays*. London: Bodley Head, 1969.

————. *A Sort of Life*. London: Bodley Head, 1971.

————. "The Town of Malgudi," *Collected Essays*. London: Bodley Head, 1969.

————. *Twenty-One Stories*. London: Heinemann, 1954.

————. "The Young Dickens," *Collected Essays*. London: Bodley Head, 1969.

Greene, Graham; Bowen, Elizabeth; and Pritichett, V.S., *Why Do I Write? An Exchange of Views*. London: Marshall, 1948.

Phillips, Gene D. "Graham Greene: On the Screen," *The Catholic World* 209 (August 1969): 218–21.

Shuttleworth, Martin and Simon Raven. "The Art of Fiction: Graham Greene," *Paris Review* 3 (Autumn 1953): 24–41.

2. Secondary Sources

A. Books

Atkins, John Alfred. *Graham Greene.* London: Calder and Boyars, 1957.

Evans, Robert O., ed. *Graham Greene: Some Critical Considerations.* Lexington: University of Kentucky Press, 1963.

Hynes, Samuel, ed. *Graham Greene; A Collection of Critical Essays.* New Jersey: Prentice-Hall, 1973.

Kunkel, Francis Leo. *The Labyrinthine Ways of Graham Greene.* New York: Sheed and Ward, 1959.

Pryce-Jones, David. *Graham Greene.* Edinburgh: Oliver and Boyd, 1963.

Wyndham, Francis. *Graham Greene.* London: Longmans, Green and Co., 1958.

B. Articles

Alexander, Calvert. *The Catholic Literary Revival.* Milwaukee, 1935. pp. 277–95.

Atkins, John. "Altogether Amen: A Reconsideration of *The Power and the Glory,*" *Graham Greene: Some Critical Considerations,* Edited by R.O. Evans. Lexington: University of Kentucky Press, 1963.

Auden, W.H. "The Heresy of Our Time," *Graham Greene: A Collection of Critical Essays.* Edited by Samuel Hynes. New Jersey: Prentice-Hall, 1973.

Beebe, Maurice. "Criticism of Graham Greene: A Selected Check-
list with Index to Studies," *Modern Fiction Studies: 3.
Graham Greene Special Number* (Autumn 1957).

Boardman, Gwenn R. "Greene's 'Under the Garden': Aesthetic Exploration," *Renascence* (Summer 1965): 180–194.

Brady, Charles A. "Melodramatic Cousin Of R. L. S.," *America* 64
(1941): 439–40.

Brennan, Neil. "Coney Island Rock," *Accent* 16 (Spring 1956):
140–42.

Cartmell, Canon Joseph. "A Postscript to Evelyn Waugh," *Graham
Greene: A Collection of Critical Essays.* Edited by Samuel
Hynes. New Jersey: Prentice-Hall, 1973.

Consolo, Dominick P. "Graham Greene: Style and Stylistics in Five
Novels." *Graham Greene: Some Critical Considerations.*
Edited by R.O. Evans. Lexington: University of Kentucky,
1963.

Cottrell, Beckman W. "Second Time Charm: The Theatre of
Graham Greene," *Modern Fiction Studies: 3 Graham
Greene Special Number* (Autumn 1957): 249–55.

Cruise O'Brien, Conor [O'Donnell, Donat]. *Maria Cross: Imaginative Patterns in a Group of Modern Catholic Writers.* New
York: Oxford University Press, 1952. pp. 119–34.

Daiches, David. *The Romantics to the Present Day.* vol. 4 *A Critical
History of English Literature.* 2nd edition. London: Secker
and Warburg, 1969. 217–24.

DeVitis, A.A. "Allegory in Brighton Rock," *Modern Fiction
Studies: 3. Graham Greene Special Number* (Autumn
1957): 217–24.

———. "The Catholic as Novelist: Graham Greene and Francois
Mauriac," *Graham Greene: Some Critical Considerations.*
Edited by R.O. Evans. Lexington: University of Kentucky,
1963.

Evans, Robert O. "Existentialism in Greene's *The Quiet American*,"
*Modern Fiction Studies: 3 Graham Greene Special
Number* (Autumn 1957): 241–48.

————. "The Satanist Fallacy of *Brighton Rock*," *Graham Greene: Some Critical Considerations.* Edited by R.O. Evans. Lexington: University of Kentucky, 1963.

Foote, Timothy. "Our Man in Gehenna," *Time* (September 17, 1973): p. 58.

Fraser, G.S. *The Modern Writer and His World.* London: 1953. pp. 109–113.

Gardiner, Harold C. "Taste and Worth," *America* 75 (1946): p. 53.

"Graham Greene: The Man Within," *Times Literary Supplement* (September 17, 1971): 1101–2.

Gregor, Ian. *"The End of the Affair,"* *Graham Greene: A Collection of Critical Essays,* Edited by Samuel Hynes. New Jersey: Prentice-Hall, 1973.

Haber, Herbert R. "Two Worlds of Graham Greene," *Modern Fiction Studies: 3. Graham Greene Special Number* (Autumn 1957): 256–68.

————. "The End of the Catholic Cycle: The Writer versus the Saint," *Graham Greene, Some Critical Considerations.* Edited by R.O. Evans, Lexington: University of Kentucky, 1963.

Hargreaves, Phylis. "Graham Greene: A Selected Bibliography," *Modern Fiction Studies: 3. Graham Greene Special Number* (Autumn 1957): 269–80.

Hayes, H.R. "A Defence of the Thriller," *Partisan Review,* 3 (Winter 1945): 135–37.

Hesla, David H. "Theological Ambiguity in the 'Catholic Novels'," *Graham Greene: Some Critical Considerations.* Edited by R.O. Evans. Lexington: University of Kentucky, 1963.

Hinchliffe, Arnold P. "The Good American," *Twentieth Century* 68 (1960): 529–39.

Hoggart, Richard. "The Force of Caricature: Aspects of the Art of Graham Greene, With Particular Reference to *The Power and the Glory,*" *Essays in Criticism,* 3 (October 1953): 447–62.

————. "The Force of Caricature," *Graham Greene: A Collection of Critical Essays*. Edited by Samuel Hynes. New Jersey: Prentice-Hall, 1973.

Hynes, Samuel. "Introduction," *Graham Greene: A Collection of Critical Essays*. Edited by Samuel Hynes. New Jersey: Prentice-Hall, 1973.

Kermode, Frank. "Mr. Greene's Eggs and Crosses," *Graham Greene: A Collection of Critical Essays*. Edited by Samuel Hynes. New Jersey: Prentice-Hall, 1973.

Kettle, Arnold. *An Introduction to the English Novel*. New York: Harper & Row, 1968. pp. 335–41.

Kunkel, Francis Leo. "The Theme of Sin and Grace in Graham Greene," *Graham Greene: Some Critical Considerations*. Edited by R.O. Evans. Lexington: University of Kentucky, 1963.

Laitinen, Kai. "The Heart of the Novel: The Turning Point in *The Heart of the Matter*," *Graham Greene: Some Critical Considerations*. Edited by R.O. Evans. Lexington: University of Kentucky, 1963.

Lees, F. N. "Graham Greene: A Comment," *Scrutiny* 19 (1952-53): 31–42.

Lerner, Laurence. "Graham Greene," *The Critical Quarterly*. 5 (Autumn 1963): 217–31.

Lewis, R.W.B. "The Fiction of Graham Greene: Between the Harror and the Glory," *Kenyon Review* 19 (1957): 56–75.

————. "The 'Trilogy' of Graham Greene," *Modern Fiction Studies: 3 Graham Greene Special Number* (Autumn 1957): 195–215.

Lewis, Theophilus. "Post Mortem Report," *America* 92 (1955): 386–87.

Lodge, David. *The Novelist at the Crossroads, and Other Essays on Fiction and Criticism*. London: Routledge and Kegan Paul, 1971. pp. 87–118.

Madden, Joan. "With Crooked Lines: Greene's 'The Living Room'," *America* 90 (1954): 600–602.

Maguire, Mother C.E. "Grace and the Play," *America* 93 (1955): 433–35.

Marshall, Bruce. "Graham Greene and Evelyn Waugh," *Commonweal* 51 (1950): 551–53.

Martin, Graham. "Novelists of Three Decades: Evelyn Waugh, Graham Greene and C.P. Snow," *The Modern Age*. Edited by Boris Ford. vol. 7 of *The Pelican Guide to English Literature*. Penguin Books, 1961. pp. 394–414.

Mauriac, Francois. *Men I Hold Great*. New York: Philosophical Library, 1951. pp. 124–28.

McCarthy, Mary. "Graham Greene and the Intelligentsia," *Partisan Review* 11 (Spring 1944): 228–30.

———. "Sheep in Wolves' Clothing," *Partisan Review* 24 (Spring 1957): 270–74.

McCormick, John. *Catastrophe and Imagination: An Introduction to the Recent English and American Novel*. London: Longmans, Green, and Co., 1957. pp. 286–89.

McLaughlin, Richard. "Graham Greene, Saint or Cynic?" *America* 79 (1948): 370–71.

McNamara, Eugene. "Prospects of the Catholic Novel," *America* 97 (1957): 505–506.

Noxon, James. "Kierkegaard's Stages and *A Burnt-Out Case*." *Review of English Literature* (Leeds), 3 (January 1962): 90–101.

Orwell, George. "The Sanctified Sinner," *The New Yorker* 24 (July 17, 1948): pp. 66–71.

Patten, Karl. "The structure of *The Power and the Glory*," *Modern Fiction Studies: 3. Graham Greene Special Number* (Autumn 1957): 228–34.

Scott, Carolyn D. "The Witch at the Corner: Notes on Graham Greene's Mythology," *Graham Greene: Some Critical Considerations*. Edited by R.O. Evans. Lexington: University of Kentucky, 1963.

Scott, Nathan A., Jr. "Graham Greene: Christian Tragedian," *Graham Greene: Some Critical Considerations*. Edited by R.O. Evans. Lexington: University of Kentucky, 1963.

Steward, Barbara. "Graham Greene: A Hint of Explanation." *Western Review 22* (Winter 1958): 83–95.

Spender, Stephen. *The Creative Element: A Study of Vision, Despair and Orthodoxy Among Some Modern Writers.* London: H. Hamilton, 1953.

Spier, Ursula. "Melodrama in Graham Greene's *The End of the Affair*," *Modern Fiction Studies: 3. Graham Greene Special Number* (Autumn 1957): 235–40.

The Tablet. 228 (December 1973): 1226.

Tonybee, Philip. *The Observer* London. (December 4, 1955).

Traversi, Derek. "Graham Greene: The Earlier Novels," *Twentieth Century 149* (March 1951): 231–40.

Tynan, Kenneth. *The Observer* London. (April 8, 1956).

Wall, Barbara. "London Letter," *America* 77 (1947): 521–22.

———. "London Letter," *America* 79 (1948): 470–71.

Wassmer, Thomas A. "The Problem and the Mystery of Sin in the Works of Graham Greene," *The Christian Scholar* 43 (Winter 1960): 309–315.

Waugh, Evelyn. "Felix Culpa?" *The Tablet.* 191 (June 5, 1948).

Webster, Harvey Curtis. "The World of Graham Greene," *Graham Greene: Some Critical Considerations.* Edited by R.O. Evans. Lexington: University of Kentucky, 1963.

Wilson, Colin. "Evelyn Waugh and Graham Greene," *The Strength to Dream: Literature and the Imagination.* Boston: Houghton Mifflin, 1962.

Wilson, Edmund. "Theodore Dreiser's Quaker and Graham Greene's Priest," *The New Yorker* 22 (March 23, 1946): pp. 88–94.

Zabel, Morton D. "Graham Greene," *Critiques and Essays on Modern Fiction: 1920-1951.* Edited by John Aldridge. New York: The Ronald Press Co., 1952.

———. "The Best and the Worst," *Graham Greene: A Collection of Critical Essays.* Edited by Samuel Hynes. New Jersey: Prentice-Hall, 1973.

3. Other Works Consulted

Bernanos, Georges. *La Joie*. Paris: Plon, 1929. *Joy*. Translated by Louise Varese. New York: Pantheon Books, 1946.

———. *Journal d'um cure de la campagne*. Paris: Plon, 1936. *The Diary of a Country Priest*. Translated by Pamela Morris. London: Boriswood, 1937.

———. *Sous le Soleil de Satan*. Paris: Plon, 1926. *Star of Satan*. Translated by Pamela Morris. London: Bodley Head, 1940.

———. *Bulletin de la Societe des Amis de Georges Bernanos*. nos. 15-16. pp. 13-14.

Berne, Eric. *What Do You Say After You Say 'Hello'? The Psychology of Human Destiny*. New York: Bantam Books, 1973.

Blatty, William Peter, *The Exorcist*. New York: Bantam Books, 1971.

Bonhoeffer, Dietrich. *Ethik*. Edited by Eberhart Bethge. *Ethics*. Translated by Neville Horton Smith. London: Fontana Library, 1970.

———. *Letters and Papers from Prison*. Edited by Eberhard Bethge. London: SCM Press, 1971.

Booth, Wayne. *The Rhetoric of Fiction*. Chicago: University of Chicago Press, 1961.

Brown, Douglas. "From *Heart of Darkness* to *Nostromo*: An Approach to Conrad". *The Modern Age*. vol. 7 *The Pelican Guide to English Literature*. London: Penguin Books, 1961.

Caldarwood, James L., and Tolivar, H.E. ed. *Perspective on Fiction*. New York, Oxford University Press, 1968.

Campbell, Joseph, ed. *The Portable Jung*. New York: Viking, 1972.

Chapman, Dom John. *Spiritual Letters*. London: Sheed and Ward, 1935.

Chesterton, G.K. *What's Wrong With the World?* New York: Sheed and Ward, 1956.

Collins, A.S. *English Literature of the Twentieth Century.* London: University Tutorial Press Ltd., 1962.

Curran, Charles. *Counselling and Psychotherapy: The Pursuit of Values.* New York: Sheed and Ward, c. 1968.

Daiches, David. *A Critical History of English Literature.* 4 vols. London: Secker and Warburg, 1969.

Eliot, T.S. *Selected Essays.* London: Faber and Faber Lts., 1955.

————. *Selected Essays.* Third enlarged edition. London: Faber and Faber Ltd., 1951.

————. *Selected Poems.* London: Faber and Faber Ltd., 1961.

Evans, Ifor. *A Short History of English Literature.* Baltimore: Penguin Books, 1963.

Forster, E. M. *Aspects of the Novel.* London: Penguin Books, 1963.

Frankl, Viktor E. *From Death-Camp to Existentialism.* Boston: Beacon Press, 1959.

Fraser, G. S. *The Modern Writer and His World.* Calcutta: Rupa & Co., 1961.

Fromm, Eric. *The Art of Loving.* New York: Bantam Books, 1972.

————. *Escape from Freedom.* New York: Discuss Books, 1969.

————. *The Sane Society.* New York: Holt, Rinehart and Winston, 1960.

Furbank, P.N. "The Twentieth-Century Best-Seller," *The Modern Age.* Vol. 7 *The Pelican Guide to English Literature.* Edited by Boris Ford. London: Penguin Books, 1961.

Gomme, Andor. "Criticism and the Reading Public," *The Modern Age.* vol. 7 *The Pelican Guide to English Literature.* Edited by Boris Ford. London: Penguin Books, c. 1961.

Grigson, Geoffrey, ed. *The Concise Encyclopedia of Modern World Literature.* London: Hutchinson, 1970.

Hebblethwaite, Peter. *Bernanos, An Introduction: Studies in Modern Literature and Thought Series.* London: Bowes and Bowes, 1965.

Heiney, Donald and Downs, Lenthiel H. *Contemporary British Literature*. vol. 2 *Essentials of Contemporary Literature of the Western World*. New York: Woodbury, 1974.

Hoggart, Richard. "Mass Communications in Britain," *The Modern Age*. vol. 7 *The Pelican Guide to English Literature*. Edited by Boris Ford. London: Penguin Books, 1961.

Holloway, John. "The Literary Scene," *The Modern Age*. vol. 7 *The Pelican Guide to English Literature*. Edited by Boris Ford. London: Penguin Books, 1961.

Hudson, William Henry. *An Outline History of English Literature*. London: G. Bell and Sons, Ltd., 1936.

James, Henry. "The Art of Fiction," *Partial Portraits*. London, 1888.

The Jerusalem Bible. Edited by Alexander Jones et. al. New York: Doubleday and Co., Inc., 1966.

Jung, Carl Gustav. *The Portable Jung*. Edited by J. Campbell. New York: Viking, 1972.

Karpman, S. "Fairy Tales and Script Drama Analysis," *Transactional Analysis Bulletin* 7 (April, 1968): 39–43.

Kettle, Arnold. *An Introduction to the English Novel*. Perennial Library Edition. New York: Harper and Row, 1968.

Koestler, Arthur. *The Ghost in the Machine*. New York: The Macmillan Co., 1967.

Kroll, Jack. "Sin and Sentimentality," *Newsweek* 86 (November 3, 1975): pp. 87–88.

Kumar, Raj. *Modern Novel*. Bhopal: Lyall Book Depot, 1967.

Lubbock, Percy. *The Craft of Fiction*. London: Jonathan Cape, 1921.

Mauriac, Francois, "An Interview given to Jean le Marchand, for *The Paris Review*," *Writers at Work*. Edited by Malcolm Cowley. New York: The Viking Press, 1958.

Muir, Edwin. *The Structure of the Novel*. London: The Hogarth Press, 1928.

Muller, Herbert J. *Modern Fiction: A Study of Values*. New York: Funk and Wagnalls Co., 1937.

"Mysticism," *Encyclopedia Britannica*. vol. 16 (1955 edition).

Nin, Anais. *The Novel of the Future*. New York: MacMillan, 1968.

Orwell, George. "The Art of Donald McGill," *Critical Essays*. London, 1946.

Piaget, Jean. "The Language and Thought of the Child," in *Classics in Psychology*. Edited by Thorne Shipley. New York: Philosophy Library, 1961. pp. 995–98.

Pound, Ezra. "A Few Don'ts by an Imagist," *Poetry* 1 (March 1913).

Rahner, Karl; Ernest, Cornelius; and Smyth, Kevil. *Sacramentum Mundi*. An Encyclopaedia of *Theology*. London: Burns and Oats, 1969.

Sastri, Shakuntala Rao, ed. *The Bhagavadgita*. Bombay: Charatiya Vidya Bhawan, 1971.

Scott-James, R. A. *Fifty Years of English Literature: 1900-1950*. London: Longmans, 1960.

Stanton, Robert. *Elements of Fiction*. New York: Holt, Rinehart, and Winston, 1965.

Symons, Julian. *Bloody Murder. From the Detective Story to the Crime Novel: A History*. London: Faber and Faber, 1972.

Thomas, Gilbert. *How to Enjoy Detective Fiction*. London: Salisbury Square, 1947.

Thompson, Francis. "The Hound of Heaven," *Poems of Francis Thompson*. Edited by Terence L. Connollly. New York: The Century Co., 1932. pp. 77–81.

Toliver, H.E., and Calderwood, James L., ed. *Perspectives in Fiction*. New York: Oxford U. Press, 1968.

Waugh, Evelyn, *Brideshead Revisited*. Revised edition. London: Chapman & Hall, 1960.

———. "Come Inside," *The Road to Damascus*. Edited by John A. O'Brien. New York: Doubleday & Co., 1949. pp. 17–20.

———. *Decline and Fall*. London: Penguin Books, 1964.

———. Edmund Campion. New York: Image Books, 1962.

Webster's Seventh New Collegiate Dictionary. Indian Edition, 1971.

West, Paul. *The Modern Novel.* 2 vols. London: Hutchinson University library, 1965.

Yeats, W. B. *Selected Poetry.* Edited by Norman Jeffares. London: Macmillan and Co., Ltd., 1962.

Zachner, R.C. *Zen, Drugs and Mysticism.* New York: Vintage Books, 1974.